GLOBAL PERSPECTIVES ON YOUTH ARTS PROGRAMS

How and Why the Arts Can Make a Difference

Frances Howard

First published in Great Britain in 2022 by

Policy Press, an imprint of
Bristol University Press
University of Bristol
1-9 Old Park Hill
Bristol
BS2 8BB
UK
t: +44 (0)117 374 6645
e: bup-info@bristol.ac.uk

Details of international sales and distribution partners are available at
policy.bristoluniversitypress.co.uk

British Library Cataloguing in Publication Data
A catalogue record for this book is available from the British Library

ISBN 978-1-4473-5710-0 hardcover
ISBN 978-1-4473-5712-4 ePub
ISBN 978-1-4473-5713-1 ePdf

Cover design: Hayes Design and Advertising
Front cover image: Getty Images / We Are
Bristol University Press and Policy Press use environmentally responsible
print partners.
Printed and bound in Great Britain by CPI Group (UK) Ltd, Croydon, CR0 4YY

FSC
www.fsc.org
MIX
Paper from
responsible sources
FSC® C013604

For Danny, Sid and Ella

Contents

List of figures

List of abbreviations

AI	Arts programs as intervention
BERA	British Educational Research Association
CAMP	Chicago Arts and Music Project
CAYW	Creative arts youth work
CCIs	Cultural and creative industries
EHV	Education in human values
EVS	European Voluntary Service
JKPeV	Jugend- & Kulturprojekt e.V. (Youth & Culture Project)
NEET	Not in education, employment or training
NYCI	National Youth Council of Ireland
PYD	Positive youth development
SEL	Social emotional learning
WA	Western Australia
YPC	Youth Planning Committee (Propel Youth Arts WA)

About the author

Frances Howard is Senior Lecturer in Youth Studies at Nottingham Trent University. She has previously worked in local authorities, arts education and youth work. Alongside her academic role, Frances continues to volunteer with local youth organisations, often contributing to the evaluation of arts programs. She is still involved as a Moderator with Arts Award.

Acknowledgements

This book draws on two different stages of my academic career. The first was the research undertaken for my PhD, funded by University of Nottingham. The greatest thanks go to Professor Pat Thomson, my Supervisor, who guided me through the PhD and set me off in the direction of this book. Additional thanks go to my second supervisor, Professor Simon McGrath, who alongside Pat awakened a new critical consciousness about my youth arts practice. I would also like to acknowledge my viva examiners Professor Jo McIntyre and Professor Pam Burnard (University of Cambridge), who encouraged me to take on the world! I was lucky enough to be surrounded by inspirational colleagues due my PhD journey – Dr Nicky Sim, Dr Ecem Karlidag and Dr Louisa Penfold – whose own work on youth and creativity inspired me.

  The connection made during my doctoral study with the TAGPALYCW group, in particular, continued to flourish as I entered the early career research stage. Meeting Dr Janet Batsleer at a TAG event opened the door for meeting like-minded colleagues, many of whom had similar youth work backgrounds to myself and enjoyed talking about these previous experiences very much. Within TAG, I felt as though I had found the 'academic community' to which I felt I most belonged. Being part of the Creative Margins network, and exploring radical youth work and socially engaged arts practice, enabled me to connect with colleagues Dr Harriet Rowley (Manchester Metropolitan University) and Dr Edward Beggan (University of Glasgow), whose research had a strong affinity with my own. In addition, the support and platforming of my research through the British Educational Research Association (BERA) Special Interest Group for Youth Studies and Informal Education, and in particular of my co-convenor Dr Ian McGimpsey, should be acknowledged as a force for collegiality.

  Finally, I would like to thank Shannon Kneiss, Sarah Bird and Isobel Bainton at Policy Press for supporting this book.

The contribution of COVID-19

Parts of this book have been written from my PhD thesis, which was well before the COVID-19 timeline. However, the data generated from the international case study programs was gathered between October 2020 and March 2021 – the time of the 'second peak' of COVID-19 in the UK. All interviews with youth workers, program leaders and managers, and young people were conducted via Zoom video conferencing. Online fieldwork, despite the time differences and late-night video calls, was actually an easier endeavour in terms of reaching and connecting with programs and their participants. Talking to people about the status of COVID-19 in their area of the world and the different stages of lockdown people were experiencing assuaged the feelings of isolation during the pandemic. Although many programs were disrupted, on hold or operating digitally with young people, youth arts practitioners enjoyed reflecting on their experiences and the highlights of their work. Together we felt connected through the time afforded by the pandemic to reconsider what was important in our lives and in our work and to champion the good work that these programs were continuing to try to achieve despite restrictions.

I would like to thank the six international programs, the young people, youth workers, arts educators, and program managers who gave their time to talk to me about their experiences, and of course, to grumble about COVID-19!

- Chicago Arts and Music Project: Lindsay Fredrickson, Nayelli Duran, Ana Marroquin and Young People R and AD
- Annantalo/Dancehearts: Pirjetta Mulari, Sanna Kuusisto and Elina
- Jugend- & Kulturprojekt e.V.: Myrto-Helena Pertsinidi, Dr Rita Sebestyén and Alvaro Sanz Lamperez
- Propel Youth Arts WA: Jamie Gleave, Cecile Vuaillat, Kobi Arthur Morrison and Grace
- Bolt FM: Neil Young, Mark Chambers, Eilidh McMillan and Young Person N
- SWAN Youth Service: Eibhlín Harrington, Dr Shireen Shortt, Darragh Flood and Tamzin Brogan
- National Youth Council of Ireland: Saoirse Reynolds

Preface

"The arts? The arts?!" replied a young person, wrinkling up their nose, when I asked them about what their interests were. "I've never thought of myself as doing 'the arts' because I wasn't into it at school and my Mum and Dad didn't pay for lessons for me," they continued. Yet this young person is part of creative collective that I have been hanging out with in Nottingham for the past few months. They define their practice as creative and recognise the artistry in what they do, however they do not categorise it as 'the arts'.

They are referring to the 'high' arts, which is seen as an elitist endeavour that is out of reach (and not to the taste) of the majority of young people. This book deals with this contested domain by drawing on a wide conception of the arts and a wide spectrum of artistic practices that young people are engaged in today. Although I hang the label of 'youth arts' over this domain, I also want to acknowledge the interchangeability of other labels, such as creativity, artistic practice, cultural interests and youth culture, which are frequently referred to in this book.

So, please do not be deterred by the label 'youth arts programs' in the title. This is not a book about arts organisations working with young people. I have no doubt that some do brilliant work, but instead the focus of this book is on young people doing arts in their communities, supported and enabled by grassroots youth organisations. All programs hold young people at their centre, and the art forms emanate from that centre, where youth arts practices are changeable, challenging and found within the everyday lives and cultures of the young people themselves.

What this book aims to bring attention to is the particular context of youth settings, whether these be youth clubs, community centres or church organisations. I want to highlight the work that youth workers, youth arts practitioners and arts educators do within these settings, acting as connectors and catalysts of youth arts programs. Through their work, the arts have the power to help young people learn about the world and others, finding a place, finding themselves.

While I do explore arguments around the social and economic impact of the arts and the measurements of youth arts programs by instrumental outputs, I strive to offer messages of hope, messages about the impact of the arts at a highly developmental time in the lives of young people. This book gives examples of self-esteem, confidence, expression, movement – all forms of humanity through which the arts support young people to see differently, to encounter, to challenge and, ultimately, to live differently. Giving young people the opportunity to question stereotypes, to question assumptions, and to create their own place in the arts landscape is vitally important.

This book tries to encompass all of this – the passion and the prejudice, the practice and the pedagogy – and offers a way forward for nurturing and growing the benefits of future youth arts programs.

Frances Howard,
July 2021

Part I

1

Introduction

How do young people develop through youth arts programs? What might the best offer of programs look like? How can we ensure that the content of these programs reflects young people's personal interests but also develops new and exciting experiences? How do we know that youth arts programs are designed in the best interests of young people? How can youth arts support participatory democracy and social change? And what kinds of cultural citizens are arts programs developing?

These questions will be addressed in this book.

Not all young people get to access arts programs. For those young people who do not take up arts education in school their experience of the arts is often through informal education and youth work settings. However not *all* young people are offered the same arts practices, experience similar pedagogies and benefit in equal measure. This book questions claims for the assumed benefits of arts programs for young people. It explores youth arts programs targeted at young people under deficit labels and presents research which demonstrates that often the most disadvantaged young people receive the weakest arts programs. I extend the discussion on deficit identities from the field of youth work to arts-based pedagogies. In addition, the book addresses current policy contexts of 'austerity', 'inclusion' and 'at-risk' youth, which are frequently drawn on to justify arts programs for young people. Therefore, I make a stand for universal youth work in the face of targeted neoliberal measures.

This book seeks to address the unequal programming and application of youth arts programs, drawing on the dichotomy between 'high' arts and 'low' culture and the classed-based take-up of youth work. Reporting on international exemplars, I draw attention to the conditions required for youth arts programs to be successful, while acknowledging the challenges of this work. I attempt to fill the gap between the discourse of the role of youth work and specifically how arts-based work can make significant contributions to a more just society. This cross-cultural and contextualised learning will help to support the field in continuing progressive directions. I also make recommendations for practitioners that are based on research. Taking the position that what is offered to some groups of young people can be seen to reinforce prejudice, this book tackles an ethical dilemma for those working with the arts and young people.

In offering a way forward, by focusing on the practices and pedagogies that 'work' in youth arts programs, three key theoretical perspectives are introduced, which engage with a sociological analysis of these programs. First, young people's take-up of *common culture* in youth work settings is explored through engagement with digital and DIY arts practices. Secondly, the ideals of *cultural democracy* are examined from the perspective of cultural responsivity and the representation of local communities. Finally, youth arts programs that hold *cultural citizenship* at their hearts are presented in order to explore what kinds of 'citizens' young people are expected to be.

Why this book? Why now?

The use of the arts is a perennial theme in youth work, yet the area of youth arts programs is underexplored. Ever since youth work began, arts-based methodologies have been used, but there is a lack of research on practices and pedagogies, with limited theorisation of these. A growing body of research demonstrates the value of youth arts work as strategies for pedagogic engagement, with a particular significance for creativity in developing new democratic spaces (Batsleer, 2011). In her research on youth work within gallery spaces, Nicola Sim observed youth workers who were deeply passionate about working with others in creative and democratic ways. She reported young people gaining access to new enriching cultural experiences that motivated a life-long engagement with the arts or changed worldviews (Sim, 2019). In Beggan and Coburn's (2018) study of two youth work programs, which engaged with the creative arts, young people were encouraged to tell their stories using newly acquired arts-based skills. They observed the application of professional youth work methodologies through informal education as a way of improving young people's experiences of, and access to, creative education outside of schooling. Here the arts were given an educational purpose in self-expression and in learning from experience, by facilitating feelings of socialisation, purpose and well-being. In contributing to this existing research, this book enables a wider dialogue about youth arts programs for social justice, in relation to positioning young people as activists and active producers, as opposed to consumers of pre-packaged cultural artefacts.

My first role within youth arts programs began in England in 2005, when I worked for an organisation called Creative Room, which was part of the local authority's arts offer for young people in the city of Nottingham. At this time, government support and funding were abundant and I enjoyed artist-led sessions, accompanying young people to national showcase events and international residentials. We had creativity and craziness 'coming out of our ears' and a steady stream of young people regularly attending our programs. However, the global financial crash of 2008 and the resulting 'austerity' policies in England brought massive cuts to both the youth and arts sectors, and the programs that had been my most enjoyable and most impactful work were devalued, de-prioritised and de-funded. I struggled through five years of restructures and redundancies, during which the number of programs and young people I had been working with dwindled. In 2013, I entered into a 'strategic' role, where I no longer got to work directly with young people or be involved in programs that attracted a wide range of young people. I began to see that these programs were no longer benefiting young people in the same ways. At this point, I decided to 'get out' of local authority youth services and applied to undertake a PhD study based on my previous practice. Focusing on arts programs for 'dis-engaged' youth was my attempt to capture and celebrate what was being lost. I was fortunate enough to be awarded funding from the University of Nottingham to explore one such program – Arts Award – which I had successfully run with over 200 young people in the local authority.

The thinking for this book began then, way back in 2013, through my desire to celebrate and share best practice in youth arts programs. However, my PhD research took me on a different journey, where I realised that some elements of my practice in working with the arts and young people were in fact problematic and that this was widespread within the sector. This book seeks to capture the problems I encountered in my professional practice and the unintentional consequences this can have for young people. While this book offers critique, partly in response to my learning journey, it also offers possibilities through a wider global picture of youth arts programs. I present best practice case studies as exemplars and conclude with recommendations for facilitating youth arts programs in future.

The rollercoaster of experiences through my PhD has not dissuaded me from working in and researching youth arts programs. I have continued my work with youth arts programs throughout and beyond my PhD, volunteering for music, film making and visual arts programs and evaluating the work that creative programs do with young people and local communities. In my academic work, I engage with creative and experiential pedagogies, which represent an extension of my youth work and arts practice within a higher education environment (Howard, 2021a). At a time when these two distinctive practices frequently come under threat, this book seeks to champion their synergies and celebrate their values.

What is a youth arts program?

As the preface to this book suggests, the title of 'youth arts' is misrecognised, misunderstood and frequently contested. The terms 'youth work' and 'arts' denote a binary set of associations – one with democracy and the working classes, the other with elitism and bureaucratic control. In combining these two terms, questions can be raised about *which* youth and *whose* conception of the arts? Historically, arts education has sat uneasily with informal education structures, whereby the arts have been offered as either a service or market (Burton et al, 2016). Gaztambide-Fernández (2020), for example, argues for the reframing of 'the arts' towards 'cultural production', whereby practices, processes, and products of symbolic creativity that are situated in particular local contexts can be shaped by specific material circumstances, and power relations can be understood. This is a useful lens through which to view youth arts programs today.

In the preface, I set out my stance that 'youth arts' represents a wide conception of the arts, one which encompasses a spectrum of artistic practices that young people are engaged in today. This label can be used interchangeability with creativity, artistic practice, cultural interests and youth culture. Therefore, I define a youth arts program as a particular offer for young people to come together to create and affirm culture, to make art in their communities and engage with artistic practices that are rooted in their own lived experiences. Through this definition, I position youth settings as offering alternative spaces and different ways for young people to engage with the arts. This may manifest in regular workshop-based sessions, creative activities that take place in the community or youth settings, and more experimental open access spaces.

My reference to 'global' within the title of this book refers not only to geographical location, spanning several continents, but also the global reach of arts practices that incorporate digital technologies. The use of the word 'global' refers to a diversity of arts practices that can be recognised and acknowledged on a world scale. While the case studies in this book might be better described as international, a key limitation should be acknowledged through the inclusion of case studies from economically competitive liberal democracies. My position is that no perspective can be truly inclusive or representative, and the reference to global alludes to the things that connect us; the ways that we can live together in the world and be part of society, and the affordances that arts practice has for this.

Why the arts are good for youth work

The synergies between youth work and arts practice, which will be further explored in this book, include an emphasis on informal education, participation and opening up new ideas and ways of understanding the world. Youth work holds shared principles with the purposes of arts engagement for young people through personal and social development (Batsleer, 2008), developing trusting relationships and opening up new opportunities for young people to express democratic voices, learning about themselves and the world around them (Davies, 2010). Characteristic practices of youth arts programs include the importance of encouraging young people's learning through creativity, engaging with everyday and experiential learning, and social and relational learning (Sefton-Green, 2006; Coburn, 2011b). They have happened in a variety of settings from schools to arts organisations, from youth clubs to youth-offending institutions. Importantly, out-of-school educational experiences can lead to beneficial advantages, which are often aligned with building cultural, social and symbolic capitals (Machin, 2006). Projects that engaged young people in cultural opportunities were universally assumed to be a good thing, with increased participation benefiting both individuals and society (Long et al, 2002). For example, arts-led urban regeneration was seen as an engaging tool for working with communities (Bianchini and Parkinson, 1994; García, 2004; Denmead, 2019) and within youth offending, the arts had been used as a mechanism to create a diversionary focus (Hughes et al, 2005).

Previous research has argued for the value of youth workers as informal educators in terms of improvisation skills for youth work (Davies, 2011). The arts are often used as a tool to approach sensitive subjects with young people and as part of their own personal 'tool box' to create activities for their settings (Kiilakoski and Kivijärvi, 2015). Seen as vehicles for engaging young people in positive activities, the arts can take them on personal and emotional journeys, but they also achieve an end product – often a performance – that a young person can take pride in. Youth arts programs can open up new spaces for young people to develop relationships and shared identities, using fun activities where different young people can mix and create common ground (Miller et al, 2015). Youth workers in my study mentioned taking young people to places they would not normally go, opening up new experiences, putting different groups of youth together, achieving goals, opening up pathways, and removing barriers to training and employment. One of the key practices of youth work is identity building through interactions with the everyday, where youth clubs provide a culture of participation and a common language, which generates a sense of belonging with other young people in the area (Nolas, 2014). Young people taking part in youth arts programs can draw on their creativity in order to negotiate their identities and to become part of proto-communities (Willis, 1990), which are viewed in a positive light.

These benefits were not new to me when I was reviewing the literature for this book. Through my previous work experience I had utilised the arts within youth work as a tool to work with young people and as part of my own personal 'tool box'. I had particularly enjoyed the shared practices of encouraging young people's decision making and creative problem solving, which working with the arts afforded. This was in addition to the shared pedagogical approaches of informal education, through dialogue and co-creation. In my work with young people, the arts helped me to build long-term trusting relationships and enabled young people to have a voice, but also brought elements of fun, collective challenge and feelings of self-worth.

Working as a youth arts worker in the 2000s, I was involved in a scheme called Gallery 37.[1] This program aimed to engage young people through youth work pedagogies and arts-based practice. Gallery 37 was historically rooted in Chicago where the Gallery 37 Centre was set up to provide a venue for youth, families and adults to participate in several innovative arts programs, including arts school and arts education programs. One of the projects I worked on was invited to contribute a case study to the National Youth Agency publication *Artswork with Socially Excluded Young People* (2009). These case studies featured five youth organisations that drew on an 'arts and culture' approach to youth work. This approach principally drew on the arts as a tool for engaging with young people, manifesting in not working with a particular arts practice per se but utilising the associated pedagogies in engaging with young people. The affordances of this approach were reported as the use of taster sessions, which gave young people 'quick win', and creative arts activities as holding young people's attention, through hands-on experiences, often in new environments. It was argued that the arts are 'accessible' and enable young people to 'engage quickly', as well as focusing on areas in which they are interested and common languages such as music. However, the reported outcomes from this approach focused solely on an economic perspective and included young people re-engaging with education or training, work experience, apprenticeships and employment, and so on. The development of 'soft skills' was also recorded, but this failed to capture young people's self-expression and creativity. These tensions led me to explore a more critical and sociological perspective on youth arts programs.

Why the arts are bad for youth work

As my fieldwork progressed, I became increasingly aware that the current pressures on youth work to produce measurable outcomes had risked instrumentalising arts programs. In her book *Grassroots Youth Work*, Tania de St Croix (2016) explores the 'market values' and pressure on youth workers to demonstrate outputs and 'value for money'. The valorisation of 'enterprise' in youth policy has resulted in short-term funding and project-based 'diversionary' youth work (de St Croix, 2016). Neoliberal education policy that highlights social inclusion and the rhetoric of opportunity has resulted in deficit terms for those young people who are viewed as not taking up opportunities and not investing in themselves (Edwards, 2009; Archer and Hutchings, 2010; Bradbury et al, 2013). McGimpsey (2018) argues youth services are better understood as an exemplar case of the reforming effects of a 'late neoliberal regime' that has enabled the emergence of a new youth sector founded on norms of investment and return. Key changes have included reforms to the distribution of capital to services; the place of social investment in policy discourse and the constitution of new notions of value and new objects of knowledge; and the reform of the field of youth provision, with increased hybridity in organisational forms in the new 'youth sector'. As a result, young people are frequently depicted as 'in trouble' or 'in need of intervention', and for them arts programs became a 'targeted' approach predominantly concerned with behaviour modification, rather than a universal program for personal development. Taking this approach, youth arts programs have been critiqued for being offered purely as a diversion, rather than a deep engagement with artistic mediums and practices (Burton et al, 2016). This deficit model, based on social investment, raises questions about the arts as process or product, and the return on investment youth arts programs must be seen to generate.

Cultural policy has also mirrored this individualist and instrumental shift in arguing for its contribution to health, crime reduction, employment and education. Research has attempted to demonstrate 'impact' in order to justify continued public expenditure (Jermyn, 2001; Long et al, 2002; Staricoff, 2004; Hughes et al, 2005). However, the improving qualities of culture and the assertions that the arts 'do good' have been critiqued. An instrumentalised viewpoint of the arts and culture has claimed social impacts through the absorption of cultural policies within existing social policies (Merli, 2002; Belfiore, 2010; 2012), while the arts are tasked with combating social issues (Jermyn, 2001). Sim's (2019) chronology of shifting ideological trends and conflicts with youth work and the arts demonstrates that the 'fields'[2] of youth work and gallery education 'emerged out of similar social and political movements and have fostered similar critical and moral values' (p 67). Therefore, Sim argues that sometimes programs set up with an emancipatory and democratic social agenda unintentionally alienate (in particular) working class young people.

The re-emergence of pedagogical expectations, where youth work becomes more 'organised' and about 'participation' (Van de Walle et al, 2010), leaves space for accredited programs, such as Arts Award, which is the focus of Part II of this book. Youth work became framed not only as informal education, but as 'positive activities', whereby 'educational principles and purposes are likely to become increasingly hard to safeguard as ones in favour of "child-saving" and youth control are increasingly prioritised' (Davies 2010, p 59). Through the Every Child Matters framework[3] and the PAYP program (positive activities for young people), assumptions were made about preventing anti-social behaviour by providing activities that were seen in a more positive light, to be character building and educational in nature. Arts-based youth work was given the task of 'social improvement' or providing young people with more positive things to do. In England, New Labour's emphasis on instrumental purposes moved arts practice away from more expressive forms enabling identity development, towards accredited outcomes and transferable skills. The voluntary and open access nature of democratic youth provision was replaced by targeted programs with measurable outcomes. Despite a wide range of opportunities, stronger approaches to youth empowerment, the restructuring of youth services under New Labour, and diversion of funding towards mainstream education resulted in unpredictable funding and the need for youth organisations to develop resilient, business-like values (Wylie, 2015). Youth work became rolled up into wider support services tasked with delivering on outcomes such as increasing youth employment and lowering youth crime. While 'the family' was forefronted in New Labour policy, through the funding of Sure Start and Children's Centres, social integrationalist discourses highlighted those 'in need' as lacking economic and moral prosperity (Bradford and Cullen, 2014).

An instrumentalised approach to arts programming was given priority by policy makers within the context of the need to evidence 'impact' or prove value for money. This instrumental shift in youth policy has positioned young people as 'problems' to be solved or 'victims' to be saved through targeted approaches (Jeffs and Smith, 2002; Davies, 2010; Wylie, 2015) and resulted in the development of programs which 'target' particular groups of young people under deficit labels such as 'at-risk', 'NEET' (Not in Education, Employment or Training) and 'hard-to-reach'. This book identifies areas of practice where youth arts programs have become instrumentalised, and maps global trends by exploring positive youth development programs, the arts as an 'intervention' and creative arts youth work. The selection of case studies that follow in Part III of the book provide a juxtaposition to deficit-based and instrumentalised programs.

Sharing 'close-to-practice' research

My research focused on young people's experiences of Arts Award – a national arts program, run in England as a 'vocationally relevant qualification'. My interest was in young people taking this up as part of youth programs in a variety of out-of-school settings, from youth clubs to alternative education provision. The research aimed to explore the educational experiences of Arts Award for young people deemed as 'dis-engaged'. This label of 'dis-engaged', despite connoting negative stereotypes, was a carefully considered choice as it also reflected young people who had elected to disengage themselves from mainstream education. Feelings of the arts 'not being for them' were prevalent. The out-of-school or youth settings also capture those who were disengaged from standard arts curriculums or activities through mainstream provision by schools and arts organisations.

Engaging with a qualitative methodology, my research methods were aligned with youth work practices of conversation, relationship building and experiential learning. I also drew on arts-based methods and artistic production within my analysis. The data throughout the book is drawn from interviews with young people, and the arts-based artefacts that they produced during the program, as well as ethnographic fieldnotes. There were also a small number of interviews that I conducted with fellow youth arts workers, but this 'adult perspective' was not a primary focus. I drew on ethnography as a suitable method due to the ability to benefit from sustained 'hanging around' (Russell, 2013) with groups of young people across five different arts programs. I selected these programs to cover a range of art forms and levels of Arts Award,[4] but also based on previous relationships I had built up with the organisers of these programs.

Having delivered the Arts Award program for many years prior to my doctorate and having a role within the program itself where I act as a 'Moderator', who visits programs and approves the qualification, gave me an advantageous insight as an insider. However, these previous roles meant that it took longer to be regarded as an ethnographer, rather than a facilitator, by the program organisers. It also took longer to see the problematic work and points of sociological critique. This feeling ran contrary to my desire to view all youth arts programs as beneficial. The specific focus of this research on a marginalised group was both a strength and a limitation and the results could not be generalised to report on the award as a whole. I was aware of other research that had been undertaken on Arts Award, which had focused on take-up from mainstream schools (Hollingworth, 2016). However, my research offered a nuanced and in-depth insight into the experience of this marginalised group, which had implications for future practice with those deemed most 'in need'.

In addition to my own research, this book explores diverse global perspectives by presenting six case study programs from around the world. These case studies were selected as some were familiar to me and others were recommended by academics within the field. Again, a wide range of art forms and approaches have been incorporated and data was generated through a series of interviews with different individuals involved in the programs. These included program organisers, facilitators and young participants themselves. The aim of this data generation was to collate practical experiences and personal benefits of these programs so that they may be shared. This case study approach engaged with thematic analysis based around the theoretical underpinnings of the book: common culture, cultural citizenship and cultural democracy. Case studies were shared with the programs involved prior to publication. The organisations have not been anonymised, whereas participants under the age of 16 are represented by initials. The learnings from these case studies have been incorporated into the final chapter, which examines implications for practice and guidance for the future creation of youth arts programs.

Structure of the book

The book consists of three Parts. The first three chapters will provide a critical perspective on youth arts programs, setting the context for youth arts work, while highlighting key tensions. Part I questions current assumptions around arts programs for young people under deficit labels and introduces the key theoretical perspectives that run throughout the book: common culture, cultural democracy and cultural citizenship. Part II is made up of three chapters, which present the data and findings from my PhD study, in particular focusing on youth work settings. This Part will explore the arts practices and pedagogies used with young people in these settings. The final four chapters, which make up Part III, will feature a range of international case studies that align to the key themes of the book. The final chapter concludes with key implications for practice, in order to argue that the arts – rather than behaviour management or social skills – should be at the centre in order to ensure high-quality and equitable outcomes for the young people involved.

The next chapter focuses on global trends within youth arts programs, exploring the different meanings and intentions of these programs across the world. I explore three diverse approaches, which include creative arts youth work (CAYW), the arts as intervention (AI), and positive youth development (PYD). This chapter introduces the three key themes that run through the book: common culture, cultural citizenship and cultural democracy, as alternative ways of configuring youth arts practice. I argue that there is pedagogical value in the way that youth arts programs can be used to challenge deficit discourses around particular groups of young people and move on to explore this further in Chapter 3, where the problematic labels which are placed upon groups of young people are explained. Following this, the impact on arts programs is examined, where I argue that for those young people taking up arts programs under deficit labels, opportunities are restricted.

In Part II of the book, Chapter 4 introduces my research, which investigated the young people's Arts Award program within youth settings. I give a synopsis of my findings in relation to the affordances of Arts Award within youth work settings and focus on the benefits of creative work with and by young people and the particular constraints of youth work settings. I argue that despite the award being a 'good fit' with the informal education practices of youth work, its utilisation as an accreditation instrumentalises the experience of working with the arts. Within youth settings, this award often became a tool for monitoring young people and offered weaker forms of arts pedagogy. Building on Chapter 3's exploration of how young people are positioned by youth arts programs, Chapter 4 focuses on the youth programs themselves and their shifting instrumental rhetoric. Alongside an exploration of the growing body of literature concerned with the arts in youth work, I propose two key findings: the arts as a 'tool' for youth work and the arts as a tool for monitoring and control. These include the tensions between open access and increasing access, and my perspective on measurement as being situated in 'risky terrain'. These findings are developed further by the following two chapters, which provide an in-depth investigation into the diverse practices and pedagogies on offer from Arts Award within youth settings.

Chapters 5 and 6 explore two particular findings from my research and focus on the different arts practices on offer through the Arts Award program and the differing pedagogies drawn upon by the youth workers. While arts practice was an opportunity for learning new things, developing new arts skills, working with artists and utilising industry-standard equipment, access to quality arts practice was restricted for some, with a failure to engage with more challenging and contemporary arts experiences. I explore the more 'subcultural' arts practices and their functioning as realignment for these young people to deviant social groupings. Consideration is also given to what pedagogies and ways of working with the arts disadvantage young people. I demonstrate that varieties in pedagogical practice can be viewed as a hierarchy depending on young people's perceived behaviour and assumptions made about their artistic ability. This is intended to highlight that the potential of youth arts programs is not being reached.

Part III of the book focuses on the six international case studies under the themes of common culture, cultural democracy and cultural citizenship. In Chapter 7, I draw on two programs: *Dancehearts* (Finland) and *Bolt FM* (Scotland) in order to explore DIY (do-it-yourself) and digital arts practices, as a way of firmly rooting youth arts programs within young people's interests, while building on their cultural funds of knowledge. Chapter 8 follows, celebrating cultural democracy through *Propel Youth Arts WA* (Australia) and *SWAN Youth Service* (Ireland) as exemplars of youth-led arts programming, and platforming young people as cultural experts. In Chapter 9 the value of youth arts programs in supporting participatory democracy and social change is explored through two case studies: *Chicago Arts and Music Project* and *Jugend- & Kulturprojekt e. V.* (Youth and Culture Program, Germany).

As well as being based upon research, this book reflects on practice and is designed to appeal to practitioners and those planning their own programs. The final chapter of the book presents a summary of best practice from around the world and incorporates guidance for practitioners, which can enable youth arts programs to flourish. I focus, in particular, on maintaining youth work principles, artistic quality, partnerships, planning and evaluation. Two models are drawn from the case studies: the youth arts festival and working with an artist-in-residence, as exemplars of how the arts and young people can be at the centre of every program. This book makes a contribution to a growing body of 'close-to-practice' scholarship and to those training to enter the diverse professions where youth work happens both nationally and internationally.

2

Current and future trends in youth arts programs

Youth arts programs benefit a wide range of young people, including disadvantaged groups, as the arts celebrate cultural difference and acknowledge diverse ways of being, doing and thinking. There is pedagogical value in the way that youth arts programs can be used to challenge deficit discourses around particular groups of young people. However, a diversity of practice, from around the world, needs to be acknowledged. This chapter explores three diverse approaches of global youth arts practice, which includes creative arts youth work (CAYW), the arts as intervention (AI) and positive youth development (PYD). Each of these trends in current practice highlights different ways arts programs function, and the affordances for and positioning of the young people involved.

Following the mapping of international trends, this chapter will introduce the three key themes that run throughout the book – common culture, cultural citizenship and cultural democracy – as alternative ways of configuring youth arts practice. Common culture, on which I draw from the work of Paul Willis (1990), highlights the value of accessible and everyday cultural practice as the foundation for youth arts programs. I engage with cultural citizenship to draw attention to the potential of youth arts to develop *justice-informed citizens* (Kuttner, 2015) who feel a civic responsibility to use their artistic practice to actively promote justice and address inequalities in society. Finally, I consider cultural democracy as a rights-based approach which acknowledges the capabilities of all young people to be not just consumers of the arts, but also producers. This chapter, therefore, not only maps the field, but also sets frameworks for the future development of youth arts programs.

Why youth arts programs work

Youth arts as a practice is riddled with historic tensions. The arts are seen as exclusive and elitist, whereas youth work is seen as taken up by communities living in poverty or from disadvantaged areas. This book purposely focuses on programs existing within this informal domain, rather than those school-based or arts organisation-run programs. Defined by participation outside of formal education, the term 'youth arts' grew out of three traditions: theatre, community arts and the youth service (Myers, 2016). Arts programs have been well documented to provide challenging and life-changing experiences for the young people involved. Youth work settings engender meaningful mentoring and initiate developmental relationships (Kane, 2014). Therefore, youth arts programs are an opportunity to engage young people with issues they care about, drawing on ethical pedagogies, enabling the creation of counter-narratives in relation to their lives and futures (Rogers, 2016). This pedagogy is also political, where the arts provide a springboard for the discussion of critical incidents within young people's lives (Gallagher and Wessels, 2013). As a new 'pedagogical imaginary', youth arts programs can offer localised, context- and culture-specific arts pedagogies and celebrate the power of difference, which holds the potential for social justice (Harris and Lemon, 2012).

The arts have been pedagogically proven to 'work' with young people in informal education settings and are frequently used as tools for informal learning in youth work as a pedagogy of the here-and-now (Batsleer, 2008). Informal learning characteristics are mirrored in youth work pedagogy, which tends to be focused around small group work and a concern with 'youth voice'. Flexibility, responsivity and the co-creation of knowledge are also key elements of youth arts programs, whereby relational learning is encompassed through building relationships and new connections within young people's social and emotional lives (Smyth et al, 2013). A large part of the process of informal learning relies on experience, experiential learning and the hands-on approach to arts learning. Youth arts programs offer quick wins, praise culture and practical learning experiences, which are recognised for attracting and retaining young people on the programs (National Youth Agency, 2009).

Research has shown that arts spaces can offer important opportunities for youth work and vice versa (Nolas, 2014; Kiilakoski and Kivijärvi, 2015). Artists and arts education practitioners are often adept at working with inventive, improvisatory practices and with youth-led engagement, so they are well placed to function as advocates for critical, creative and democratic youth work. Particular elements of strength include the personal and social development of young people through taking part in arts activities, but also the development of youth workers' practice through the experience of engaging with the young people on the programs (Howard et al, 2018). The arts can accommodate different cultural considerations and knowledges and can promote the acknowledgement and acceptance of difference. As such they are vital to thriving future communities. Pedagogical engagement through the arts develops diverse dispositions, which include motivation, social and emotional well-being and attitudes, as well as cognitive ability and skill. Gadsden (2008) reminds us that

> [t]he arts – neither the panacea to ameliorate all that troubles us in education nor the beacon of all possibility – offer us a lens through

which to examine long-standing questions, provocative ways to (re)consider creativity, opportunity to reimagine engagement, and a renewed sense of possibility that can lead us to the formation of new epistemologies. (Gadsden, 2008, p 54)

In terms of informal education, youth arts offer a pedagogical style that mirrors the behaviour, techniques and values evident in those professionals who work with 'at-risk' young people (Kinder, 2004) and are regarded as useful for other sites of learning and in particular emotional well-being and therapeutic outcomes (Karkou and Glasman, 2004). Youth arts pedagogy can promote radical democracy, critical citizenry and agency, while addressing power relations, critical pedagogy and the politics of representation (Villaverde, 1998). For example 'hip-hop' pedagogy (Gosine and Tabi, 2016) affords the construction of counter-hegemonic identities and critical consciousness raising. In this way, the pedagogical value of youth arts programs offers an opportunity to challenge dominant discourses, as a way of transcending the disconnection and stigmatisation of marginalised youth (Altman and De, 2010).

Youth arts practice can work to disrupt patterns of racism and other forms of exclusion. For example, the anti-oppressive practice of youth workers becomes a site of struggle for young people in relation to oppressive institutions that deal with the social control of young people. Batsleer (2021) argues that valuable experiential learning starts from these forms of 'discontent', as 'collective community groups become powerful in challenging hegemonic power in everyday life, whilst building the collective agentic power of participants' (p 6). Anti-oppressive practice, therefore, is a grassroots strategy for opening up spaces of possibility alongside young people and communities to work creatively to disrupt knowledge-making practices and deficit-based policy discourses (Bowler et al, 2021).

Finding a safe place to 'be yourself' is another reason why youth arts activities benefit young people (Trayes et al, 2012). The well-being benefits of youth arts programs have been well documented as a space for social and emotional gains, and other benefits from participation and the development of skills (Ennis and Tonkin, 2018). Youth arts activities are known to contribute to self-confidence and self-esteem (Bungay and Vella-Burrows, 2013). These include improvements in artistic and communication skills, and the creation of positive social connections, feelings of belonging, and sense of identity and community (Anwar McHenry, 2009). Music making, in particular, offers significant psycho-social benefits for young people, particularly when combined with mentoring support (Parker, 2018).

It is important to understand creative approaches within the changing landscape of youth work. While highlighting these benefits of youth arts programs, this book aims to show that not all young people benefit in equal measure. In order to do so, I explore and critique three international trends in youth arts programs, namely creative arts youth work, arts programs as intervention, and positive youth development, which differ in their implementation and positioning of young people.

Creative arts youth work

Edward Beggan and Annette Coburn's research on arts-based youth work programs proffered the term 'Creative Arts Youth Work'. They argued that combining creative arts with youth work developed an authentic and participatory means for young people's expression of voice (Beggan and Coburn, 2018). The participants in their study came from two diverse Scottish programs and acquired arts-based skills developed through informal education approaches, which enabled young people to tell their stories. These findings aligned with previous research which has highlighted the use of creative arts as a focus for development of critical youth work (Coburn, 2011b) and as a catalyst for emancipatory practice and to offer a counterbalance to contemporary social issues (Coburn and Gormally, 2019). CAYW draws on the shared characteristics of both youth work and the creative arts, which incorporate the importance of improvisation, flexibility and the opportunity to be creative. CAYW is therefore a pedagogical approach to youth arts programs, based on a synergy of creative practice, informal education and critical pedagogy.

CAYW draws on strategies of pedagogic engagement, which encompasses the use of symbolisations, expression of feelings and the exploration of meaning (Batsleer, 2011). Practices of creating safe spaces, taking risks and giving permission to be free like a child are facilitated and negotiated by skilled creative practitioners and informal educators. Batsleer further argues that arts-based creative approaches are a means of challenging tokenistic versions of participation and deficit identities by drawing attention to who is involved in the framing of their depiction. In response, CAYW emphasises a strength-based model of practice that focuses on the young people's existing capacities and positive qualities. Brown and Jeanneret's (2015) study explored one such program, which had a central commitment to relationship building, mediated through art practice. Particular pedagogies derived from CAYW will be explored further in Chapter 6 of this book.

CAYW consists of arts practices that can be engaged with in a youth setting. However, Nicola Sim's exploration of youth work in gallery spaces reversed these elements where she observed the youth work pedagogies being practised within visual arts settings (Sim, 2019). She argues that there is the need for a more critical, less instrumental intersection between youth work and the arts, and a 'need to move beyond the stereotyping of DJing, spray painting and street dance as "typical tropes" or arts-based youth work' (p 9).

Sim (2019) highlights the complicity of youth work in sustaining damaging practices of 'symbolic violence'. She reminds us how different communities interpret culture and creativity, whereby different tastes and levels of creative confidence signify social disparities. While the middle classes receive arts education and appreciate aesthetics, the arts for the working classes are tasked with improvement and tainted by instrumentalism. Yet, despite finding elements of unintentional alienation of different class cultures and capitals, Sim found that young people might gain access to new enriching cultural experiences that could motivate a lifelong engagement with the arts.

While the arts remain a powerful tool for youth work through this approach, increasingly target-driven youth settings and the influence of neoliberalism have resulted in an arts offer which is often no longer voluntary, thus eroding a core principle of CAYW. Open access and drop-in sessions, for example, and the structured nature of certain arts practices (such as performance rehearsals), are shown to be sometimes in tension with the voluntary principle of open access youth work (Howard et al, 2018). Using drama practice as a particular example, Brocken (2015) reports encountering several challenges with the politics of running a venue, structural constraints and young people's behaviour. At times these ran contradictorily to her pedagogical approach to CAYW. Therefore the creative and critical power of CAYW in relation to refocusing society's gaze on young people needs to be further explored. This will be taken up in the following chapter, which addresses how young people are positioned by arts programs.

Arts as intervention

Arts programs offered as an intervention for young people have shown cultural relevance and have demonstrated life-changing outcomes (de Roeper and Savelsberg, 2009). With music projects, for example, a love of performance, a shared unity of purpose and the quality of relationships developed and sustained has been well documented (Barrett and Smigiel, 2007) as well as improved attitudes towards teachers and peers, feelings of calm, and better communication skills (Parker, 2018). With drama, the experience of 'being other' is important for the development of young people's ability to self-regulate, empathise with others, and work collaboratively (Tawell et al, 2015). Visual arts are often credited for their therapeutic benefits, which can bring about emotional expression and promote social change in young people's communities (Talaina Si'isi'ialafia, 2018). Participation in youth arts activities has well-supported outcomes for mental health and well-being, in particular through 'emotional development', with youth settings acting as a safe place for expressing and sharing as 'exercise for the soul' (Ennis and Tonkin, 2018). Some arts intervention programs may focus on the effectiveness of tutoring or mentoring and developing relationships (Rapp-Paglicci et al,

2007), however, these often short-term and more diversionary approaches are problematic.

Despite compendiums of evidence on the benefits of the arts for young people, these programs are most frequently aimed at those deemed more disadvantaged, less able and in a deficit positioning. De Roeper and Savelsberg (2009) argue that these interventions highlight a 'binary divide' between those young people identified as 'high-functioning' and those who are offered a remedial experience. As a consequence these programs focus more on keeping youth 'on track' and often ignore young people's deeper developmental needs. These kinds of arts programs are more likely to have a limited time frame and a focus on behaviour modification, rather than artistic creativity. Research has shown that arts programs for young people in the UK and Australia, for example, which have targeted particular groups of young people, have often been much more instrumental in their approach (O'Brien and Donelan, 2009; Howard, 2017). Through this perspective, the arts have been applied not as a universal learning offer or an entitlement, but as a result of criminal behaviour, poor mental health or living in conditions of disadvantage. Therefore, these programs can be seen to reinforce stereotypes that accompany inequality.

Dominant discourses of youth arts have fixed particular values to creativity as a means of 'adding value' to young people (Hickey-Moody, 2013b). Anna Hickey-Moody's book *Youth, Arts and Education* critiques the popular use of youth arts as forms of social governance. This is closely connected to the particular arts practices that programs offer and the pedagogies through which young people engage with the arts in youth settings. She argues that 'the inclusion of arts in assemblages of governance not only produces impoverished arts practices; it can also (but does not always) take away young people's voices through imposing adult tastes on the lives of youth' (Hickey-Moody, 2013b, p 14). For example, the Arts Award program, which is the focus of the Part II of this book, is an arts-based qualification taken up by youth settings due to both its flexibility and its accredited outcome. However, these programs often emphasise economic benefits over educational value, drawing clear distinctions between quantifiable or 'hard' measures of impact and those described as 'soft', less tangible and lacking a strong evidence base (Robinson et al, 2019).

Within the area of youth offending, arts programs are frequently used as an intervention. For example, the Centre for Youth and Criminal Justice (Vallance, 2017) reports that while the arts should not be considered as a replacement for specialist arts interventions such as therapy or treatment, incorporating creative processes into day-to-day practice can be a useful and meaningful way of engaging young people, offering a positive distraction and facilitating dialogue. The key evidence built through this report was in relation to the affordances the arts present to work towards more 'positive' identities. Through involvement in arts-based interventions participants demonstrated considerable changes in 'perceptions of themselves, how they behave and, in some cases, improving aspirations'. These outcomes lean towards behaviour change and it is questionable as to how these 'negative' identities or aspirations arrive in the first instance. Antithetical to social 'norms', weighty labels are unknowingly ascribed to young people's identities.

Positive youth development

The third trend explored in this chapter is positive youth development, which is an approach mainly taken up in the US. As a growing area of community arts education that spans both youth development and arts education, PYD is an intentional, holistic practice that combines hands-on art making and skill building in the arts with development of life skills to support young people in successfully participating in adolescence and navigating into adulthood (Delgado, 2018). Similar to the AI approach, the arts are used as diversionary activities in steering young people away from crime, drugs and deviant behaviours. Based on an empowerment model, music programs, in particular, have emphasised diversity and collaboration and demonstrated young people's development of a sense of dignity and achieving outside of a school environment (Mantie, 2008). PYD programs therefore claim social justice aims and have intrinsic and personalised outcomes such as confidence, identity and collaboration.

Common benefits of this approach are reported as increased levels of artistic skill, and increased self-esteem, sense of belonging and sense of pride (Travis and Leech, 2014). Much emphasis has been placed upon the pedagogical value of the arts in engaging young people in their local communities through community building, public engagement, and social change (Lin and Bruce, 2013). PYD programs have also been characterised by positive staff–youth relationships, positive peer relationships and the development of team building (Wright et al, 2014). Best practice within PYD has been defined as engaging with professional artists to deliver high-quality arts programs, consideration of young people as artists in their own right, public and performance events, use of current equipment and technology, and an investment in decision making for the participants. Longitudinal research through the National Endowment for the Arts has shown the transforming ways that young people have engaged with the arts (Hager, 2010). However, as with the previous trend (AI), this agency has often argued for the value of the arts in terms of non-arts goals (academic, social, economic, and so on). Despite using longitudinal research to argue for the importance of 'sustained involvement', there is an overemphasis on the instrumental impacts of the arts and normative assumptions about young people based on a deficit model.

Youth arts programs, as part of PYD, have become a significant feature of urban spaces throughout the world (Poyntz et al, 2019). This has led to the emergence of new artistic and cultural practices which often support marginalised communities. However, this approach has been appropriated by urban regeneration schemes and is subject to forces of gentrification. Tyler Denmead's book *The Creative Underclass: Youth, Race, and the Gentrifying City* (2019) presents a critical exploration of PYD as an approach which supposes 'soul-saving' processes of transforming 'troubled youth' into 'creative youth'. Focusing on the 'performance' of creativity and its relationship to youth, class and race, Denmead argues that 'creatives' are the most desirable kind of urban youth. While he highlights the importance of these programs for activism and the importance of arts practice for social justice movement, his ethnographic study draws our attention to the often unintended adverse effects of cultural policy on young people. Through 'creative youth development' programs, young people are learning to perform particular dispositions such as adopting 'privatised' orientations and accepting personal responsibility. Denmead's research highlights the taken-for-granted assumptions about arts programs as 'positive activities' through which young people can 'better themselves', as a form of moulding the ideal young person (Denmead 2019, 157).

Having explored current trends within youth arts programs, this chapter now goes on to explore alternative ways of configuring youth arts practice. It examines the three themes of common culture, cultural citizenship and cultural democracy, which run throughout the book and are applied analytically to the data from my study on Arts Award (Chapters 4 to 6) and also to the international case study projects (Chapters 7 to 9).

Common culture

The conceptual framework of 'common culture' was coined by Paul Willis (1990) in order to question the distinction between high and low arts. Rather than being a new form of cultural practice, Willis suggested that common culture is a process, whereby young people draw on their available cultural resources as an input for their own cultural productivity in the contexts of their everyday lives. Common culture has a dual significance of being frequently found everywhere, in the everyday, as well as being shared among individuals and groups (Willis, 1990). Willis criticised education and cultural policy's narrow view of culture (Laermans, 1993) and argued for more democratic cultural policies that stimulate the possibilities for all to become cultural producers. He rejected ideas of cultural populism, suggesting instead that we are all artists: 'Let's look to the streets, to the common culture, not to the towers, for what is to be learnt' (Willis, 1990). In arguing for the need to recognise the 'new diversity' and meaning-making from below, Willis emphasises the creation and consumption of different forms such as mass media, fashion, language and the arts.

Willis argued that the arts should no longer be the preserve of these institutions, but instead recognised as part of everyday and ordinary cultural experience, part of our common culture. He highlights 'the hidden continent of the informal' (p 16), where young people significantly participate in cultural practices, focused on their leisure time as 'bedroom culture' (Willis 1990). Rather than seeing people as 'labour power', meaningful only in work, Willis regarded them as full creative citizens who undertake symbolic activities in the construction of their own identities. He argued that young people use symbolic creativity and have learned how to interpret the codes within this media and learned how to play with and reshape them. In arguing that we need to rethink and reclassify what counts as culture, Willis shifts focus onto the cultural activities that are accessible and of real interest to young people. Young people utilise symbolic resources from cultural media and new screen-based technologies in order to be active producers. Therefore, the focus of this book on youth arts programs is through the lens of particular experiences within youth settings that afford the production of artistic works which encompass digital, DIY and everyday arts practices.

Young people today engage with a diverse range of arts practices that include digital technologies and DIY techniques. These arts practices draw on social media as a key stimulus within youth arts. The focus of the everyday in DIY and digital arts practices facilitates connections with young people's existing interests but also others within connected communities. We know that young people locate their own cultural participation in their everyday experiences, with many drawing on the home sphere and bedroom culture as the main sources of artistic activity. Recent research has documented the richness of bedroom culture for arts activities such as lyric writing, music production and gaming (Manchester and Pett, 2015). Technology is a key mechanism, with many young people utilising their personal phones, computers or iPads to undertake these practices and connections made through social media networks rather than physical groupings (Livingstone, 2007). Previous research (Sefton-Green, 1999; Green, 2003; Buckingham, 2008) has demonstrated the centrality of digital practices in young people's experience of culture, including the use of social media in marketing culture as a social endeavour.

Common culture, as well as representing consumption and production, denotes a shared space – be this either physical or virtual – where people come together as a community with a particular shared cultural interest. A 'cultural commons' is defined by the confluence of three dimensions: culture, space and community (Bertacchini et al, 2012). Knowledge, practices and rituals are shared and produced (and reproduced) within this group. Youth arts programs develop shared attitudes, values and cultural resources. Cultural commons in relation to youth arts programs should emphasise principles of open access or universality, democratic values, engaging in cultural and creative activities that can enrich life, offering educational value, social cohesion and global awareness. Within a cultural commons spaces are formed around groups of young people who create together. Aligning with Hickey-Moody's concept of 'little publics' (2013b), young people as audiences of performances develop a sense of 'materiality' of their arts practices, which constitutes a form of citizenship. These draw from everyday practice such as religion, race, the arts and sport. In the case of arts practices for youth run by adults, these little publics are often groups invested in 'the power of the arts' to better society through the inclusion of marginalised young people.

Youth arts programs that draw on sources of everyday creativity are most likely to be engaging for young people. Processes of symbolic creativity (Willis, 1990) are vital for understanding arts education within informal settings. However, as the exploration of key trends has shown, these settings are caught amidst the tension between the benefits of the aesthetic experience (Eisner, 2002) and the instrumentalist perspective (Gaztambide-Fernandez, 2013). Mirroring the AI and PYD programs considered in this chapter, instrumentalist approaches argue that the arts can improve academic achievement, employability, educational engagement and attainment. Whereas intrinsic arguments assert that the presence of the arts enhances individual experiences and perceptions of the world (Thomson et al, 2019a). Common culture, therefore, is a valuable framework through which to engage with youth arts programs as it emphasises intrinsic values, symbolic creativity and a foregrounding of community within youth arts programs.

Cultural citizenship

Cultural citizenship recognises and celebrates difference as part of the diversification and fragmentation of the cosmopolitan tastes of global society (Stevenson, 2003). Not only are these cosmopolitan dispositions displayed through engagement with everyday cultures, but they also acknowledge the less visible and more marginalised groups in society. Cultural citizens are active and choice driven, and are more likely to develop entrepreneurial dispositions and symbolic presence (Pakulski, 1997; Stevenson, 2010). A rights-based approach, where young people have rights to produce and participate (Mai and Gibson, 2011), can claim co-authorship and develop activist practices against cultural exclusion (Boele van Hensbroek, 2010), is upheld. Through this lens the rights to culture are embedded with notions of entitlement, the right to be different and to celebrate diverse identities, where those previously stigmatised are revalued and those marginalised are legitimated (Pakulski, 1997). Practised through everyday life, leisure, critical consumption and popular entertainment, cultural citizenship is embedded within 'practices of identity construction and representation and implicit moral obligations and rights' (Burgess et al, 2006). Both online international social network and offline local programs, in this regard, are designed to engage youth in representing themselves and interacting with the representations of others (Hull et al, 2010). This concept, therefore, holds the possibilities for youth arts programs to offer alternative perspectives, not only on the world around them, but also on what counts as 'culture'. This involves a critical awareness of how the arts are used in processes of opposition and resistance, which can be found in the fields of social justice arts education, community-based arts, youth participatory action research and community cultural development among others.

Recent calls to reframe arts education as a process of developing cultural citizenship (Thomson et Hall 2019b) echoes the value of the arts in supporting participatory democracy and social change (Kuttner, 2015). There is a responsibility of these programs for supporting young people in demonstrating activism, agency and engagement within their cultural lives. Sharing values of the arts for learning about their localities, experiencing citizenship (Talaina Si'isi'ialafia, 2018) and the materiality of arts practices as a form of citizenship (Hickey-Moody et al, 2010), cultural citizenship within youth arts programs puts young people in a strong position to become active in the practices of meaning-making through their own diverse cultural identities (Stevenson, 2003). Much like Hart's ladder of participation (Hart, 2013), Kuttner has developed a scaled typology of cultural citizenship (Kuttner, 2015). He defines three categories of cultural citizenship: (1) *informed cultural citizens*, who have the capacity to understand, appreciate, and critique works of art as an active consumer; (2) *participatory cultural citizens*, who see themselves as active participants who can produce, remix and share work created; (3) *justice-orientated cultural citizens*, who feel a civic responsibility to use their artistic practice to actively promote justice and address inequalities in society. These frameworks will be revisited later on in the book.

However, the term 'citizenship' also denotes particular assumptions (Young, 1989), within 'citizenship education' (Davies et al, 2005) in particular, which raises important questions about what kinds of citizens arts programs prepare young people to be. How do young people create themselves as 'good' or 'bad' citizens? Forms of cultural action are key as they implement forms of active negotiation with the dynamics of social transformation they encounter (Leccardi, 2016). Young people can take an active interest in various manifestations of artistic and art-oriented cultural processes from street art to contemporary digital arts, drawing on a democratic and rights-based approach. The concept of cultural citizenship, in this sense, addresses the right to full participation in the cultural sphere, together with recognition of experiences and identities that are connected to this participation. Citizenship rights are currently expanding towards a new domain of cultural rights that involve the right to symbolic presence, dignifying representation, propagation of identity and maintenance of lifestyles (Pakulski, 1997).

While citizenship has been criticised as a governmentalised version of learning and social control, cultural citizenship has a transformative role in terms of learning processes and impact upon individuals and society (Delanty, 2003). A cultural understanding of citizenship denotes young people working through the arts in their communities, playing strong leadership roles, identifying social needs and calling for a sustainable community. Of primary importance to young people working in the arts across national boundaries are issues related to health, environment, social justice, and human rights (Heath and Robinson, 2004). The struggle for a democratic and autonomous society as opposed to a society ruled by neoliberalism or an authoritarian state is central to the concerns of cultural citizenship (Stevenson, 2010). As such, cultural citizenship is closely linked to educational democracy (Rosaldo, 1994) and raises questions about the impact of capitalism on cultural practices and democratic forms of participation.

Cultural democracy

Cultural democracy is wider than simply access; it relates to production. Therefore, through cultural democracy, everyone can be a producer. This is an important position from which to understand youth arts programs. It is vital that youth arts programs encompass 'meaning-making' from below (Willis, 1990), which incorporates a range of digital and DIY arts practices. Willis' criticism of policy's narrow view of culture evokes genuine democratic cultural policies that stimulate the possibilities for everybody to become fully developed cultural producers. As opposed to the 'ripple effect' mode of communication from centre to periphery proposed through democratisation of culture, cultural democracy leans more towards networks of independent units and is more relevant to the structure of the cultural and creative industries (CCIs), technology and digital arts practices today. We know that the 'better-quality' programs are those that engage with professional artists, and for those programs to be meaningful for the participants, young people need to be positioned as artistic producers, rather than passive consumers.

From an arts policy perspective, cultural democracy resists dominant models of commissioning art to effect social change. Jeffers and Moriarty (2017) argue for cultural democracy as a critical practice, which disrupts expected forms of participation and communication of culture. Through the Campaign for Cultural Democracy and The Manifesto (1986), the ideas of cultural democracy played a key role in thinking about the relationship between art and people and critiqued the source of cultural authority. The value of youth arts programs through this perspective is in challenging preset cultural, social and economic values, and instead focusing on the individual's right to express themselves. This theoretical concept is most aligned to CAYW as an approach and can oppose the instrumentalised approaches of AI and

PYD. Therefore, cultural democracy is a policy approach to providing broader public opportunities for creative engagement, which enables the expression of artistic ideas and the acknowledgement of diverse values within society.

Writing in relation to the Australian context, de Roeper and Savelsberg (2009) argue that instead of focusing specifically on the development of young artists or youth audiences, youth arts programs are intended to challenge young people by offering them opportunities to develop new skills and abilities and change their lives. The focus, therefore, is on an outcome for the young people themselves rather than outcomes for the arts (by producing new artists) or for artists (by developing new audiences). When UK cultural policy opened the door to making the arts accountable for social and economic goals (Jancovich, 2011), cultural democracy was identified as a key discourse offering a counter-formulation of what the aims of cultural policy could and should be (Gross and Wilson, 2020). While Hadley and Belfiore (2018) argue that hierarchies of cultural value have always been, and always will be, embroiled within our cultural lives, the value of cultural democracy is in questioning the power and authority of those positions. Pools of cultural resources historically exclusively accessible for society's elites are now opened up for everyone (Gripsrud, 2000).

Historically, the shift from 'community art' to 'cultural development' was a policy initiative and political discourse intended to reposition the arts within mainstream social and economic aims. Sim (2019) explores an interlocking and often jarring history of the arts and youth work, drawing on the history of community arts as a contested space with shared emancipatory and democratic ideals with youth work. She tracks the shift away from voluntary participation towards coerced and targeted approaches, where the arts are tasked with combating social issues. Sim argues that the fields of youth work and gallery education 'emerged out of similar social and political movements and have fostered similar critical and moral values' (p 67). She reminds us that whereas youth work has fallen out of favour with successive UK governments, the arts – based on the democratisation of culture model – have not. Therefore, cultural democracy represents a new arena for youth arts programs to share democratic aims and community-responsive approaches. Beneficially for youth arts programs, cultural democracy has developed as a way to acknowledge a variety of cultural activities and recognise all young people as artistic producers. Therefore, youth arts programs that seek to expand cultural opportunities for young people hold value.

Conclusion

Through exploring three global trends in youth arts practice – CAYW, AI and PYD, this chapter has identified how youth arts programs are positioned differently across the world. CAYW can be seen to enhance practice because it challenges what counts as learning, youth work and creativity. This approach draws on the arts as a tool for the holistic development of young people by taking part in arts activities and the development of youth workers' practice. AI and PYD, on the other hand, incorporate wider educational, social and economic aims, which, while being important objectives of some programs, lend themselves to instrumentalisation in others. This has opened up criticisms towards assumptions of these programs to 'transform' troubled youth. The conflation of intrinsic affordances with extrinsic social and economic impacts was also highlighted. This chapter has demonstrated that these trends within current youth arts programs highlight different ways arts programs function and the differing outcomes for the young people involved.

The key theoretical frameworks for the book were also introduced, in an attempt to offer alternative conceptualisations of youth arts programs. I explored common culture as the 'new diversity' and meaning-making from below, including symbolic creativity through different forms such as mass media, fashion, language and the arts. Cultural citizenship was examined as the development of diverse cultural practices and identities alongside full participation in cultural and political life. Finally, cultural democracy provided a lens through which to acknowledge a variety of cultural activities and recognise all young people as artistic producers. It must be acknowledged that cultural citizenship and cultural democracy bear many similarities to the tradition of social pedagogy: a strong focus upon relationships, increasing engagement and agency, and drawing upon the rights of the individual in challenging social problems and social injustice (Jones and Brady, 2022). However, for the analysis within this book, cultural citizenship and cultural democracy were selected for their application to arts programs in particular. While there are synergies in relation to bringing to public consciousness major global issues such as xenophobia and social exclusion, and campaigns such as School Strike 4 Climate and Black Lives Matter, my arguments within the book suggest that arts practices should not be valued for social outcomes only. These frameworks will continue throughout the book, first within my analysis of Arts Award, a UK-based arts program; and secondly, in Part III of the book, which presents six international case study programs.

Having investigated the emergent practices and conceptual landscape of youth arts programs today, the following chapter will explore how young people are positioned by such programs.

3

Knowing young people

Getting to know young people is a key skill of youth workers. However, a youth worker's perception of a young person, or group of young people, may differ, for example, from that of government bodies and local agencies, youth program funders they work for, and managers and project organisers they work with. At some point a young person's lived reality becomes translated into a statistic, a funding bid, a policy document that contains a generic description where they are frequently assigned a 'label'. This was a key piece of personal learning that I faced in my fieldwork, through the realisation that in colluding with these labels, usually for the purposes of levying funding to run youth arts projects, I may have disadvantaged the young people that I worked with on a longer-term basis. This is a tension that many youth arts workers may face in their practice today.

In response, this chapter will examine the problematic labels which are placed upon groups of young people. I starting by unpacking the definition of *deficit* in relation to youth and considering the implications for social governance and assumptions of negative difference. I explore a variety of labels that have been assigned to young people whose social backgrounds, behaviours and educational attainments have been considered less desirable. While these labels have changed over time and differ according to professional context, I focus on three prevalent labels: 'at-risk', 'NEET' and 'hard-to-reach'. I argue that underpinning these labels is an economic focus, such as young people as an economic risk, and instead, I explore intersecting social, political and cultural perspectives.

Through charting the proliferation of deficit discourses in society, a link can be drawn to a variety of moral panics across the decades. A critique of deficit frames of youth work is given, which provides an important position to challenge the quality of arts pedagogies offered to disadvantaged young people. Following this, the impact upon arts programs is examined, where I argue that for those young people taking up arts programs under deficit labels, the opportunities and offer are restricted. Where young people access arts programs often dictates what kind of practices and pedagogies they receive (Howard, 2022b). This raises issues of social justice about the conditions of learning, cultural recognition and entitlement that can become aspects of oppression for young people under these categorisations.

The deficit model of youth

Understanding the deficit model of youth is one of the key objectives that I aim to achieve through my teaching. For students to understand that the conditions which young people face are not individualised, they are not of their own making and are in fact structural, is a key piece of learning for all students wanting to go on and work with young people. How we can contest this model, which is firmly embedded within benchmarks and measurements related to young people, is an ongoing debate. Schnorr and Ware (2001), for example, recommend that educators should consider developing environments within which 'at-risk' youth can develop positive self-appraisals, while recognising that this does not mean devaluing their peers or the social groups from which they come. Emphasis should be placed upon individual growth and development rather than social comparisons. Te Riele (2006), however, prefers the use of 'marginalised' as a label, arguing that the marginalised are no longer a minority, with risk being capable of reaching every young person. These alternative perspectives and perceptions are often overlooked within an economic viewpoint on young people.

In the UK since the days of New Labour, policy initiatives have focused on young people's 'services' as an intervention and this was explored in the previous chapter in relation to a key trend in youth arts programs that take an interventionist stance. Through this approach, the UK government has been one of the worst offenders in demonising young people, and the landscape of previously democratic and emancipatory forms of youth work has been superseded (Davies, 2013). In response, there has been a clash between the emergence of more interventionist policy, which is based on the deficit model of youth and more established practices of working with young people (Nolas, 2014). Youth 'at risk' in Australian education policy and programs has tended to simplistically focus on personal attributes of the young people, positing a supposed problematic minority versus a 'normal' majority (Te Riele, 2006). Young people defined as socially excluded through deficit policy are regularly depicted as deviant, drawing attention to individual young people, rather than the wider society.

The different professions that work with young people, from education to youth work to youth offending, invoke diverse 'standards' by which deficits are judged. Particular attributes are 'normalised' against categorisations of 'loss', 'lack' and 'failure' (Candlin and Crichton, 2010). This is often without the knowledge and actions of the young people involved. These categories are ascribed to them. Data collected on young people under these categorisations is often inadequate and misleading as the deficit model of youth focuses on what is 'wrong' with people or rather what they lack. This approach fails to investigate the factors in a young person's life that lead to healthy development (MacDonald and Valdivieso, 2001). Therefore, a key criticism levelled at the deficit model of youth is based around the underlying assumption that young people, in particular those from disadvantaged areas, are uniformly deficient and in need of development (Nols et al, 2017). As a result, where categorisation of young people is done by social background, rather than individual needs, which is reliant on stereotypes and assumptive profiling, these programs rarely achieve their intended objectives.

In relation to youth arts programs, which is the particular focus of this book, Hickey-Moody (2013b) critiques the popular use of youth arts as forms of social governance that tend to be connected to particular media practices of representing and characterising young people. In addition to this, she highlights the development of knowledge systems through which young people are encouraged to understand themselves as being 'at risk', highlighting problematic implications for youth arts programs in the reproduction of clichés and stereotypes. This approach to programming takes for granted the lived experienced of young people and their valued arts practices. In identifying and calling out these deficit discourses of youth, it is possible to carve out an alternative reality in which the cultural lives and cultural values of all young people are acknowledged and celebrated.

Labelling youth

A variety of labels have been assigned to young people whose social backgrounds, behaviours and educational attainment have been considered less desirable. These labels have developed in response to particular political regimes and policies, which differ according to professional context. Macdonald's (2008) key text on the 'Underclass' highlights an inherent weakness with social exclusion policies, prompting us to ask who or what is doing the excluding and excluding from where. Fahmy's 'Tackling youth exclusion in the UK: challenges of current policy and practice' (2008) echoes this paradox of the social integrationist agenda, where in an economically driven society, where education and work are positioned as the only ways out of poverty, a narrative of young people as young workers but not necessarily as young citizens is upheld. Therefore, if a young person is deemed unsuccessful in either of these areas, they are further excluded, reaffirming the underlying assumptions driving policy.

Labelling theory, as the theory of how the self-identity and behaviour of individuals may be determined or influenced by the terms used to describe or classify them (Goffman, 2003), has implicit associations with notions of self-fulfilling prophecy and stereotyping. Previous research has demonstrated that the stigma of a powerfully negative label changes a person's self-concept and social identity (Yardley, 2008). Therefore, the labels that are placed upon young people represent a form of social constructionism, whereby youth are unknowingly categorised, which has implications for a young person's future life. This chapter contributes to the growing body of evidence from research about the adverse effect of labels upon young people. The following section considers this literature under three common labels found in youth arts programs: 'at-risk', 'NEET' and 'hard-to-reach'.

Youth 'at risk'

The policy framework surrounding 'at risk' places the individual under a spotlight of blame and does not take into account surrounding social and economic situations. This terminology does not recognise the complexities of life, and how many or multiple 'at risk' factors may overlap in a young person's life. Turnbull and Spence's article 'What's at risk? The proliferation of risk across child and youth policy in England' (2011) argues that these labels are used as 'tools of blame' for different social problems. They list factors of risk, such as poor parenting, truancy, exclusion or underachievement, aggressive or hyperactive behaviour, peer group pressure, lack of training and employment, drug or alcohol abuse, being raised by criminal parents, and so on. The language used in policy documents reflects a language of danger and surveillance, where young people who are 'putting their own futures at risk' are in need of protection, intervention and preventative measures. Te Riele (2006) argues that young people 'at risk' are perceived as being disconnected from family and society (a lack of social capital), as not knowing what to do with their lives (a lack of identity capital), and as not valuing or even rejecting the importance of education (lack of cultural capital). Taking a preventative approach to working with young people classified as 'at risk' focuses on the negative, on a deficit model, which has become a fascination of policy makers (MacDonald and Valdivieso, 2001). The logic here is predicting patterns of future behaviour based upon a set of indicators, which are not based upon current behaviours but rather on membership in a demographic category with which trouble has been associated.

Within the education field, 'at risk' is used interchangeably with labels of poverty and ethnicity. Hickey-Moody (2013b) argues that

[f]or almost two centuries, poor children, who were often non-white and/or from non-dominant cultures, were perceived to be 'at risk' because of the financial drain they posed to society. This fear of increased state spending on welfare and prisons resulted in the establishment of public schools and the implementation of laws for compulsory schooling. Through educational discourses, risk was located within the individual or family, rather than society or culture. What is implicit in this characterization of risk is the impetus for society to take control of the individual or family who is possibly at risk, in order to avert future costs to society. (Hickey-Moody, 2013b, p 53)

'At-risk' students, therefore, are statistically more likely to leave secondary school early and be unable to transition into the workforce. This is often conflated with the psychological connotations of risk as those young people who are seen as having the potential to develop emotional and behavioural problems. From a Foucauldian perspective, this label represents a new form of governance of youth, further illustrating the ways moral panics contribute to the governability of society through the deployment of strategies for the attribution of risk (Kelly, 2006).

Young people 'not in education, employment and training'

Similar criticisms have been directed towards the label NEET in signifying negative difference and projecting disadvantage onto those labelled. NEET is a policy discourse, which promoted education and employment as a way of tackling social exclusion and driving the economy. Schemes were developed to engage young people in work or training programs, in order to combat youth unemployment, situating NEET within economic discourse. These schemes offered low-level, non-academic qualifications, which were seen as more suited to those who had not succeeded in a mainstream education environment with a traditional curriculum. Again, this label has a focus on individualisation (the individual standing on their own two feet and finding their own way), rather than acknowledging underlying social and economic issues. Simmons and Thompson (2011) argue that NEET young people are seen as *in* trouble but also *as* trouble as many 'churn' between participation and non-participation, while alternative causes of unemployment such as a lack of job opportunities, low levels of demand for skill, or economic policy tend to be ignored.

Particular sub-groups are identified within this category: those seeking work, young parents, and those with disability or illness (Simmons et al, 2013). This highlights the transitory period of the NEET categorisation, however the longer-term impacts of this label are rarely acknowledged. A common identifier in NEET young people is poor educational experience and low aspirations. However, these identifiers are misconceptions; as Finlay et al's (2010) research demonstrates, young people's expectations, rather than aspirations, are low and these expectations were based on their empirical observations of the life chances of people 'like them'. In tracing the genealogy of NEET, Wrigley's (2019) research highlights that the label has become a key concern in media discourse, social welfare, academia and globalised policy concerning young people. Drawing on the work of Diane Reay (2017), Wrigley explores the label as part of a 'neoliberal vocabulary', which effectively ignores the structural disadvantages that young people face. His research exposes how young people identified as NEET have been reconstructed as agents of self-action and self-management, tasked with becoming self-governing citizens in an era of austerity. In critically analysing the assumptions that underpin these labels, the damaging practice and perspectives these vocabularies leave can be explored.

'Hard-to-reach' youth

Whereas the categorisation NEET is derived from discourses around education and employment, 'hard to reach' is located within the realm of community and participation. This label is most frequently applied to young people in the domain of local politics and is often used in health campaigns or social marketing in targeting 'hidden populations'. Local governments find some groups in society more difficult to engage than others, due to one or a combination of factors, which include disengagement, difference, disability or lifestyle. Young people who are 'hard to reach' are often described as disinterested, disadvantaged or facing particular barriers to participation, whereas it could be argued that what makes people hard to reach is not their distinctive characteristics, but simply the inability of local authorities to reach particular populations (Brackertz, 2007). This raises questions about who is doing the 'reaching' and how they are doing it.

Therefore, the 'hard-to-reach' label can be viewed as a political issue, whereby groups who are considered 'hard to reach' or disengaged from society are simply not interested in participating in local politics. In terms of youth arts programs, 'hard to reach' is interpreted as those who do not usually participate in the arts or those who have barriers which prevent them from participating. Assumptions are made about 'access' to arts programs, equating to 'inclusion' and an overemphasis on the social impacts of the arts as a vehicle to include all young people. Publicly funded arts and culture have been positioned by policy as integral to a civilised society and a flourishing economy, where an established connection between education and culture serves economic and social inclusion agendas (Buckingham and Jones, 2001). Therefore, those young people who are not engaging with the 'high' arts and culture are seen as not participating.

By examining the theoretical underpinnings and inherent assumptions in the terms 'at-risk', 'NEET' and 'hard-to-reach', I have been able to raise some important questions about the political and governance dimensions of these attributions. With an ever-growing policy focus on prevention and intervention, could the net be cast so wide that it encompasses every young person at some stage in their life? Each of the three labels explored contributes to a deficit discourse on youth, which has adverse implications for the future of individuals and particular groups. Deficit discourses, as exposed by the work of Foucault (1975), highlight practices of discipline and governance of young people which produce young people in similar ways, whether that be moral panic or risk. They are discursive structures fuelled by media, political stereotypes and universalising assumptions. Having explored the deficit model of youth, I move on to consider what happens when labelled youth or young people facing deficit discourses engage with arts programs.

Impact on youth arts programs

Research on arts programs targeted at young people under deficit labels has shown that these programs have had life-changing impacts on participants, have engaged and empowered young people from all social backgrounds and have demonstrated long-lasting psychological, social and ultimately economic benefits (de Roeper and Savelsberg, 2009). Arts activities have been employed to attract and retain the young people, and reduce offending behaviour and social exclusion by keeping them 'out of trouble' (Arts Council England, 2004). They have impacted upon 'soft outcomes' such as confidence and communication skills, which can be seen as contributing towards hard outcomes such as employment (Jermyn, 2004). Research has demonstrated that engaging young people in productive activities such as arts programs can contribute to altering offending behaviour (YJB, 2008), offering an 'affective experience' which includes feelings of self-satisfaction and achievement linked to desistance from crime (Arts Alliance, 2013). Arts programs can enhance and extend provision of educational, developmental and therapeutic programs across the criminal justice sector (Hughes et al, 2005). However, despite there being compendiums of evidence around the value of arts programs for 'at-risk' youth, the quality of the programs they receive has never been questioned.

Claims made in previous research around the assumed benefits of arts programs with young people under deficit labels can now be questioned. For example, several research reports, including 'Doing Well and Going Good by Doing Art' (Catterall, 2009; 2012) have reported that arts-involved young people with low socio-economic status have improved 'academic' and 'civic behaviour' outcomes compared to those who are not arts involved. Programs that engaged young people in cultural opportunities were assumed to be a good thing, for both the individuals involved and wider society. However, the assertions that the arts 'do good' have been critiqued, based on an instrumentalised viewpoint of the arts, whereby culture becomes tasked with social impacts (Merli, 2002; Belfiore, 2010; 2012). This chapter argues that labelling young people has an impact on the kinds of arts programs they receive. This raises questions of equity, highlighting which groups of young people have access to particular practices and pedagogies and how this can impact their future pathways. For example, those who demonstrate 'talent' are often deemed worthy of 'platforming', and those who demonstrate obedient behaviours are deemed worthy of reintegration within mainstream schooling.

As arts programs, such as undertaking a graffiti mural, offer alternative modes of citizenship practice (Baker, 2015) for young people, the involvement in hip-hop culture also serves as a source of identity formation. Rap and the artistic production of self-imagery provide alternative cultural forms for young people to express themselves, which is currently absent from mainstream schooling contexts (Brooks et al, 2015). Globally, youth programs have increasingly turned to music for young people likely to be or already convicted of criminal behaviour, as described in the AI approach in the previous chapter. Earlier research has argued that there are implications of drawing on hip-hop music, with its themes of deviance and resistance, as a creative vehicle within a broader environment of 'offender to citizen' discourses for the youth involved (Baker and Homan, 2007). Tyler Denmead (2019), for example, argues that 'creatives' are the most desirable kind of urban youth, and his critical exploration of the supposed 'soul-saving' processes of transforming 'troubled youth' into 'creative youth' highlights who benefits from their human capital. The preparation of the underclass to be ideal 'subject-citizens' (Bansel, 2015) through arts engagement is investigated alongside an expectation that creative young people will be successful, upwardly mobile and ready to serve the labour market. There is a need to destabilise the taken-for-granted assumptions about arts activities as 'positive activities', through which young people can 'better themselves'.

Previous research has highlighted a 'binary divide' between 'high-functioning' young people and others who face 'remedial orientation'. These sociological divisions have implications for attending arts programs under deficit labels which frequently 'ignore the different biases of identity among young people' (de Roeper and Savelsberg, 2009). Labelled young people are more likely to receive a limited offer of arts practices and pedagogical processes that are aligned to monitoring, tracking and performativity. Under these conditions the arts become viewed as a deviant rather than 'culturally sanctioned' activity:

> The provision of cultural programmes for 'at-risk' young people is often viewed as premature and a waste of resources, as these young people are deemed developmentally unready. Indeed, there is evidence that the art of 'at-risk' young people may be actively shunned and discouraged. That is, popular arts such as rap music, breakdancing, and spray painting and graffiti are deemed to promote an unhealthy, confrontational and sometimes illegal subculture. Here the 'moral panics' about feral youth come into play, while the school-based education and development of those young people deemed 'on track' is augmented with extra-curricular engagement in culturally sanctioned activities and programmes. (de Roeper and Savelsberg, 2009, p 220)

Where young people arrive at (or are referred to) arts programs under deficit labelling, decision making and agency are notably absent. Program Managers may well recognise the tensions in their policies of targeting 'at-risk' youth, while those young people may be actively discouraged if it is seen 'to promote an unhealthy, confrontational and sometimes illegal subculture' (Rimmer, 2012). Funders who target 'at-risk' youth in order to provide structured activities, which are viewed in a more positive light, could stifle the young people's creativity, which engagement with those art forms is seeking to encourage. In addition, assumptions that youth arts programs can make up for 'gaps' in publicly funded arts and culture by enabling 'access' may simply result in the affirmation of those groups who are deemed to 'lack' possession of culturally valued resources. Due to the misrecognition of everyday forms of cultural activity, 'official' provision of culture both excludes and relegates those groups to a status associated with lower positions in the social structure (O'Brien, 2010). Therefore, from a sociological perspective, it is troubling that arts programs can claim to include *all* young people. Anna Hickey-Moody (2013b) has previously argued that arts programs run for young people by adults can often offer an extension of deficit discourses that uses the arts as a way to responsibilise their subjects. In this way youth arts practice is presented as a form of self-improvement, when, in reality, the programming and application of youth arts programs for labelled youth is unequal and leads to disadvantage (Howard, 2022a). Part II of this book will demonstrate that access to arts programs is often socially streamed and what is offered to young people facing deficit terms is a social justice issue. It is important to raise awareness of this risky terrain so that prejudice is not reinforced as this represents an ethical dilemma for those working with the arts and young people.

Risky terrain

Where youth arts programs have been given the task of 'social improvement' or place an emphasis on instrumental purposes, the value of engaging with the arts is shifted away from expressive forms, identity development and well-being towards accreditation, hard outcomes and transferable skills. This instrumentalised emphasis becomes hard to substantiate and puts both youth work and the arts in risky terrain (Howard, 2017). Previous research has questioned whether the desire to 'do good' has actually obscured the most innovative and engaging approach to arts programs with youth 'at risk', focusing instead on instrumental benefits (O'Brien and Donelan, 2008). However, we know that for young people one of the most appealing features of CAYW is arts experiences through 'everyday creativity'. Jones (2014) argues that the 'everyday' deserves more recognition as reductive and deficit models fail to 'notice' how young people are being resourceful and creative, and succeeding within their own spheres of everyday life. In addition, when value judgements were removed, along with pressure to create something 'good', and when the level of skill became irrelevant, young people were more likely to become engaged (Karkou and Glasman, 2004).

Where youth arts programs are frequently positioned as mechanisms of 'self-salvation', the arts become a tool for self-evaluation and self-management. Hickey-Moody (2013b) argues that programs specifically designed for at-risk young people often problematically replicate prevailing neoliberal logics of individualisation, responsibilisation and the naturalisation of deficit. Therefore youth 'at risk' are simply recreated through these programs as 'subjects of their practice'. Expectations of transformation for youth under deficit terms means that youth arts programs can become sites of governance where young people, under the spotlight of moral panic due to perceived deviant behaviour, are expected to 'perform' a new form of constructed youth subjectivity (Denmead, 2019). This critical questioning of the purposes and intentions of labelling young people accessing arts programs extends particular critiques of risk discourses, which actually enable such discourses, namely through the mobilisation and mediatisation of moral panics (Kelly, 2011).

In this chapter I have considered the impact of labels on young people but also on the arts programs they experience. Those that depicted a negative view of these young people held detrimental and potentially stigmatising representations. Despite the successes of arts programs with 'at-risk' young people, they continue to exacerbate an educational and sociological divide. I argue that these programs enter risky terrain when it is not 'the arts' that are valued, but rather other outcomes such as access to services, educational and employment outcomes, and 'transferrable skills'. These kinds of programs, which have to demonstrate instrumental benefits, could be viewed as much less effective than those that simply value the impact of arts learning and participation. Remedial programs designed for 'at-risk' youth led to stereotyping of this group as non-academic, having lower-value forms of culture and gaining soft skills, which are of little value to employers. The arts are often considered as secondary outcomes of these programs, with a large amount of participants' time spent on behaviour management and mentoring. Numeracy and literacy targets can dilute arts provision, with the instrumental assumptions of policy that underpin these programs recognising only economic and social outcomes. It is important that we interrogate these assumptions about the arts as a social project and that we consider how to influence future policy so that it begins to value more holistic and human perspectives as 'measurement'.

Conclusion

This chapter has explored the labels which are placed on groups of young people and the problematic implications of these. The deficit model has emphasised social comparisons rather than individual growth and development. I offered an analysis of 'at-risk', 'NEET' and 'hard-to-reach', in particular, which have tended to focus on deviance amplification in order to justify need for intervention. Youth policy has had implications for social governance and assumptions of deficit, which has developed a 'risk rhetoric' where discourses are universalised and fundamentally negative. Arts programs have been caught up in this tangled web and tasked with 'doing good' by targeting young people with undesirable characteristics through a form of creative transformation.

I have made the case for the need to be more critical about the arts' claims of impact with labelled youth. There is real danger that the sustainability and future funding of youth arts programs becomes based on measurable outcomes and instrumental values. What youth arts programs do really well, and what this book will draw upon later, is the expression, articulation and often interrogation of young people's personal journeys. What is good about youth arts programs is the process rather than the product, the experience rather than the end point, and the overcoming of obstacles rather than an outcome. Viewing the value of youth arts programs as 'hard' outcome driven situates them in risky terrain, not only due to their future sustainability, evidence and claims making, but also because of the impact of reproduction of stereotypes and labels for young people.

In this chapter I have argued that for those young people taking up arts programs under deficit labels, the opportunities and offer were restricted. Research has shown that there are many beneficial affordances of arts programs within youth work settings, despite the instrumentalisation of the arts by programs that take a 'targeted' approach, such as working with 'at-risk' youth. This chapter has highlighted a social justice issue, by which the most disadvantaged young people get a lower-quality offer. Positioned on this spectrum by adults, a misrecognition about young people's behaviour and assumed creative ability meant that 'at-risk' youth were offered the least opportunities. A key failure within policy is the lack of acknowledgement of how arts programs, which are practised differently in different settings, can be reproductive in nature. This will be further explored through the example of Arts Award in Part II of the book, where an in-depth example is given through my own doctoral research into the UK-based program.

Part II

Part 1

4

Researching Arts Award in youth work settings

Part II of this book focuses on my research on a British-based arts program – Arts Award – within the context of youth work settings. The desire to undertake this research was prompted by my own background as a youth arts worker, working for local authority youth services within Nottingham. In this chapter, I introduce the Arts Award program and my ethnographic methodology and describe the three diverse settings in which I had the privilege of being a participant-observer for a year. Drawing on qualitative data from my study, I seek to capture the young people's diverse experiences of the Arts Award program within youth settings. In addition, I share initial interviews with a small group of youth workers conducted at the beginning of my study. Methodologically, I recount the tensions within 'insider ethnography' and argue for the synergy of youth work values and ethics in conducting research.

In the second part of this chapter, I give a synopsis of my findings in relation to the affordances of Arts Award within youth work settings and argue that despite the award being a 'good fit' with the informal education practices of youth work, there was a real danger that this program would instrumentalise the experience of working with the arts. In support, I demonstrate the alignment with youth work practice, which includes dialogue, relationship building, a sense of ownership and the co-production of knowledge. In addition, I highlight the value of the arts as a 'tool' for youth work. However, I also show how the program was used as a tool for monitoring and controlling behaviour of some young people. Practices of austerity youth work are presented in order to explore how the arts can be translated into instrumental and measured forms of youth work.

What is Arts Award?

Arts Award is a national qualification that is growing in popularity, in particular within youth, community and informal education sectors. Anyone aged up to 25 can take part in Arts Award Explore, with Bronze, Silver and Gold open to ages 11 and above. Not only a school-based program, young people can work towards the award at an arts and cultural organisation, a youth club or anywhere that registers itself as a 'centre'. These centres must employ a trained 'Adviser', who can be any adult with a minimum of three years' experience in working with young people. Within youth settings the Advisers are principally youth workers, who may or may not have arts interests and skills and be practising artists. Their key role is to design the program for young people to follow and to support them in gathering 'evidence' for their portfolio. In youth work settings, this program most frequently takes the shape of weekly drop-in sessions, conducted over a term or a year, depending on the level of award undertaken.

As Arts Award recognises a wide spectrum of art forms and activities that make up the arts within small groups and youth groups, young people are more able to set their own scheme of work in art forms of their choice. This is a key strategy of Arts Award in terms of inclusion. However, there are common threads to each part of the award, which grow in complexity, total qualification time (Bronze 60 hours, Silver 95 hours, Gold 150 hours), level of responsibility and self-guided learning required by young people with each level. These include:

- *Arts Practice:* this is a practical and artistic activity. Some undertake a one-off workshop, whereas others work at developing a specific art form for many months. Key to this part is reflection from the young person on how their art form knowledge and skills have developed.
- *Arts Research:* this is a learning and researching activity. Young people are encouraged to learn about artists who inspire them, to be the audience for 'live' arts events, and to participate in opportunities hosted by local arts organisations. Key to this part is reflection from the young person on what they have found out.
- *Arts Leadership:* this is a skills development activity. Young people take up a leadership role, with an emphasis on planning activities and the role of communication. This varies from a simple 'skill-sharing' activity to more complex leadership projects, including managing a whole performance, workshop series or public event. There is usually a performance or sharing element to this activity.

Once the Adviser has assessed the portfolios, a visiting Moderator then moderates these. At the time of writing, the cost per individual portfolio is Bronze £24.50, Silver £30 and Gold £45, however there is a minimum moderation charge of £490.[1] The other costs of Arts Award, such as practical activities, visits to arts events, support for the young people and moderation costs, are usually covered by the centre through arts or education funding and occasionally by financial contribution from parents. Arts Award does have an open application Access Fund, of up to £1,500 per centre, which is available twice per year for work with 'disadvantaged' young people. Funders of youth arts programs, such as Arts Council England and Youth Music, look favourably on proposals with an Arts Award component as they provide a measurable accredited outcome for young people. However, this has frequently led to the award becoming an 'add-on' rather than a stand-alone program within youth work settings.

Launched in 2005, Arts Award is a major initiative set up by Arts Council England and is now accredited by Trinity College London. Historically, following the Children Act 2004, Arts Award is one of the initiatives created to afford universal access to the arts for young people living in poverty, and is tasked with the inclusion of *all* young people. In the National Review of Cultural Education (Henley, 2012), the award is heralded as a 'valuable and valued qualification' (p 45), designed to 'support access' (p 13) and raise cultural capital in all young people through publicly funded arts and culture. Fleming (2008) described the approach as 'a government-initiated programme, … charged with developing an arts learning framework for all young people, and especially those less likely to engage in the arts or benefit from existing cultural provision'. By its 15th year, 563,973[2] awards had been achieved by young people. As a 'vocationally relevant' qualification, the award can support young people to progress into further education and employment. It holds an unusual hybrid position as an award which incorporates academic knowledge that can afford entry to higher education, in addition to offering vocational practice, in the form of work experience, which holds value for employment in the arts and CCIs. This hybridity as a qualification is designed to address a classed take-up for the arts, by seeking to develop audiences for the arts and routes to employment for young people.

Arts Award's inception, in the political context of New Labour, saw a new funding landscape for both youth work and the arts, which resulted in new contracts, outcomes and forms of measurement. Davies (2013) argues that the already low standing of youth work as a distinct educational practice was superseded by a preoccupation with 'protection' and 'safeguarding'. In Chapter 3 of this book I explored how shifts in youth policy towards 'targeted support' for 'at-risk' or 'vulnerable' young people has had a negative impact on arts programs. Underpinning this policy was an assumption that the arts and creativity would magically somehow transform society. The political context within which Arts Award was developed is significant in the context of the shifts in cultural policy and the 'sidelining' of youth work. Despite New Labour's good intentions in embracing the 'Every Child Matters' policy (DfES, 2003), youth work as a profession became reframed as a complement to others, such as education, mental health and employment (Wylie, 2015). Furthermore, New Labour's 'cultural turn' (Buckingham and Jones, 2001) established a connection between education and culture, in particular with economic and social inclusion agendas. Top-down 'managerialist' agendas further shifted the provision of youth arts work to focus on 'prevention', targeting deficit-labelled groups (Davies, 2013), and measurement by 'bums on seats' and defensive instrumentalism (Belfiore, 2012; McDonnell, 2014).

Within my research on Arts Award, I took the decision to focus on its application and utilisation within youth work settings. This included both open access youth clubs and targeted programs aimed at 'labelled youth'. Stemming from my previous experience working with the award, I found that it had been an effective tool for engaging with small groups of young people, developing their arts interests and providing an opportunity to undertake more personalised one-to-one work. Therefore, my focus was on a small cohort of young people, from non-arts backgrounds, who generally did not engage with arts education in schools and often faced other forms of marginalisation such as living in poverty, being in care, being unemployed or being outside of mainstream education. Nationally, this group makes up a small but growing percentage of the total take up of Arts Award at 11 per cent.[3]

Aim and objectives of the research

This research aimed to explore the varying arts activities and how they impacted upon the experiences of young people on Arts Award programs. In investigating both the opportunities and constraints of Arts Award for young people experiencing it through youth work settings, I intended to demonstrate the different offerings and experiences of the program for young people accessing the award through these settings. The objectives for the research were as follows:

- to explore the award within the context of current debates about the arts and culture, youth work and education;
- to describe the first-hand individual experiences of this particular group of young people undertaking the award;
- to investigate what arts practices young people chose to engage with from the different programs;
- to examine the differing pedagogies on offer from youth work settings; and
- to consider the implications for the design of future arts programs.

Working across three different youth settings enabled me to develop a multi-sited perspective and to compare the sites of study and the differing offer for young people. Beatboxers[4] was a contemporary and street dance program that ran one evening per week. It was funded by the local authority and took referrals of young people categorised as NEET. The FRESH program was a music and visual arts scheme run by a local education charity. Funded by Youth Music,[5] young people could access the program three times a week, if they were considered as 'facing challenging circumstances'. The Youth Media program was a national youth charity scheme working with digital art forms, including music, radio and film making. As an open access youth arts program young people could drop in to different art form sessions after school on different days of the week. These three sites were based in the East Midlands of England, a geographical location which enabled my travel, as a researcher, to attend on a weekly basis. There were a total of 46 participants for the research, who took part in varying degrees from one-off interviews to frequent interviews, shadowing days and the creation of collaborative arts-based work. The participants were recruited through the youth workers leading the projects, and not all young people within the Arts Award programs took part in the research. The ages of the participants ranged from 14 to 23 and they participated in the research on a voluntary basis and self-selected following a briefing session. In addition, three youth workers were interviewed for this research. Fifty interviews were undertaken, but some participants were interviewed several times throughout the programs, which lasted up to a year. A total of 432 hours were spent undertaking fieldwork in these youth settings.

A previous impact study has been commissioned on Arts Award, which had been primarily limited to quantitative data, with additional interviews with Advisers and other stakeholders (Hollingworth, 2016). Some young people were followed up for case study, however these were deemed 'high arts achievers' with notable and inspiring arts pathways to higher education or arts employment. The findings focused on 'hard' and 'soft' outcomes, without challenging the connotations of these for different groups of young people taking up the award. One of the future recommendations of the impact study was further investigation into the unconventional educational trajectories facilitated by Arts Award, given the potential openings for disadvantaged young people. Arts Award literature has argued that the award offers greater impact for 'harder to reach' (Arts Award, 2014, p 6) young people and in contexts outside the school environment. Addressing these limitations and in an attempt to fill these gaps, my ethnographic study produced rich individual stories, as a significantly different approach from that which had previously been taken.

An insider ethnographic study

My methodological strategy for undertaking the research was to generate data in order to present case studies based on the differing sites of study. I drew on a qualitative methodology, which included interviews and arts-based methods, and took the decision to undertake an ethnographic study so that I could enjoy a long time in the field and observe the practice of others. However, my focus was not on the Advisers directly; I was more attuned to the experiences of the young people undertaking the award as I acted as a participant-observer (Hammersley and Atkinson, 2007). I willingly took part in the arts activities alongside the young people in order to foreground an embodied experience and the participants' perspective (Howard, 2021b). The ethnographic methods for this study consisted of participant observation, participation in arts activities and one-to-one interviews, alongside arts-based research methods such as photography, collage, lyric writing and filmmaking. These activities were embedded within the young people's Arts Award programs from the outset and were supported by the youth workers working on these programs. The artistic methods produced a range of creative data, which was frequently used as a springboard for conversation and as a dataset in itself, alongside other arts-based artefacts such as the young people's Arts Award portfolios. Artistic work created by the young people such as music, lyrics, films and visual artwork were also analysed, as well as attendance at performance events and informal arts networks. Using this assortment of methods captured additional dimensions in order to generate a greater depth of data and allowed for an exploration of the particulars of young people's experience.

My approach to ethnography was influenced by my background as a youth worker and involved sustained 'hanging around' in various youth settings, building rapport with young people and adapting to different environments as they did (Russell, 2013). I engaged with these ethnographic research methods because they enabled an approach in youth settings that necessitated spending time with young people and joining in activities (Curtis et al, 2004), utilising informal learning experiences found in the everyday (Batsleer, 2008), and developing human relationships with participants as a reflexive and participatory approach (Atkins, 2013). However, as a participant-observer within ethnographic research, there was often a tension between participation and observation, knowing how much to get involved and when to sit back. A background in youth work guided some decisions about when to take part in creative activities and when to become less visible, in particular during difficult situations. In addition, being an insider in the Arts Award program meant that I had strong prior knowledge and personal investment in the field, with experience of delivering programs. However, this held disadvantages in relation to assumptions based on my practice and the ability to take an objective view, as someone who was there as a researcher and no longer a program organiser.

Ethnographic fieldwork and qualitative methods afforded continuous spirals of data collection, hypothesis building and theory testing through a grounded theory approach (Charmaz, 2014) rather than simply recording one-off events. Data was then coded and categorised under the four components of Arts Award, which made up the analysis of themes within my study: policy, practice, pedagogy and pathways. Part II of this book reflects on two key categories of data: practice, which included an exploration of what art forms young people took up; and pedagogy, which involved an analysis of the different ways that youth workers worked with the program.

The quotations and visual data used throughout the book come from these two areas of analysis.

Youth work values and ethics

The approach to the research and the view of the participants was influenced by an axiology of youth work values and previous work experience with Arts Award and young people. The particular dispositions I brought from my previous experience as a youth worker included an understanding of young people's lives, an emphasis on the importance of building relationships and trust with young people, as well as the use of informal conversation to facilitate learning. Familiarity with youth work processes and settings developed my cultural competence, which enabled a quick understanding of the research context as a sound starting point. Youth work practice can easily be aligned with participatory research, which youth workers are in a 'position of strength' to undertake (Gormally and Coburn, 2014). Shared values included an assets (rather than deficit) view of young people, engaging in conversation, acknowledging the co-creation of knowledge and enabling young people's voices to be heard.

Taking part in the same activities as the young people gave a shared frame of reference for discussions and gained respect through mutual creativity. Joining in practical sessions, such as dance, demonstrated my lack of skills compared to many of the young people, but this helped to develop a sense of trust and understanding, and balance (as much as possible) the power relations. This enabled an 'ethics–of–care' approach (Noddings, 2013), which holds the development of relationships as central in alignment with youth work ethics, and manifested in taking a genuine interest in the work that they were producing for their Arts Award, often undertaking new arts learning experiences alongside them. Arts-based methods offered not only an ethics–of–care approach, but also a strategy for enabling 'voice' through alternative means of expression.

This research study, as well as taking into consideration the standard ethical concerns in the planning stages of informed consent, avoidance of harm, confidentiality and anonymity, had extra considerations due to the age of participants (14 to 18 years old) and the fact that some of them were considered vulnerable. Ethical approval was sought and granted from the School of Education Ethics Committee, University of Nottingham, prior to commencing fieldwork, which covered the former concerns. In the field, the most effective way of gaining informed consent was to speak to the young people about the research, as a group at first and then individually, about how they might want to be involved. It was optional for them to engage with the research, and some of those who did were able to take some ownership and suggest ideas. At the research design stage, it was intended to use the gatekeepers to the various programs to guide the levels of consent required for the young people. Letters were issued in advance to each of the projects, which were addressed to parents and then followed up with individual consent forms for those young people who expressed an interest in taking part. However, each program wanted a different approach to consent. Some wanted parental consent, some wanted the young people to give consent as a way of giving them responsibility, and some wanted both. Therefore, in reality, informed consent was sought on a situated and reflexive basis, which ensured each setting was comfortable with the nature of participation. In the writing up of the research, and this book, the names of the participants and programs have been changed to protect anonymity.

Research findings

My research on Arts Award sought to explore young people's experiences of the program within youth settings. In my findings, I demonstrate the different offer for young people accessing the award through these settings. First, I celebrate the synergy between arts practice and youth work pedagogies. Secondly, I highlight the opportunities of Arts Award and explore its value as a 'tool' for youth work. My third finding takes a more critical perspective of this particular program, by demonstrating the use of Arts Award for monitoring and controlling behaviour. I argue that due to pressure to provide 'measurable outputs' and demonstrate impact, youth arts programs can often find themselves in risky terrain. These findings have implications for arts programming, practice and pedagogies across the youth work sector.

Arts Award's synergy with youth work settings

Within youth work settings, in particular, the arts have been proven to work by encouraging the holistic development of young people (Mills and McGregor, 2013). Pedagogies such as praise culture (Kinder, 2004), journeys of self-discovery and 'small-step' learning (Daniels and Cole, 2010), often associated with learning in the arts, have been drawn on. In these youth settings, Arts Award was seen as a vehicle for engaging young people in 'positive activities', with the arts taking young people on personal and emotional journeys as part of identity building. Through observing the program in a variety of youth settings, I observed that Arts Award worked well because of its flexibility as an award that can be designed around young people's interests and that is flexible in timescale, with an informal education focus. It was a program that could be 'picked up and put down' and engaged with when young people chose. It was also a good mechanism for stimulating individual interests and creativities and engaging young people in working together, which was often in collectives or collaborations. Some young people demonstrated entrepreneurial sensibilities when they set up their own promotions companies and record labels and organised gigs and events, meaning that participants in the program were able to engage in a wide variety of cultural activities that appealed to them (Howard, 2022a).

Experiential learning was a key practice of Arts Award within youth settings as much emphasis was placed on 'doing'. This was either through arts activities organised by the youth workers, or by shadowing artists in other contexts. Working with artists in this way was a part of gaining real-life work experience on which many young people reported positively. There were also other opportunities organised by the youth workers such as special events and workshops, which enabled young people to develop informal arts networks. This encompassed the 'induction' of young people into these practices and included the use of artists' languages, professional production equipment and resources, and performance practices. These enabled young people to choose to act in ways which allowed them to gain a new embodied understanding of working as an artist. There follows an example of an opportunity organised by one of the youth workers for a young person to 'get recognised'. Although opportunities such as these were only offered to those participants considered as 'talented', they did offer advantages by placing young people in new social situations. The young person describes being selected for the Ultimate Artists Scholarship:

Tyler:[6]   Basically, Martin [youth worker] told me about this opportunity where some people from London were coming here to look for like raw talent and stuff, so we sat down and had a chat about it, like what songs to perform, and we decided on a song and I like changed the song at the last minute, to a different one. And I wasn't really prepared for it, but like they really saw something in me and they took me for the scholarship and that. So that's happening soon.

Frances: So, what is the scholarship? What is it?

Tyler: It's called Ultimate Artists scholarship. It's basically like an eight-day course, where people going there are like, singers, spoken word artists, like everyone whose going, it's a chance to prove yourself and prove that you actually really want it. And basically, make your mark on the music industry to be fair.

                    (Interview with young person, FRESH program)

Diverse forms of 'youth arts', outside of gallery contexts, were noted as youth arts programs drew on everyday forms – music, street art, performance – as well as the digital. Arts practices were those that could be picked up in a youth setting – not requiring specialist equipment or trained practitioners – despite many youth workers being artists and many youth clubs having facilities such as recording studios. Within youth work settings, I observed the youth workers fulfilling a dual role – that of artist, musician, dancer, filmmaker or arts practitioner, alongside youth worker. This was often interdisciplinary and responsive to whatever arts practice the young people wished to engage with. Undertaking a dual role of youth worker and Arts Award Adviser enabled them to draw on both their artistic abilities and their youth work practice. Workers found Arts Award a useful framework for youth sessions, as an opportunity to engage with something new, access culture, develop artistic skills and for young people to feel a sense of achievement.

Within youth settings, young people are encouraged to make decisions and take ownership of ideas, activities and local spaces. Arts Award offered an extension of this whereby young people were supported in their own creative choices and were able to forge their own pathways. These included activities such as organising their own events, setting up bands and collaborations, creating record labels and promotion companies and utilising social media to promote their own work. These pathways were advantageous for young people joining collectives outside of the projects. The arts within youth settings exhibited a potential to build social and cultural capital, through border pedagogy (Coburn, 2011a), in synergy with youth work practice. Delivery of Arts Award in youth settings enabled young people to use cultural practice to build resilience, negotiate their identities and develop social connections, which would sustain their interest beyond the life of the projects. The following excerpt shows how one participant was able to extend this practice beyond the youth work setting and form a collective with others:

Tyrone: Erm, I got something in the line, cos me and Jackz got picked up by this crew.

Frances: What like an agent?

Tyrone: Called Baxters. Cos they want me to be the DJ and obviously like Jackz rapping and there's two Producers who said 'don't worry about Producing right now'. Just you focus on the DJing. And all the beats that they produce they're gonna send to me. But when they get two, three years down the line, they're gonna show me everything. Obviously not right away, but through those three years, they're going to show me everything about producing. Then that's me producing, and they're just going to step back.

Frances: So, they're like a record label, are they? Kind of?

Tyrone: Yeah, they're basically a label

Frances: I do know there are quite a few people getting picked up round Nottingham at the moment by different labels. It's exciting.

Tyrone: So, I've got that in the line. And they just said focus on
             DJing for now.
Frances: Have you got any gigs lined up for the summer?
Tyrone: I don't know yet. But I'm in the studio today.
             (Interview with young person, Youth Media program)

This example highlights how arts programs within youth settings can support the development of agency and entrepreneurialism (Howard, 2022a). I regularly observed youth workers supporting young people with social connections, the development of knowledge of self-promotion, branding and commercialisation of their arts practices. These kinds of resources and social capital made available to young people through the program enabled them to configure alternative pathways into the arts, whether as a life-long hobby or potentially a career. However, despite these commonalities between youth work and arts practice, I noted several tensions between the way that youth workers view these kinds of programs. The arts are often seen as vehicles for engaging young people in positive activities and for taking them on personal and emotional journeys, but they are also valued as an end product that a young person can take time and pride in achieving (Davies, 2011). I asked the youth workers what they felt that young people valued the most about arts practice, whether this was the process or the final product and young people valued more highly the time to develop and work on their arts practice. One youth worker reported: "I'd probably think actually that they'd value the certificate more. … Yeah, cause my first thought was that they value the process but actually, I think it's been a bit of a bind for them to do it and they just want to come down and work on their songs, so yeah." (Youth Worker, FRESH program).

Many young people reported the process of collating 'evidence' for the award as a distraction from the enjoyment of simply undertaking their arts practice. At times the accredited element, despite often being used to justify funding the program, seemed like an unwanted aspect to the sessions. This was echoed by youth workers in that some felt that the accreditations meant a loss of focus on the actual work with young people. But others had witnessed the value for that young person in gaining a certificate and gaining an accreditation:

'I think you'd struggle to get them to say "I've really enjoyed the qualification", however, when we do the celebration events and they are called up to get their certificates, we've had big lads, 16, 17, 18 who think they're really tough on youth offending orders, who've been really humbled by getting a certificate and actually going "wow I've achieved something". And they're about to leave at the end of the celebration event and they come and give you a hug. And they're really really overwhelmed by the fact that they've got a certificate and that they've achieved something. So, whilst they may verbalise it in different ways, I think they demonstrate how much they do value getting that qualification.' (Youth Worker, FRESH program)

As well as the contested place of accreditation in youth work, another tension was the delivery of an arts program within targeted provision. From the three sites that I selected, there was a range of open access and specialist provision. Often youth workers saw these as a committed program, however their organisations had labelled their sessions 'drop-in'. One youth worker described young people coming to the centre to hang out but being coerced into undertaking the program, as that was the session running on that particular evening and there were reports of young people being steered into activities. If young people were coming down in the evening and just 'for a laugh', being taken out of that environment for an hour, into a separate room was detrimental to the young person's experience of the open session and the distraction from peers was too great. However, some youth workers felt that it was very useful to have dedicated sessions for the arts because it separated out the informal education and the youth work, which enabled more intensive and creative work with the young people. One worker argued that he did not consider the work that his organisation offered to be open access at all:

'Open access is exactly that. Young people just come and go as they please and as soon as you get a sheet of paper out, they just walk off, don't they? It's really tricky. Because you can't really build ... well it's a challenge to build relationships with the young people and that's what we're here for, to build the relationships with the young people and then engage them for sustained periods of time. Whereas open access, my experience of it is, that you've either got two youth workers in a corner somewhere and the young people are just running riot.' (Youth Worker, Beatboxers)

Despite these tensions, the youth workers all valued the diverse ways of working with young people that the arts offered in these contexts. In a similar fashion, the young people on the programs valued the experience of doing their Arts Award, whether that was for the process or the certificate at the end. If we consider youth settings as important site of cultural democracy, where everyone can be a producer, the arts play a key role in forging relationships between people (Jeffers and Moriarty, 2017). The focus is on an outcome for the young people themselves, rather than outcomes for the arts (such as new artists or audiences) (de Roeper and Savelsberg, 2009). The synergy between arts practice and youth work, therefore, is in acknowledging a variety of cultural activities, recognising all young people as artistic producers while questioning power and authority (Hadley and Belfiore, 2018).

A 'tool' for youth work

Previous research has argued for the value of youth workers' skills in terms of improvisation for youth work, using the arts as a tool to approach sensitive subjects with young people (Davies, 2011) and their own personal 'tool box' to create activities for their settings (Kiilakoski and Kivijarvi, 2015). Youth workers interviewed as part of this research viewed the arts as part of their 'tool box' for facilitating youth sessions. They also reported that youth arts programs helped young people reach some goals, raise their aspirations and realise that they could achieve something. Youth workers saw it as a great opportunity for young people to do something they were interested in, to develop their skills, confidence and interaction with other people, to feel valued, to feel that they could achieve, and to gain something from it at the end. In particular, Arts Award was suited to young people who were reward driven and who struggled with education in other environments due to its inclusivity and non-reliance on writing. There was also a sense from the young people that this was an environment where they could make mistakes and it was 'OK' to fail.

Young people build resilience through youth arts programs with the development of person-level protective factors such as self-efficacy, improved emotional regulation, social skills, coping skills and ethnic pride (Rhodes and Schechter, 2014). Youth workers were able to use the arts as a way of being responsive to young people's interests, often reacting quickly and positively to their needs and ideas. The arts were considered a useful tool for getting to know young people, and building relationships and springboards for conversation. Some youth workers developed techniques around using different arts practices for exploring and developing shared interests with the young people. They reported that they valued the program for the opportunities that it afforded young people for decision making and creative problem solving, as well as the importance of conversation, negotiation and co-creation of knowledge. Youth workers considered using the arts as a way of bringing people and communities together, but also enabling signposting to other services:

> 'And that's opened up the door for us to actually be able to work with them and mentor them with other areas of their lives as well. And once you build up a relationship with some of them through the arts, helping them to achieve they do come back time and time again. I'm helping quite a few of them now, look for volunteering opportunities

or college or things like that. I don't think we would have built up those kinds of relationships in the first place, had we not used the Arts Award as a creative vessel to be able to work with them and build up those relationships.' (Youth Worker, FRESH program)

One of the key values of youth work is identity building through interactions with the everyday, where youth clubs provide a culture of participation and a common language, which generates a sense of belonging with other young people in the area (Nolas, 2014). This was one of the effects that I observed develop in the young people, who, despite their diverse backgrounds and arts interests, felt an affinity as a group within the youth settings. Young people were using their cultural practice to negotiate their identities and to become part of certain communities, which were viewed in a positive light by the youth workers, as opposed to deficit groupings. Part of this identity work was discovering and joining informal arts networks, getting to know where their art form happened and how to take this forward beyond the life of the projects. Making social connections with youth workers, local artists and other young people afforded some young people access to opportunities that did or could lead to future arts practice. Tapping into locally held knowledge, through the connections of the youth workers, was a key offer of the programs for participants. Many young people reflected on their experience of attending local events and how this influenced their dispositions, with some being inspired to organise their own events. These social connections were a mechanism for building capitals, in particular for those with non-arts backgrounds. The following excerpt highlights the diverse nature of these informal networks, which are key to maintaining young people's arts practice beyond the life of the projects:

'There are so many informal and formal networks. So, for something that I concentrate on in delivery, the music tech, people just go round each other's houses and if they've got a laptop and a keyboard, that's how people tend to make music. Hip-Hop and Grime people tend to gather in warehouses and have battles and stuff like that. And those are the networks, that's where people practise their art. And however, you feel about it, its where it happens. And you can't really steer people towards that. They find those avenues themselves.' (Youth Worker, Youth Media program)

Here, the youth worker explains a typology between informal networks and different art forms, identifying the different practices of each: house-bound practices with electronic equipment for house DJs and warehouses and rap battles for Grime and hip-hop. These forms of expression, experimentation and identity formation were welcomed, becoming part of certain communities of practice, which included joining informal arts networks, getting to know where their art form happened and how to take this forward beyond the life of the projects. Building upon the connections of local artists or youth workers was important to the young people as they were able to develop shared interests, experience and understandings, as well as shared languages and resources. The sharing of work and creation of collaborative arts practice is key to young people's identity development and learned ways of being.

Working with youth workers who were also artists was one of the key benefits of the award, whereby young people directly benefited from youth workers' 'tool boxes'. Young people had the opportunity to 'try on' identities and frequently made affiliations through music and style, using the arts as a badge. The creation of rap lyrics, in particular, enabled young people to have their voices heard and get their messages across. The language that young people chose to use was significant, exploring their multiple and inherited identities and the stories they chose to tell about their lives through their work, whether that was film or music or dance. Arts activities developed a strong sense of collective identity, with the benefits of 'feeling part of something'. Overcoming barriers with young people from non-arts backgrounds, who often state that they 'can't draw, dance or sing', do not consider themselves creative, was facilitated and negotiated by youth workers as skilled informal educators.

However, this is not without the problematic reproduction of youth stereotypes – as discussed in Chapter 3 – and the creation of issue-based work, which can compound notions of poverty and marginalised youth. For example, I found that the educational purpose of youth arts programs was frequently lost within messages of transferable skills, skills for employability or addressing young people's own risk-taking practices. Therefore, there is the need for a more critical, less instrumental intersection between youth work and the arts, which includes moving beyond the stereotyping of DJing, spray painting and street dance as 'typical tropes' of arts-based youth work. Anna Hickey-Moody (2013) argues that 'the inclusion of arts in assemblages of governance not only produces impoverished arts practices; it can also (but does not always) take away young people's voices through imposing adult tastes on the lives of youth' (p 14). Building upon this critique, my research found that the arts were used as a 'tool' for youth work practice, but also as a tool for monitoring and control in youth work settings.

A tool for monitoring and controlling behaviour

Within youth settings, in particular, assumptions were made about young people as unsuited to more challenging arts practices. In the case of some young people, they received restricted practices and dumbed down pedagogies, and the award was used to monitor and control their behaviour (Howard, 2022b). The program was pitched as a CV builder rather than an offer of intensive and creative work with short-term instrumental values compared to the longer-term impacts of identity development and self-expression. I observed a moral imperative placed upon some programs towards changing the young people and behaviour modification. As well as a different offer within youth settings, throughout my fieldwork I noted a language of danger and surveillance which surrounded 'labelled' young people on the programs. This use of language was used to justify strategies of performativity as ways of monitoring and controlling. These often focused on 'character' and 'resilience' as ways of developing young people as ideal citizens, in neoliberal terms (Miller, 2007; Edwards, 2009). An ideal citizen is one who takes responsibility for themself, gets involved, can learn independently and is successful by progression through various recognised levels of achievement, such as Arts Award. Narratives of performativity manifested in the award being used to measure individuals' 'progress' and to focus on measurable outcomes and accreditation. This was at odds with youth work principles of voluntary participation and informal education. These narratives of performativity have particular implications for arts programs of this nature, including a focus on ability-oriented goals rather than learning for the sake of it, short-term, goal-focused, product rather than process, skill rather than enjoyment, good practice as improved 'outcomes' and skills over knowledge as lists of competencies and standards.

Arts Award was often used as a benchmark for the program's success to obtain future funding. Although within youth settings Arts Award gave the opportunity for young people to undertake more intensive and creative work, the structuring of sessions was an issue for those who just wanted to come and 'hang out', sometimes being turned away from provision as they were not undertaking the accreditation. This frequently resulted in coercion of young people to undertake the award and youth workers pushing young people into the programs to help boost their numbers. Showcasing and performance events were 'measurable outcomes' for youth projects and drew attention to the outcomes of young people undertaking positive activities, increasingly needing to be demonstrated as part of targeted work. The award was used to provide a measurable outcome in return for funding particular youth projects and in return a culture of record keeping and 'box ticking' was visible.

Stemming from the deficit position of young people on targeted and referral-based programs and the stereotypes aligned with particular art form practices, my analysis showed that some participants experienced more diluted and remedial arts practices. These were designed to 'repair' young people rather than to inspire and empower them. There were tensions in how the arts were viewed by program managers, with Arts Award being championed for its instrumental purposes as a measurable outcome. There was a dissonance between the current economic and social focus of youth policy and the relational and well-being approach that the youth workers found much more valuable in practice. Viewing the arts as instrumental reiterates the rhetoric of arts for social good, as well as demonising those who take up places on these programs. The impact of these targeted programs and measurable outcomes on youth work may be detrimental to its democratic and responsive nature. I give further examples of this often subconscious and unrecognised distortion of the program in the following two chapters.

Conclusion

Through introducing my research on Arts Award and sharing three key findings, my aim has been to bring the previous theoretical chapters to life. I shared my positionality to highlight the dual role of youth worker and arts practitioner that many youth workers hold today. There is clear value in this duality in terms of youth workers' 'tool boxes' and what they bring to the role as vehicles for engaging with young people. In particular, I explored the synergies between the award and youth settings, such as dialogue and experiential learning. I used my findings to argue that despite Arts Award being a 'good fit' with informal education settings and the practices of youth work, there was a real danger that this program would instrumentalise the experience of working with the arts.

Despite arguing for the value of Arts Award as a 'tool' for youth work, I also shared a more critical analysis whereby the instrumentalisation of the arts by youth work programs resulted in the monitoring and behaviour control of young people. I argued that there is a need to be more critical about youth work and the arts' claims of impact and that an emphasis on achievable measurable outputs and value for money can put them both on risky terrain. There is real danger that the sustainability and future funding of both youth work and the arts, becomes based on measurable outcomes and instrumental values. Therefore, it is important that we interrogate key assumptions about the arts and young people as a 'social project' and that we consider how to influence future policy so that it begins to value more human factors in its measurements. What youth arts programs do really well is to express and often interrogate young people's personal journeys. Why the arts are good for youth work encompasses the process rather than the product, the experience rather than the end point, and the navigation of obstacles rather than an outcome.

I develop this analysis further over the next two chapters, with an in-depth exploration of the particular 'practices' and 'pedagogies' on offer for young people taking up Arts Award in youth settings.

5

Youth arts practices

This chapter explores the different arts practices on offer through the youth arts program in my study on Arts Award. Drawing on Paul Willis' (1990) framework of 'common culture', examples of the artistic practice undertaken by the young people are given as incorporating everyday practice, symbolic resources and bedroom culture. Arts practice was an opportunity for learning new things, developing new arts skills, working with artists and utilising industry-standard equipment. However, access to quality arts practice was restricted for some, with more challenging and contemporary arts experiences not being offered. In this chapter, I explore 'subcultural' arts practices and their functioning as realignment for these young people to deviant social groupings. I draw on case studies of two young people – Tyler and Jamie – to exemplify the opportunities and constraints of these practices.

Having explored the shared practices of youth work and the arts in the previous chapter, including cultural responsivity, enabling identity work and forms of meaning-making that enabled a sense of inclusion for the young people, this chapter investigates the affordances of these practices. I give examples of digital and DIY practices that underpinned young people's identity development. These arts practices, which I observed flourish within youth work settings, are not always recognised as 'the arts'. Digital technologies are clearly part of young people's everyday lives and artistic production, however they are rarely taken into consideration in discussions of cultural value (Manchester and Pett, 2015). I also share practices which excluded young people. These included stereotyping, issue-based work and school-like obedience for labelled groups of young people. However, the practices explored in this chapter do not exist in isolation as they function alongside a range of pedagogies employed by youth workers. These will be explored in the next chapter.

What arts practices were on offer?

Youth arts programs engage with a wide range of art forms. These arts practices are not always recognised as part of officially funded arts and culture. Previous research exploring arts-based youth work has focused on visual arts (Beggan and Coburn, 2018; Sim, 2019) and in particular graffiti art (Lombard, 2013; Hillman, 2018; Fransberg, 2019); music (Rimmer, 2010; Travis, 2013) and specifically rap and hip-hop (Baker and Homan, 2007);

dance (Hickey-Moody, 2013b) and in particular street dance (Petracovschi et al, 2011); theatre (Lee and Finney, 2005; Beswick, 2018; Howard et al, 2018); and film making (Coles and Howard, 2018). This chapter builds on this body of previous research and focuses in particular on digital and DIY arts practices within youth settings. I will argue that these practices are culturally responsive to how young people experience the arts today and that they offer a key vehicle for identity work.

Widening the possibilities for arts participation is a key strategy of Arts Award. As well as incorporating traditional cultural activities such as working in museums, libraries and heritage sites or working with artists and arts organisations (institutionalised versions of arts practice), the award also encompasses popular culture. Young people are positioned as arts producers in various ways, not only as creators of their own work, but also as performers, backstage team members, front-of-house staff, technicians, camera operators, writers, editors, promoters, DJs, costume designers, prop makers and so on. Within youth settings, I observed young people taking up arts practices such as lyric writing, music production, film making and digital art/design work. These arts activities were how young people used their leisure time and symbolic resources from media and music alongside assertions of their style and peer group to situate themselves. These everyday arts practices recognised 'meaning-making' from below, which is grounded in bedroom culture, symbolic creativity and proto-community (Willis, 1990).

Doing arts digitally

Digital technologies are key to youth arts programs. The use of technology is significant for the young people in terms of opportunities to get inspiration, create work, and 'get their work out there'. Digital art forms that young people worked with included radio, sound engineering, music production, DJing, filmmaking, working with photography, image manipulation, and music videos. Use of symbolic resources from electronic and cultural media are a powerful stimulant for the creativity of young people (Willis, 1990). New screen-based technologies have their own practices and new spaces for interaction (Livingstone, 2007) as well as being a key site for leisure consumption, where access to technology represented a willingness to try new things (Finney and Burnard, 2010). Young people have learned particular codes for this interaction, learned to play with them and manipulate them using electronic media as cultural commodities (Willis, 1990). Digital practices became intertwined with the hyperreal (Baudrillard, 1994), through the saturation of images, quick and easy availability of sounds and film clips, and ready-mades from the internet that many young people used to create their own work. Embedded within the fields of commerce and consumerism, these cultural resources were readily available to participants. Young people are actively engaged with these resources in the production of new work.

'Digital' referred to physical things, for example using computers, equipment and technical kit, as processes of creating art. In addition, digital also refers to the artificial, the ethereal and the hyperreal, in the form of digital networks, ways of communicating and sharing work, disseminating work through various social media, for example Soundcloud, Facebook, Twitter. These platforms for participants' creative work were closely linked to their symbolic creativity and identity work as well as new kinds of collaborative practice through online environments. Young people were also fluent in digital languages, proficient with the codes of communicating through electronic systems, and expert in the ways of being that digital arts practices enabled. These included social media practices such as vlogging and other forms of content creation. Within digital practices, in particular, young people drew on and revised existing media, messages and languages in order to construct (and reconstruct) their own linguistic codes and to make choices about how they wanted to be in the world (Gadsden, 2008). Digital production, so common within youth settings, offered situated learning, the possibility to develop the agentic self and an exploration of meaning-making and symbolic creativity (Willis, 1990).

Digital arts practices are a rich domain for young people, with activities such as lyric writing, music production and gaming. Many young people in my study utilised their personal phones, computers or iPads to undertake their arts practice. Some young people created lyrics during their time at the projects working with youth workers, however others used their mobile phones to write lyrics at home and then brought these to the settings to share with others. A further motivation was the recording spaces that many of the youth clubs had, where young people could record their lyrics and turn them into a music track. As an example, Figure 5.1 is a photograph taken of a participant's mobile phone, where they had written their lyrics at home, and then brought them to the project to share with others and to record a track.

Technology most frequently used was mobile phones and video cameras, together with use of the internet on both computers and phones. Resources included use of software for music and film production, search engines and YouTube to download instrumentals for songs and clips for films. Young people composed lyrics on their phones, created EP[1] covers and artwork using image manipulation, recorded their voices, took photos, edited videos and used midi systems. Many creative tasks were undertaken digitally, such as producing music, sound recording for a radio show and designing album covers. The mobile phone was an important resource for young people creating work, by writing and reading lyrics on their phones, downloading music, and making recordings. At the fingertips of the young people, these

Figure 5.1: Lyrics on a mobile phone

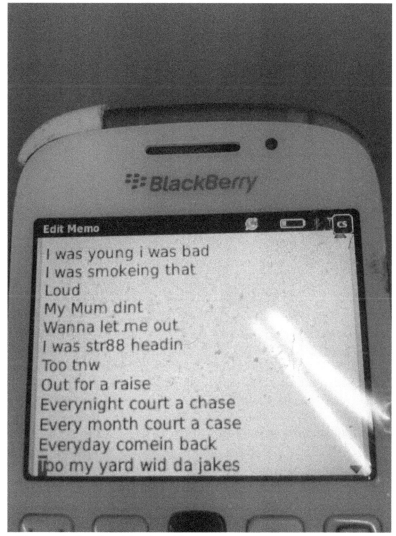

Note: Photograph taken of participant's mobile phone, FRESH program.

transformative digital practices made symbolic resources quick to access and were a key affordance of youth arts programs. A key affordance of the emphasis on digital arts practices within youth arts programs, such as Arts Award, was the positioning young people as both consumers and producers of the arts (Howard, 2022a).

The prevalence of digital arts practices within youth work settings aligns with the rapidly expanding field of digital youth work. The European Union Work Plan for Youth 2016–2018 (European Union, 2016) defines digital youth work as proactively using or addressing digital media and technology in youth work, which can be included in any youth work setting (open youth work, youth information and counselling, youth clubs, detached youth work and so on). This mixture of face-to-face settings and online environments positions digital media and technology as a 'tool' within youth work. Therefore, digital arts practice, which forms part of youth workers' 'toolkit', can be considered an extension of digital youth work. Lauha (2019) argues that the digitalisation of youth work is an absolute requirement for keeping up with the times and developing the civic skills and social relationships of young people. Within this emerging field of practice, youth-centred digital literacy initiatives have become prominent in Europe in recent years, whereby youth work has become tasked with developing the competencies, skills and knowledge required for critical digital literacy (Fernández-de-Castro et al, 2021). However, the social impact of this work remains increasingly difficult to capture (Pawluczuk et al, 2019).

In relation to digital and social media, any youth worker engaging with young people through the internet, via social networking sites such as Facebook or mobile technologies for group communication such as WhatsApp, can be said to be participating in digital youth work. During the Coronavirus pandemic, youth workers relied on these means of communication, when youth centres were shut or lockdowns restricted detached youth work. However, if the role of youth worker problematically shifts to 'checking in' (Batsleer et al, 2020), the notion of digital youth work as *only* meeting online becomes fraught with ethical, moral and structural complications (Melvin, 2019). Recent research has highlighted the value of online group activities alongside one-to-one offline youth work for more targeted counselling-based interventions (Kivijärvi et al, 2019). This blended approach to youth work offers a positive affordance of digital technologies in further supporting young people to address the risks, opportunities and challenges that they face in the world (Cohlmeyer, 2014). The place of digital arts practices within this, with activities such as giving young people the opportunity to use video cameras and film-editing software, enables them to explore issues in their lives.

DIY arts production

Digital arts practices supported by screen-based interaction, corresponded to an arts engagement pattern of 'alone-together-alone', which is symptomatic of bedroom culture (Willis, 1990). This was demonstrated by the range of previous arts experiences with which young people began their Arts Award programs, which were further developed through a CAYW approach (Beggan and Coburn, 2018). DIY refers to 'creating, repairing and/or modifying things without the use of an expert craftsperson' (Bennett, 2018).

Often young people's variety of skills had been home grown and existing work had been self-crafted using DIY practices. DIY arts practices focus on the everyday, as embodied forms of 'doing', learning and knowing that facilitate a multiplicity of connections (Martin and Hickey, 2016). Youth arts programs are an important site of DIY artistic production and youth cultures, as Peppler and Kafai (2007) argue: 'DIY production provides opportunities for personal expression, creativity, and critical reflection on media culture, expressed through visual instead of oral or written discourse, and allows youth to reflect on their knowledge of culturally meaningful texts and dominant discourses and formulated a response through their work' (p 114).

DIY practices as home-grown or self-taught artistic skills engaged with a focus on the here-and-now, using innovative and original processes that were easily available. Within common culture, the lines between consumption and production are blurred, so that young people draw from the cultural resources around them to inform their arts practice. DIY methods of creating new artistic work relied heavily on reusing or rehashing of existing material, for example sound, images, or footage found on the internet. This included sampling, image manipulation and film editing, where young people made new work from things that they regarded as ordinary and freely available. Cutting and pasting from the resources available, often through digital media, created new combinations, where young people experimented with putting things together in a new way for the first time. In particular with music making, young people often downloaded backing tracks, instrumentals or samples from the internet as a way of deconstructing and reorganising commercial music (Finney and Burnard, 2010). These were then collated in a new track, as an original piece of music. Within youth settings, young people needed little or no previous arts education to undertake their own arts practice, which has significant implications for widening 'access' to the arts.

Filmmaking was also another popular art form which drew on DIY practices. Young people used their own phones to record footage and also used video cameras if they were available in the youth settings. The films they created ranged from music videos to documentaries which explored their own perspectives on being young. They drew on assemblage techniques, collating downloaded music from the internet, film clips from YouTube and other sources, in addition to the footage they recorded. Figure 5.2 is a screenshot of a film made by a young person called 'Life as a Youth'.

'The riots clips were linked to Life as a Youth cause it was talking about ... how the media kinda describe youths. How they only show footage of young people throwing stuff and thinking "oh, yeah, those are bad kids". I bet you that there was one youth who spoke up, but they didn't wanna put it in there. So, I was thinking to maybe put this is there but to ask the youths what they think as well about the media and how they portray them.' (Young Person, Youth Media program)

This hour-long documentary was analysed as part of my study and interviews were conducted with the young people involved. As well as demonstrating the DIY assemblage manner of creating digital work, the accompanying interview text describes the young person's artistic intentions for the use of news coverage of the Nottingham riots in this film. This excerpt communicates how the media can misconstrue the actions of a minority for the majority and the prejudices young people can face. On another level this film represents a form of resistance, where young people are using their arts practice, and drawing on everyday forms and available resources, in order to speak back to deficit discourse on youth. However, within filmmaking in particular, there was a tendency for young people to create 'issue-based' films as a way of taking responsibility for their previous risk-taking behaviours (Coles and Howard, 2018). Constraints such as these will be explored later in this chapter.

The opportunities of youth arts programs

The arts practices explored in the previous section have offered an insight into the affordances of youth arts programs and the value of their cultural responsivity to the young people in my study. In this section I develop this further by exploring the particular opportunities that Arts Award afforded young people in youth settings. I focus, in particular, on access to professional spaces, languages and ways of being, alongside the influence of

Figure 5.2: Introduction to 'Life as a Youth'

Note: A documentary film created on the Youth Media program, alongside interview transcript discussing the use of news footage found on the Internet.

technologies and utilising industry-standard equipment. Identity work and social networking opportunities were also important as arts practice within youth settings was an opportunity for learning new things and developing new arts skills alongside youth workers, who were often arts practitioners as well.

It is important to note that young people came with their own prior cultural experiences and the youth workers were able to work with those experiences and to build upon them. This was an extension of the relationship-building work that is a key affordance of youth work. The Arts Award program was accommodating of individuals' interests and practices, but it was also used as a tool to encourage new experiences and develop new dispositions. The strongest offers of programs for young people were those that engaged their interests in everyday art forms, but offered something new, challenging and inspiring. Young people also liked a shareable product at the end of their Arts Award program, such as a film uploaded to YouTube or an EP or track uploaded to Soundcloud.

Arts practice represented exciting opportunities for many young people to develop and improve their creative skills. Working on individual projects, often dictated by their own interests, afforded participants short-term success in arts-based tasks. Learning new things was a key affordance of the program alongside improvement in specific art forms, some of them familiar, some of them new. For example, in the following excerpt a young person is talking about developing new skills in music production, which she did not previously have, but also about improving the bass and drumming skills that she already had. This suggests that Arts Award can encourage new arts practices for young people, as well as nurturing existing ones:

'It definitely improved my nothingness of producer-skills [laughs]. So, from nothing to a little bit of something. And Paul [musician and youth worker] helped me improve my bass skills, well start my bass skills and he also like helped me improve my drumming skills a lot. So, we've jammed a couple of times where he's like played the bongos and I'm on the drum kit or where he'd playing guitar and I'm playing bass. It's really improved my confidence in those.' (Young Person, FRESH program)

Young people were able to develop creativity, originality and expression through their arts practice. Youth settings offered a key space for this personal and artistic development of young people. They benefited from the space and time given to creating work on the programs and the freedom to choose, explore and experiment. There was a clear sense of experimentation with some projects, where young people could play at working with new art forms as a process-driven, rather than outcome-focused experience of pushing the boundaries. In the following excerpt a young person talks about a series of short improvised comedy sketches that he created and filmed. He is drawing on popular culture, what has influenced him, and demonstrates Willis' notions of common culture where he argues that anything can be art as it is found all around us:

'No, there was no real purpose behind them. We just … it was a long time ago that we first thought about the idea. … I don't know if you've ever seen The Trip on BBC 2, with Steve Coogan and Rob Brydon. Which I absolutely love, I think it's so good. And we wanted to do something like that. It is basically those two and they go round different restaurants in the country and the back story is that they're reviewing the restaurants, but it is just about the conversation at the table. And so, we wanted to do something like that. And we thought, cafes in Nottingham, why not? … I think it can definitely be considered art. When I sit down and watch one of those episodes … when I watch The Trip with Steve Coogan and Rob Brydon, that are absolutely amazing. That is art, it's real art. Some of it is because of the scenery, they go to Italy on some of the episodes and its absolutely amazing scenery. But most of it is because they're just sitting there talking and obviously these are famous people, they're playing themselves, they're playing celebrities, who know each other from shows or whatever. And we wanted to do the same thing but it's not being dressed up in a big fancy show, it's not scripted. This is a conversation between two people. And I think that's the best type of art sometimes. Which is why we did it.' (Young Person, Youth Media program)

Furthermore, Arts Award gave young people the opportunity to take part in arts activities for the love of it – art for art's sake. Many young people reported that the programs gave them the opportunity to do things they enjoyed and my observations recorded uplift in mood, sustained attention and personal determination when young people were undertaking arts practice. The following excerpt describes the transformation in a young person who was dealing with difficult issues outside of the program and their sense of escape and enjoyment when they were engaging with their arts practice of lyric writing and rapping.

'A young person has been working on their own for over an hour. They came in, as usual, under a dark cloud, sat down at a computer, head down and did not talk to anybody. They put their instrumental on the studio computer and spit their new lyrics out loud. The youth worker is there to support them. They make mistakes and try again, but they are beaming. This is the first time I see them smile. They laugh, they are pleased. Suddenly they have opened up and are talking freely to the youth worker, discussing the content of the song, the lyrics, the meanings. They have been boosted up by just this small exercise.' (Fieldnotes from Beatboxers)

This passage demonstrates the emancipatory and fulfilling capacities of arts practice in terms of well-being within youth arts programs, whereby what young people valued about working with the arts was their development of well-being and sense of self-belief.

Youth identity work

Youth cultures, historically, have had a large role in cultural production (Gaztambide-Fernandez, 2013) and the arts represent opportunities for young people to make sense of the world and their place in it (Thomson et al, 2019b). The digital and DIY practices explored in this chapter afforded young people in youth settings authentic modes of artistic production. Engaging in forms of symbolic creativity through subcultural practices was an attempt by some young people to reinvent themselves at both the centres and the margins, through the real and virtual, through both the local and the global. Youth arts programs have affordances for identity work through the use of symbolisations in order to open up a wider range of communicative possibilities, including those of advocacy, recognition and compassionate witnessing (Batsleer, 2011). These are important elements of identity work for young people frequently facing deficit labels and blame cultures, as argued in Chapter 3.

Arts practice afforded young people opportunities to experiment, develop and communicate identity. Certain art forms offered through youth programs such as rap music and filmmaking allowed young people the opportunity to express a particular form of cultural creativity connection with their existing music and artistic interests (Baker and Homan, 2007). The young people in this study brought rich and diverse experiences, life stories and inherited influences with them to the projects. This was often reflected in the lyrics, films and images that young people produced, which told stories about their lives, for example, with Figure 5.1 showing the story of a young person's experience of being in court. Many young people demonstrated multiple identities, being part of several groups at the same time – family and friendship groups, school and so on – and undertaking these arts programs enabled young people to develop a sense of group affiliation. This was often seen in a positive light as 'the Arts Award group' in contrast to the deficit groupings of young people on the program. These opportunities to reconfigure identities enabled a refocusing on young people being seen to do something positive, constructive and creative. This form of collective identity can be considered a proto-community (Willis, 1990) where people come together with shared concerns, to carry out informal learning and develop a body of knowledge in which others in the collective have an interest.

The Arts Award program within youth settings afforded young people the opportunity to use the arts as a marker of identity, which was linked to the kind of artwork young people chose to make. A key example of this was working with visual art through digital platforms such as photoshop, as many young people created album covers. Drawing on these created images through interviewing young people, I was able to carefully consider the ways young people were expressing particular modes of identity in relation to particular youth cultures. For example, Figure 5.3 shows an EP image that a young person created, and the following fieldnotes describe the design process. They clearly draw on symbolic resources to play with particular subcultural codes of identity, while symbolising their own representation.

Figure 5.3: First Time E.P.

Note: Album artwork.

'The young person has uploaded their album EP to Soundcloud. It's a striking and high-quality professional image. I can remember when the initial photograph was taken with the young person wearing their special hat and black hoodie with "gang" name on. These elements stand out, as well as the explicit lyrics label. This is a symbol that the content may be offensive, and this is seen as a good thing. The colours are dark and brooding. Red paint drips down the background and the darkness of the hoodie, hat and skin blends together. The white writing of the title is in graffiti style lettering. You cannot see the young person's face. I ask if this is deliberate and it is.' (Fieldnotes, FRESH program)

This album artwork has intentionally drawn on traditions of gangsta-style imagery. Great thought and attention to detail from the young people went into creating this image, including consideration of the use of parental advisory logo, dark and unrecognisable figure, gang logo, particular hand gesture, use of certain colours and effects, and artefacts such as hoodies and chains. All these elements were significant and were specifically chosen as influenced by branding and consumption. Symbolic creativity is evident in this kind of image making but this young person is also drawing on subcultural capital, which, as this chapter will shortly argue, positions them as deviant (Howard, 2022a). Despite the 'safe spaces' of the youth settings, the development of subcultural identities only served to realign young people facing deficit labels with deviant behaviours.

Access to professional spaces and equipment

Many youth settings included, or provided access to, a sound recording studio or 'booth'. For other programs there were dance studios and computer suites for visual art and video editing. Offering these 'professional spaces' meant that young people engaging with youth arts programs had access to industry-standard equipment, which enabled higher quality of artistic output, a fast turnaround of a finished product, and professional levels of production. The following excerpt positions the studio space as a stepping stone, from which the young person is able to be picked up by a 'label' for example:

'It gives you studio time innit. Trying to do all your music and sort all your stuff out. Because before I was in a studio, I could mix it but I couldn't bring it out. I didn't have a label or nothing. Now I can move on to a label, get it copied and actually get it out there. Like I've been able to work with the right people to get it in shape. Get it airplays and that. Get it out there and promote.' (Young Person, FRESH program)

As well as physical spaces, electronic spaces or social media platforms were key to the young people's experiences. Drawing on social media practices such as vlogging and platforms such as Soundcloud, young people often felt in control of the process of platforming their work, making decisions about where it would go, who they wanted to see it and why this was important to them – choices often unavailable to them in mainstream arts education. The following case study is presented as an example of a young person drawing on the opportunities of the program, not only to work with professional spaces and technology, but also to develop their identity and social network.

Case study: Tyler's track

Tyler had been attending the Youth Media program for several years and had taken on a mentoring role for some of the younger members. He tells me that when he first came to the youth setting he lacked any confidence in lyric writing or performing in front of others. He knew that it was something that he wanted to do to develop his music, however he lacked the tools and confidence to do so. Two years later and he is happy to write and record lyrics as part of the youth sessions. He is undertaking the highest level of Arts Award – Gold – having progressed through Bronze and Silver. He has engaged with the arts leadership section of the award to develop his leadership skills and has been leading younger members in music-making activities as part of an apprenticeship-learning approach. As part of this process, I observe Tyler play a new group member one of the very first recordings they did with the program. He explains how their voice and their performance have developed over the last two years. Tyler confidently explains that when he first started to record music, he would try to emulate the voice of other recording artists, but now he has found his own 'style' within his own voice.

Tyler is proficient in the digital arts practices on offer through access to professional standard music production and recording equipment but also languages. Vocabulary used in referring to working with their digital art forms, and in particular with music, included: "create beats", "spit bars" and "lay down tracks". Young people who were new to these programs had to become accustomed to these languages as a way of being accepted within the group. Often these were defined by musical style, with the most popular two being Grime music and House music. Figure 5.4 is made up of some of Tyler's lyrics. We can see Tyler's use of language contains digital references: "hashtag", "screenplay", "beat play". In my ethnographic description of the creation of these lyrics using first a mobile phone, then a computer and a recording studio, Tyler is using his mobile phone for reading the lyrics as part of his recording session, and he draws on other digital devices – computer software and instrumental tracks from YouTube – to

Figure 5.4: Tyler's track

Wanna chat to me you better hashtag DeeKay
I'm on the screen watch the screenplay
9-5 on a weekday I graft hard for my p gotta get that, anyway
Catch me free on a freeway living life like a birthday
Get it on a Monday and its gone by Friday I spit the truth spitting fire at greenway
I got the beat watch the beat play I got popping like a bottle and I'm onit and it's all layed
Bar4bar I got it and it's all sprayed I ain't
Got no type but they all grade
I ain't got no plans but they all made
I got creps but they ain't all suede
Beats fresher when I'm onit and if I got it the I gotta get it gone like market

Note: Lyrics containing digital language highlighting digital practices and the affordances of technology.

be able to create his own music track. The following fieldnotes explain the meaning and process of recording these lyrics onto a music track:

'Tyler reads lyrics from the screen on his mobile phone. He has written these lyrics at home since the last session and now he has come to the project to record them – to "lay them down". I watch him type these lyrics onto a nearby computer and we talk about what they mean. He then downloads the instrumental he has found on YouTube for his backing track and makes his way to "the booth" with his phone in hand.' (Fieldnotes, Youth Media program)

Tyler's story exemplifies the affordances of youth arts programs for young people's creative and arts practice through accessing high-quality equipment and support to create work. His case study is one that demonstrates the value of youth arts programs for confidence and leadership. However, not all young people undertaking Arts Award within youth settings have the same experience. As explored in Chapter 4, the award can also be used as a tool for monitoring and controlling behaviour. The following section explores some of the constraints of these programs, in particular in relation to subcultural arts practices and realignment to groups viewed as socially deviant.

The constraints of youth arts practice

Previous research has shown that arts practices are frequently the site of cultural and social inequalities (Savage et al, 2013; Friedman et al, 2015; Brook et al, 2018). Everyday practices or ways of doing things often contain taken-for-granted dynamics of power, which have implications for social positioning (De Certeau and Mayol, 1998; Grenfell, 2011). With youth workers as the gatekeepers to the arts practices, there were examples of exclusion and further marginalisation of young people. Within youth settings the act of 'programming' different arts practice activities for young people can have an adverse effect (Howard, 2022b). This correlated to the hierarchies of value within different arts practices. As an example, Bull and Scharff's (2017) research on classical music demonstrates the highly ritualised production of arts practices as how people make classifications according to their own position within social space. Rap music, for example, cannot be measured against the same hierarchy of classical music.

While it is important that youth arts programs are culturally responsive and engage with common culture, many activities planned failed to acknowledge young people's funds of cultural knowledge and offered poor-quality practices and dumbed-down pedagogies. Poorly programmed and supported engagement with subcultural arts practices served, for some young people, to simply realign them with deviant youth practices, for example 'at-risk' young people making hip-hop-style album covers, such as the one shown in Figure 5.3, which drew on gangsta-style imagery. There is a need to move beyond graffiti art, rap music and street dance as typical tropes of youth arts programs.

Realignment to social deviance

The way that youth workers introduced new experiences was often dialogic and skilful, however others failed to encourage knowledge sharing and collaborative approaches. For example, Beatboxers, the dance program, which was intended for NEET young people, had a high drop-out rate. Having followed the program for several months, I could see a pattern to this disengagement and that the young people who completed the program were those with the most prior knowledge and experience of the dance practices on offer. The group's name – Beatboxers – was contrived by the funder to appeal to a certain group of young people who were affiliated with dance styles that were considered 'street' or deviant. The actual style on offer did not fit some young people's frame of reference and did not meet expectations. For example, the only male in the group reported that the feminised dance styles alienated him. However, the ritualised practices of dance were only known by those who held a position of privilege to be able to be considered cultural omnivores (Peterson and Kern, 1996; Warde et al, 2007). The omnivores consumed all styles of dance: contemporary, Bollywood and street. Those targeted by the deficit labelling were left to feel like 'fish out of water' (Tranter and Palin, 2004) and were further marginalised by this grouping through 'dropping out'. A previous study (Beswick, 2018), which explored young people engaging in a theatre production that played up classed stereotypes, found that labelling worsened their position. Beswick argued that asking young people to embody stereotypes closely related to their 'real' identities caused significant tensions and exacerbated the label of social exclusion for that group. This practice became a delicate balance between freedom to explore and guiding the young people in response to their ideas, and heavy leading and over-direction – an issue that will be taken up later in the next chapter.

Subcultural practices

The arts practices programmed were often representative of assumptions made about the young person, their abilities or their social grouping. Access to quality arts practice was restricted for some, which in turn defined how they viewed their own practice. More challenging and contemporary arts experiences were not introduced or engaged with. Through seemingly unbiased selection of arts events for participants to visit, class-based inequalities were reproduced by unconscious rules and values. Music practices, in particular, aligned to marginalised youth, often reflect themes of deviance and resistance as a creative vehicle within a broader framing of 'offender to citizen' discourses for the youth involved (Baker and Homan, 2007). With filmmaking, in particular, there was a tendency for young people to create 'issue-based' films as a way of taking responsibility for their previous risk-taking behaviours (Coles and Howard, 2018). Here we see arts practice being mobilised as a tool for responsibilising young people and behaviour modification rather than creative expression (Howard, 2022b). Involvement in arts programs was often positioned as a second chance or 'salvation' for the young people involved.

As part of arts practice, young people not only participate in arts activities, but are required to explore the arts as an 'audience member'. This involves observing the practices of others as 'being the audience' and often has an impact on the young person in terms of how they view their own creative practice. It can be inspiring, challenging and at times unfamiliar. The young people are required to reflect on their experience, what they enjoyed, the creative elements of the event, the art form involved and then share their views with others. This was frequently done through discussions on the experience. To give an example, the photographs in Figures 5.5 and 5.6 were taken when the FRESH youth program took a group to visit a street art exhibition. Despite the symbolically deviant and subcultural practices of street art on offer, some of the young people shared feelings of discomfort and lacked confidence within the environment of the gallery space. The young people on the visit had been creating their own large-scale spray-painted boards within the basketball court of the youth club. Being taken to a gallery space to see work in a similar vein was an alienating and uncomfortable experience for them, as many held negative identities of themselves as learners and as artists. The group were not prepared for visiting the gallery as there was no social or historical consideration of street art and lack of

Figures 5.5: "It's shit, don't go"

Note: Photograph of young people visiting a street art exhibition, FRESH program.

Figure 5.6: "It's shit, don't go"

Note: Photograph of young people visiting a street art exhibition, FRESH program.

discussion about its value or place within a gallery context. As a result, the young people were disconnected and lacklustre.

Previous research (Sim, 2017; 2019) has demonstrated a disconnection between the diverse fields of youth work and the art gallery due to 'symbolic violence' on offer (Bourdieu and Passeron, 1977). Sim (2019) argues that youth arts programs are sometimes set up in a way that unintentionally alienates particularly working class young people whose own cultures and knowledges are not represented or valued. Going to experience an arts event first-hand could be inspirational for young people and often gave them ideas on how to develop their own practice and the new directions to take their work. However, there were examples where young people felt alienated by these experiences. Frequently young people demonstrated indifference to the practice they were experiencing, for reasons of being unprepared or feelings of being out of place, and resisted the experience, as the following case study will demonstrate.

Case study: Jamie's first theatre visit

Youth arts programs are frequently funded because of pledges to introduce young people to new experiences. Going to the theatre is not something that all young people get to experience, outside of the annual school trip to the pantomime. One of the young people who went on the gallery trip also got to experience two more arts events as part of their Arts Award. While the opportunity to attend diverse arts events is undoubtedly an advantage, the arts practices on offer and the way they are introduced can be limiting. For his Arts Award, Jamie visited three different arts events – a rap battle night, a street art exhibition and a piece of contemporary theatre – and we discussed his experience of each:

Frances: Arts Events. So, what did you go and see?
Jamie: Clash Money and Surface Gallery and The Dog in the Night-time.
Frances: Actually, in the four or five months you've been to three different arts events. You've been to a theatre thing, a live music thing and you've been to an art thing. So, from your kind of first impressions of those, which did you feel most at home in?
Jamie: Erm, I preferred the Clash Money one.
Frances: The Clash Money one, why was that?
Jamie: Well, I like that sort of music and it was just a good environment there.
Frances: I didn't feel very at home in that environment. Maybe that's because I'm a woman. [starts to laugh at photo of Clash

Money Event]. … So out of those three events, would you
be inclined to go to any of them again?

Jamie: Erm, I'd go to the Surface Gallery and Clash Money again,
but probably not The Dog in the Night-time.

(Young Person, FRESH program)

The contemporary theatre performance was most alien to Jamie, yet the least work had been done by the youth worker to support Jamie to understand and engage with theatre as an art form. The lack of theatre-based arts practices within each of my sites of study was striking. In addition, what was notable from his experience what that he had no choice of the events he visited. Assumptions were made by the Adviser that he would feel an affinity with the outsider art exhibition, that he would be comfortable with the culture of the rap battle and that a piece of contemporary theatre would challenge and inspire him. But when I discussed this with Jamie afterwards, it was clear that these experiences had actually reinforced the idea that theatres and galleries were 'not for the likes of him'.

The two case studies in this chapter have shown the differing experiences of Tyler and Jamie. For Tyler, arts practice was culturally and personally responsive, and enabled identity work and forms of meaning-making which were inclusive. His experience of the arts program offered both a space to play with and reconfigure identity as well as to develop creativity, originality and expression. However, for others such as Jamie, practices of stereotyping, issue-based work and subcultural practices served to exclude him as a young person. In particular, for labelled groups of young people, school-like practices of obedience and the deemed lack of cultural knowledge were alienating. The differing experiences of Tyler and Jamie highlight both the opportunities offered by youth arts programs in terms of digital and DIY arts practices and access to professional spaces and equipment, and the constraints of hierarchised and subcultural arts practices and realignment with deviance. What was programmed for the young people within youth settings directly affected their artistic, personal and social development. The choice of arts practice and access to quality arts practice was restricted for some. There was a lack of cultural awareness around more challenging and contemporary arts experiences and this correlated with the differing arts practices on offer.

Conclusion

Diverse artistic practices within youth arts programs offer both opportunities and constraints. Within my study on Arts Award, arts practice was an opportunity for learning new things, developing new arts skills, working with artists and utilising industry-standard equipment. In addition, the practices were accommodating of individuals' interests and prior cultural knowledges.

The majority of this practice was through the common culture, drawing on funds of creativity within their personal spheres, using symbolic resources, which were available to young people in their everyday lives. This enabled participants to draw on their own life stories and previous experiences to create work. Authentic and accessible modes of artistic production were afforded by the youth work settings. Taking a common culture 'approach' through engaging with arts in youth settings, my research has demonstrated the importance of digital and DIY arts practices and the offer of identity work for young people today.

However, what was programmed was often representative of assumptions made about the young people, their artistic abilities or their social backgrounds. Access to quality arts practice was restricted for some, which in turn defined how they viewed their own practice, in a reproductive cycle (Howard, 2022a). Subcultural dispositions simply realigned some young people with deviant arts practices, for those who unconsciously experienced stereotyping and streaming. Despite the 'safe spaces' of the youth settings, the development of subcultural identities only served to realign young people facing deficit labels with deviant behaviours as ways of 'playing to type' (Beswick, 2018). Despite arts practice offering a form of resistance and change for young people, often the content that was encouraged, such as 'issue-based' work, was a way of responsibilising young people for their previous risk-taking behaviours. Youth arts programs can enable young people to imagine 'outside of themselves' and to envisage new identities, to feel as thought they 'fit-in' as part of a group or collective. But youth arts programs can also, inadvertently, make young people feel as though they 'don't fit' and they become socially excluded. However, arts practices do not work in isolation. They work alongside a range of pedagogies deployed by youth workers, which will be explored in the next chapter.

6

Youth arts pedagogies

This chapter investigates the differing pedagogies drawn upon by the youth workers in my study on Arts Award. Findings from my research demonstrated that young people in youth settings experienced diverse pedagogies, some of which were beneficial and some of which had implications for disadvantage. Drawing on the notion of *cultural citizenship*, I question what arts programs 'prepare' young people for. I argue that youth arts programs have the potential to develop young people as *justice-oriented cultural citizens* (Kuttner, 2015) who feel a civic responsibility to use their artistic practice to actively promote justice and address inequalities in society.

Building on the diverse art forms explored in the previous chapter, this chapter will focus on the commonalities in the pedagogical approach of youth work and arts practice. The affordances of the Arts Award program will be explored in relation to its 'fit' with youth work, as a way of exploring alternative pedagogies for arts learning. I demonstrate that youth arts programs can offer a pedagogy of empowerment, which holds transformative potentialities. Examples are given of collaborative work, the arts as a vehicle for inclusion and border pedagogy (Coburn, 2011a). These accord with the potentially liberating and oppositional affordances of working with the arts, as a way between the rhetorical and structural constraints for the young people in my study.

However, this chapter also explores a counter-argument, which demonstrates that these affordances were not consistent for all young people. Varieties in pedagogical practice can be viewed as a hierarchy depending on young people's perceived behaviour and assumptions made about their artistic ability. Consideration is given to what pedagogies and ways of working with the arts can in fact disadvantage young people. While arguing that the potential of the youth arts programs is not being reached, I problematise assumptions made about the power of the arts to 'transform' young lives, without recognising the cultural values and interests young people bring with them.

Shared pedagogies

Previous research (Ruiz, 2004) has argued for the potential of the youth service to widen young people's access to the arts, and case studies have demonstrated the value of the arts as methods for engagement within youth work (Davies, 2011). The arts are frequently used as tools for informal learning in youth work as a pedagogy of the here-and-now (Batsleer, 2008) and as a means to re-engage reluctant learners (Sefton-Green, 2006). Flexibility and responsivity are other elements that unite youth work and the arts. This looseness of learning is mirrored in youth work pedagogy, which tends to be focused around small group work and a concern for young people's 'voice'. With Arts Award in particular, the structure of the award is such that each young person can follow a personalised program and have control over their direction through their own interests. In the following excerpt a youth worker describes how they engage with the award due to its flexibility and enabling a response to what the young people wanted to do:

> 'It changed our delivery in a positive way, so they're [the young people] gaining new experiences and we can be flexible with it. So, if we get to the session and the kids wanna do dance, then they can do dance around their Arts Award. We don't have to go back and start trawling through, looking for something that's near dance in the NOCN[1] folder and then build up schemes of work and lesson plans.' (Youth Worker, Beatboxers program)

Conversation, negotiation and the co-creation of knowledge are also shared elements between Arts Award and youth work. The basic principle is that the youth worker asks the young person what they want to do for their Arts Award, they discuss it, they negotiate and then the youth worker facilitates and tries to make it happen. In this way, youth arts programs enable young people and youth workers to collaborate, through critical and reflective dialogue, in the construction of knowledge. However this is sometimes restricted by time and resources (Gormally and Coburn, 2014). On the programs that I attended, this ranged from making a music track, to creating an album cover and from teaching someone to play the guitar, to writing song lyrics. A large proportion of the youth work that I observed during the Arts Award programs was conversational and a way of learning through dialogue between youth worker and young person. In order to facilitate this dialogue for learning, close relationships were developed with young people and in this way, knowledge was co-created through the young person's experience, as opposed to learning a fixed body of knowledge. The following excerpt demonstrates the value of this dialogical approach for artistic practice:

> 'It was really nice to get them [the young people] out and take them down to the [art gallery] and I don't think that they ever really went there to be honest with you. ... So that was nice and we went on a day which was a black history event, and they knew very little about

that as well. So that kind of gave us a stimulus for conversation on the way home, and that was quite surprising as some of them were mixed race as well. They had very little information about their heritage and migration and stuff like that. And that's something we probably wouldn't have explored, had we not gone down to the [art gallery].' (Youth Worker, Youth Media program)

Relational learning, which refers to the 'social' aspect of learning, is a key tool for building relationships and new connections within young people's social and emotional lives, which encourages cooperation rather than competition between young people (Smyth et al, 2013). This shared pedagogy refers to more of an individualistic approach to learning that focuses on the conditions and interests of the young person. Through my observations, I found that the young people's educational experience through Arts Award was effective because these relationships and the content were relevant to them. As I have already explored earlier, building relationships and communication are key practices of youth work, and data from the youth workers demonstrated how these were developed through the Arts Award programs:

'Because I felt that that it was really important for that group of young people to begin to trust adults from a diverse background and to start to understand how to interact with people. ... And trusting adults, I think is really really important for them. So that communication they had with us as adult and supporters, the whole team, I think was a massive impact on them.' (Youth Worker, FRESH program)

Social pedagogy (where care and education meet) and social learning (learning through participating in a social group) were also shared approaches of youth work and the arts. Social pedagogy is a view of learning that foregrounds relationships, listening, dialogue and co-construction of knowledge (Bryderup, et al, 2011). This often manifested itself in the giving of time to a young person by the youth worker and the young person feeling the youth worker had a belief in them. The value of youth arts practice through the lens of social pedagogy highlights affordances for the transcendence of social justice into the wider society. Empowering and supporting relationships are key to social pedagogy (Batsleer, 2008), and social pedagogical thought is enabled as a consequence of holistic learning (Hämäläinen, 2003). Meaningful forms of 'citizenship and democratic agency' exist where individuals come together through a shared concern and/or issue in challenging where the power of citizenship lies, as well as who determines what meaning is defined as (Biesta, 2014). The following excerpt highlights the affordances of informal education in relation to social pedagogy:

'When you are doing informal education, the young people that you are working with feel like you care about how they want to learn or their education … you often get to give them a lot more time and attention than they normally receive. And that's the time of youth work, that successful youth work is about making young people feel that they are cared about.' (Youth Worker, FRESH program)

In their exploration of higher education students in the UK, Jones and Brady (2022) signposted their participation in professional practice settings as part of their learning experience, or working/volunteering additionally to their academic learning, as situations where social pedagogies were drawn upon in developing citizenship. They labelled their participants as 'social justice champions', whose acts of agency may create and develop this sense of purpose through a mixture of new knowledge and previous experiences, in oneself as well others (p 17). Through this lens, combining social pedagogy with arts practice – often termed as 'socially engaged arts practice' – enables young people to raise major global issues such as climate change, Black Lives Matter and forced migration through addressing injustices and perceived prejudices within institutions, focusing in particular on how citizens are perceived and treated. Youth arts practice offers a window into and vehicle out of these important conversations. These pedagogical practices are intrinsic to ways of working that youth arts programs encompass. Two key pedagogical practices of collaboration and border pedagogy (Coburn, 2011a) will now be explored further.

Collaboration

Young people undertaking their Arts Award were often positioned as active agents in their own learning (Kiilakoski and Kivijarvi, 2015) through their social interactions with youth workers and the resulting learning opportunities. Through a *community of practice* (Wenger-Traynor, 2003) youth workers and young people came together to share a passion for their art forms and creative practice and to learn how to do it better as they interacted regularly. There were many examples of young people working in collaboration with both youth workers and other young people to produce new work, in particular music. This kind of collaborative creativity (Burnard and Dragovic, 2015) represents a democratic approach to production through co-influence in meaning-making. Engaging with the concept of cultural citizenship, co-production is upheld as a normative social ideal, in particular in young people's leisure-time spaces (Boele van Hensbroek, 2010). The practice of collaboration frequently manifested in the logic of a shared frame of reference between the young people and youth workers, often based around similar understandings of popular culture. While sharing their ideas and experience, youth workers also engaged young people with ideas for the development of their own work: a delicate balance between freedom to explore by guiding the young person in response to their ideas, and didactic over-direction – an issue that will be taken up later in the chapter. Much of this dialogue happened during the practice of listening to music or watching films together, developing shared repertoires. The 'track-share' described in the following fieldnotes was an opening ritual of one of the programs as a way of collaboratively sharing practice:

> 'The day usually starts with a "track-share" – young people and youth workers can choose to put a track on YouTube and they sit and listen together. Discussion follows this. Things they particularly liked, and the meaning for them. The youth worker seems to counter the young person's offering with something that is different but familiar. It seems that everyone's got a video or knows someone in a video. Several of the young people aspire to create their own music videos and go into a detailed description of what their video would be like.' (Fieldnotes, FRESH program)

When youth workers had skills as musicians, this was valuable to improvisation and co-production with young people, as they were able to facilitate the 'sounds' that young people desired to create. For example, 'jamming together' was a frequent practice of co-production for the music-based projects, as well as large-scale collaborative graffiti artwork with the visual arts. Many collaborations happened on a spontaneous basis, based on who was present at that session, and with a sense of experimentation; vocalists singing each other's lyrics, layering up their sounds, playing with the arrangements. Co-production enabled a dialogic two-way learning process by sharing knowledge and undertaking activities together. Arts Award afforded a spirit of collective endeavour through the contribution of both youth workers' and young people's artistic skills and their aspirations for the production of their own work, as the following excerpt from my fieldnotes demonstrates:

> 'The young person is working with a sound engineer [youth worker] listening to various parts of songs they like. The engineer makes notes and gives advice so that they can build their track the way they want. They are sharing knowledge and creating together – the young person on music preference, scope and their experience and the youth worker on technicalities and composition. They are working together, co-producing the track.' (Fieldnotes, Youth Media program)

Collaboration alongside DIY and digital arts practices, described in the previous chapter, were key affordances of this youth arts program within youth work settings. These practices and shared pedagogies enabled a cultural responsivity which encompassed young people's tastes, influences and resources, as well as accommodating previous arts experiences and identities. Within society the arts are used as part of symbolic creativity as a way of defining particular social groups. Working with youth arts programs affords cultural democracy, a key theme of this book, which provides a more positive lens that acknowledges working class culture. Youth arts pedagogies often involve engaging with questions that matter deeply to young people, recognising the knowledge that they bring with them and the acknowledgement of their learning lives, through tapping into everyday knowledge. The following excerpt provides an example of a young person who is sharing their skill in playing the guitar through explaining and demonstrating, but also reacting and adapting. This demonstrates practices of self-discovery, self-guided learning and also trust of the young people to guide their own experiences:

'A young person is working with a youth worker on their "arts skill share".[2] They are teaching the youth worker how to play the guitar – carrying on from last week. They use an app on the iPhone to tune the guitars before starting. Last week the young person was very confident at leading and has set the youth worker a task during the week to learn the chords. They use letters, phrases and acronyms to help learn chord patterns/strings. The young person is mature in their approach, coaching and pushing their participant, explaining things and pointing out problems confidently. The young person is advising on how to hold the guitar, and reach each of the different chords. The youth worker is struggling with something, and says they "can't do it". The young person shows different ways to do something and then changes to something easier. They swap guitars so that the youth worker finds it easier. There is some confusion about moving up the strings higher and lower. "It's just about practising," the young person says. The youth worker is starting to get it and seems pleased. They are discussing learning harmonies and strings and the young person says they will teach the youth worker how they were taught – they are going to start with learning to read music. The young person goes off to get some sheets of paper, while the youth worker practises strumming chords.' (Fieldnotes, Youth Media program)

These powerful real-life experiences manifest from experiential learning derived from informal education pedagogies, which were encompassed within Arts Award. Collective learning (Thomson et al, 2012; Burnard and Dragovic, 2015), working with practitioners, shared experiences, and learning as a social rather than individual process are all particular strategies within these youth arts pedagogies (Hayes et al, 2017). For example, the arts leadership element afforded young people opportunities to undertake activities and events that they would not have been able to do previously. Some young people demonstrated being able to manage complex processes and engage with detailed planning. Empowerment is an underpinning value of youth work, and the following example describes the process as giving them 'power':

Young Person:	There was an event we helped plan … the event at [arts venue] last April and I would never have done that if I hadn't of come down here. And maybe if I hadn't of been doing my Arts Award, I wouldn't have presented it, which I did. But I never would have helped plan it if it wasn't for the Arts Award.
Frances:	[points to folder] and these are all the phone calls that you did to the press and a press release. This is like a real-life experience, you know if you were going to put on your own music gig.
Young Person:	Yeah, it was. Yeah, we've got the lady that came in from the press department, she did press releases. She passed it on to the press people and we did our own little press thing. The radio station gave us a shout out and gave the event a sort of nod. And things like that … it does do something very different because it's sort of … it really is giving you the power. It's saying 'here you go, you go and do some workshops' or 'you go and do a debate, you go and lead and take part in a debate'. So, there's no teachers telling you what to do. It's very different. It really is very different, now I think about it.

(Young Person, Youth Media program)

Engaging with popular culture through youth arts programs, such as Arts Award, was a way to mobilise young people's everyday cultural knowledges. This served a democratic purpose to the extent that young people from all classes possess these knowledges, which can be activated through youth arts programs (Hickey-Moody et al, 2010). The inclusion of popular culture in the pedagogy of Arts Award is a strategy that incorporates the tastes of marginalised social groups. Therefore, cultural knowledge is brought into the realm of the everyday as a way of recognising diverse cultures. Building on real-life experiences and young people's interests is one of the pedagogical strategies of Arts Award. It is popular with young people as it is culturally responsive and can be used to follow up particular interests and develop new ones. Youth workers can program activities for the young people which have strong links to their personal spheres of interest. They also create new opportunities for the young people such as working with professionals, meeting and interviewing people, the experience of going to live events and self-promotion, as these fieldnotes demonstrate:

> 'The youth workers are talking to the young people about promotion and the use of social media. They get advice on how to promote themselves as "artists" and why it is important – "to get your work out there". They proceed to set up email accounts, not in their real names, but in their artist names: Sir Dee Productions and Marshall Productions. The youth workers explain that there are many things that artists can do now themselves using the internet in the place of managers and record labels.' (Fieldnotes, FRESH program)

These shared pedagogies demonstrate Arts Award's culturally democratic potential, creating more opportunities for young people to get involved and become recognised in the arts. Here youth arts programs support dispositions of self-expression and self-efficacy, with young people making an investment in their own artistic practice by following individual projects in which they had vested interests (Howard, 2022a). In this way, the arts were utilised for personal, social and cultural development of young people accessing the programs.

Border pedagogy

Informal education is a powerful catalyst for learning, which encourages young people to be inquisitive and questioning and problem-solve creatively (Batsleer and Davies, 2010). As part of youth arts programs these practices often include the provision of creative or cultural activities as opportunities to create learning within these environments. Previous research has demonstrated the advantages of these kinds of social and symbolic capital in terms of educational decision making (Heath et al, 2010), social media networks (Ahn, 2012) and music festivals (Wilks, 2011). A form of social capital accrual, border pedagogy is acknowledged as a form of youth work capital. Border pedagogy (Coburn, 2011a) is a practice that encompasses the building of bridging and bonding capitals as part of social advantage within the field (Morrow, 2001; Putnam, 2001; Bottrell, 2009).

In particular within youth settings, Arts Award was seen in a positive light in terms of affording border pedagogy. The pedagogical approaches which included conversation and dialogue, shared values and experiences, being role models and building relationships boosted the social and cultural capitals for the young people on the program. For example, youth workers were utilising Arts Award programs to explore future opportunities with the young people and to link them into informal arts networks. Youth workers were key to this experience, using their connections and peers in the industry or local scene to bring in other arts professionals to either work with the young people on their arts practice or to talk to them about their work. There were also opportunities for young people to organise events and to perform. The program meant that youth workers could 'give time' to the young people for creative work, alongside the 'pick it up, put it down' nature of the award suited to more transient groups. This notion of 'giving time' to the young people is an important pedagogical approach of youth work practice:

> 'But when you are working informally, you often get to give them a lot more time and attention than they normally receive. And that's the time of youth work, that successful youth work is about making young people feel that they are cared about. And that you've got their best interests at heart. So that's why you're able as a youth worker, you can do the fun things with them, but you can actually take on a much more paternal role. Where you can, not discipline, but you can give some pretty stern advice. And they actually, it's more likely, that the young people will take note of that. It might actually have more of an impact, because you've been through the kind of fun positive stuff and built that respect where they feel like you care.' (Youth Worker, FRESH program)

Through the lens of border pedagogy, Arts Award represented opportunities for young people to develop artistic dispositions of self-expression and creativity. One way that young people were able to develop these dispositions was through the production work such as films and lyrics around personal issues. Young people also drew on the wider place of arts in life and called on their own experiences and interests. This resulted in individual projects and work being pursued by the young people under the Arts Award framework. Young people enjoyed the informal education offer and benefited from a non-school environment and a more relaxed ethos, where they could try new things. These kinds of non-school environments engendered capital building, which was valuable to the young people.

Deficit pedagogies

Having celebrated the valuable pedagogies of youth arts programs, I now explore a range of pedagogies that receive lesser attention and created a reductive experience for the young people involved. A key aim of this book is to raise researchers' and practitioners' awareness of deficit pedagogies, of which, like myself before starting my research, they may not have experience. This exploration is offered to help strengthen the value and purpose of youth arts programs. My research found that there were varieties in pedagogical practice, in particular for young people taking up the program under deficit groupings.

There was a hierarchy of pedagogy, which manifested in more working class young people not only being offered different opportunities for engagement, but also experiencing different pedagogical approaches (Howard, 2020).

Running contrary to Arts Award's agenda of widening access to the arts for *all* young people, my research highlighted particular deficit pedagogies, where young people's behaviour is monitored and they are more likely to learn in a tightly controlled environment, was also monitored (Howard, 2020). Some young people were more likely to receive didactic instruction with low-level work, being assigned a passive learning role with little scope for interaction. Arts programs within youth work settings were also more likely to deal with 'issue-based' work where young people were required to develop self-managing and responsible ways of being. To exemplify this, I draw on the *pedagogy of poverty*, which is an instructional style that relies heavily on teacher direction, controlling behaviour and student compliance (Haberman, 2010). This was the experience of several of the young people in this study, often due to the unconscious assumptions youth workers made about their ability, behaviour or social background. While Arts Award is presented as an open and flexible award where young people are free to make choices and follow up their own interests, my research has shown that their experience is often controlled and confined by the youth worker. Positioned on this spectrum by adults, the more disengaged or disruptive young people were offered the least opportunities. Deficit pedagogies are deeply embedded within the pedagogical strategies of the settings in the study, which has implications for young people arriving at Arts Award programs under deficit labels receiving a less engaging and lower-quality arts education.

To give an example, drawing on the pedagogy of poverty, particular arts experiences were organised for young people in which they could 'succeed' without becoming either involved or thoughtful (Anyon, 1980). For some, this resulted in a highly 'spoon-fed' and directive experience as the following dialogue demonstrates. It is drawn from an interview with a young person who recounts their experience while looking through their Arts Award portfolio. They describe the planning process, which they undertook through 'worksheets' that were already prepared for them and they describes a step-by-step approach, simply following orders. For them, this kind of arts activity was reduced to a box-ticking exercise where the young person believed they had achieved by simply following instructions. This leaves little scope for utilising new skills or ideas learned within new contexts:

Frances: Let me have a look [flicks through folder]. So here, in your leadership section.
Young Person: I just remember planning where I had to share my skill, and do Photoshop with people. That's all I remember doing planning that one.

Frances:	So, you've got like … erm … that looks like a set of reminders to yourself. Like a set of rules. And you've got something here about ground rules. So, is this like the worksheet that you had here to help you?
Young Person:	Yeah, I had to write it in steps to make sure that I didn't forget anything and that I was doing the steps properly. And this was just boundaries for the kids on what to do and what not to do.
Frances:	And look, you've got some step-by-step instructions here on how to create a CD cover on paint.net. So, what did you do before you did this leading? It looks like you've had quite a few things to think about. How did you plan this leading?
Young Person:	I sat down with Lena [Youth Worker] at first to see if it would be possible to do it and then she gave me a sheet, that sheet, to fill out and I thought of what I was going to do, I decided how many children I needed and what equipment was needed and some stuff like that pretty much.
Frances:	That's quite a few things there. So, you've got here things to talk about, your potential participants, sign-up sheet. So, you've got a series of workshops and times, feedback sheets. Did you design these?
Young Person:	No, I just had to give them to the kids.

(Young Person, FRESH program)

In my fieldwork, I observed some arts activities had been broken down into step-by-step simple processes or 'dumbed down' for certain groups of participants. Through these kinds of pedagogical practices young people were more likely to be corrected, receive simple explanation and then be instructed to repeat activities in order to encourage dispositions of obedience. Young people enjoyed less freedom to learn and less creative freedom to explore with more time on workbooks, worksheets and copying, as Figure 6.1 demonstrates. This logic of measurement is constructed to demonstrate young people's progression through an evidenced paper trail, which is arguably the result of a growing emphasis on measurement, outcomes and the impact agenda within youth services (Youdell and McGimpsey, 2015; de St Croix, 2018). As an accredited outcome, Arts Award is valued within youth settings as a 'hard outcome', irrespective of the potential life-changing experiences that working with the arts offers to young people.

In addition, as an evidence-based award, often young people's arts experiences were reduced to paperwork. Several programs avoided a written approach from the outset and instead gathered evidence through

Figure 6.1: Worksheets

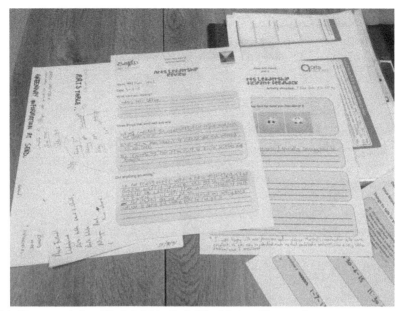

Note: Young people found the 'administration' of the Arts Award heavy going.

video cameras set up in the corner of the room to capture conversations, in line with Arts Award's encouragement of 'creative evidencing'. While Arts Award can be considered a useful tool for youth work, it can be seen as an example of how youth work has become more 'organised' and about 'participation' (Van de Walle et al, 2011), with pressures to prove 'value for money', which focuses on accreditation and recorded outcomes (Ord, 2014). The narrative of performativity has particular implications for arts programs of this nature, including a focus on ability-oriented goals rather than learning for the sake of it; short-term, goal-focused; product rather than process, skill rather than enjoyment; good practice as improved 'outcomes'; and skills over knowledge as lists of competencies and standards. Therefore, targeted programs and deficit pedagogies of youth arts programs can be detrimental to their democratic and responsive nature (Howard, 2017). Simply viewing the arts as instrumental reiterates the rhetoric of arts for social good, as well as demonising those who take up places on these programs.

Many young people accessed Arts Award through projects (either voluntarily or compulsory) under deficit groupings. This impacted upon the youth workers' attitudes towards them and assumptions made about them. This frequently manifested in low expectations, misrecognition of behaviour and viewing young people as projects to be worked on. Young people were frequently defined in a deficit view by these programs and this resulted in demonstration of reluctant behaviour by some young people towards learning and their capacity to learn. Several of the programs sought to engage the young people in creative tasks not only as a diversion, but also as a way of understanding their own accountability and responsibility – through issue-based work as a way of exploring their previous 'risk-taking practice' (Baker and Homan, 2007). Pedagogies that sought to control behaviour manifested in engaging with the arts as a way of alleviating previous offending or antisocial behaviour, where these practices offered the opportunity to 'get things off their chest' (Parker, 2018).

Through deficit pedagogies youth arts programs can be used to construct 'orderly youth' (Thomson and Pennacchia, 2015). This manifests in both tight policies of non-toleration of misbehaviour and also reward schemes or 'carrot and stick' regimes. Often these pedagogical approaches deal with the young person's behaviour first, and their learning second. Tyler Denmead's (2019) study of a youth arts studio highlights the often unintended adverse effects of arts programs on young people. His auto-ethnographic exploration critiqued the supposed 'soul-saving' processes of transforming 'troubled youth' into 'creative youth' and highlights exactly who benefits from their human capital. Focusing on the 'performance' of creativity and its relationship to youth, class and race, Denmead argues that 'creatives' are the most desirable kind of urban youth. His studio became a space where young people 'learnt' creative lifestyles, becoming co-opted by creativity as 'state orchestrated racialized class-warfare' against the underclass. Despite the young people in his study using arts practice to trouble the logic of the underclass, the arts were tasked with transforming these groups of young people from troublemakers into creative citizens.

While these critical reflections emerged from my post-fieldwork analysis and writing up of my thesis, the young people on their programs took a much less instrumental view of this experience. For them, there was real value not only in creating and sharing the work they had made, but also through experimenting with different art forms and their own ideas through being part of a collective group. To close this chapter, I explore cultural citizenship in relation to youth arts pedagogies in order to offer a route for future practice to avoid this dichotomy.

Pedagogies for cultural citizenship

Returning to the concept of cultural citizenship, the shared pedagogies of youth work and the arts explored in this chapter highlight an engagement young people have in practices of creativity through their own diverse cultural identities (Stevenson, 2003). Using this approach contributes to an ongoing dialogue about the role of arts education in supporting participatory democracy and social change (Kuttner, 2015). There is a responsibility of youth arts programs to generate a particular set of conditions through which young people can demonstrate activism, agency and engagement with cultural life as competent members of their cultural communities; a rights-based approach, where young people have rights to produce and participate (Mai and Gibson, 2011), and can claim co-authorship and develop activist practices against cultural exclusion (Boele van Hensbroek, 2010). Through this lens the rights to culture are embedded with notions of entitlement, the right to be different and to celebrate diverse identities, where those previously stigmatised are revalued and those marginalised are legitimated (Pakulski, 1997). This is opposed to neoliberal notions of citizenship which depict young people as responsible, obedient and able to progress through meritocracy (Osler and Starkey, 2005; Lawy and Biesta, 2006; Hart, 2009). Cultural citizenship, therefore, is an approach to youth arts programs that positions young people as connected members of both local and global communities.

Kuttner (2015) defines three categories of cultural citizenship:

1. *informed cultural citizens* who have the capacity to understand, appreciate, and critique works of art as an active consumer;
2. *participatory cultural citizens* who see themselves as an active participant, who can produce, remix and share work created; and
3. *justice-oriented cultural citizens* who feel a civic responsibility to use their artistic practice to actively promote justice and address inequalities in society.

My research found that Arts Award was mainly developing informed cultural citizens. The program is designed for young people, often lacking arts backgrounds and prior knowledge, to have the capacity to understand and appreciate works of art without feeling alienated. As explored in the previous chapter, the participants in my study sometimes found themselves feeling at odds with the practices on offer and were disadvantaged by deficit pedagogies, as argued here. However, there were some young people in the study whom I considered to be participatory cultural citizens as they saw themselves as artistic producers who drew on common culture (Willis, 1990) to create work.

However, youth arts programs have the potential to enable young people to develop as *justice-oriented cultural citizens.* This represents young people who feel a civic responsibility to use their artistic practice to actively promote justice and address inequalities in society. This involves a critical awareness of how the arts are used in processes of opposition and resistance and aligns with CAYW. In my study on Arts Award, there were a select few examples of art works created that represented activist and radical work, through which marginalised groups might attempt to gain control over their representation in the media. Youth arts programs, therefore, have the potential to contribute to social justice arts education, youth participatory action research and community cultural development in future manifestations.

Conclusion

This chapter has explored the shared pedagogies of youth work and the arts and a way of theorising youth arts pedagogies. This included the importance of collaboration, co-creation of knowledge and relational learning. The affordances of youth arts programs for border pedagogy (Coburn, 2011) were also examined. However, for those young people under deficit labelling, there were varieties in pedagogical practice, which were viewed as a hierarchy depending on young people's perceived behaviour and assumptions made about their artistic ability. While Arts Award is presented as an open and flexible award where young people are free to make choices and follow up their own interests, this offer was counteracted by the restricted offer of the programs and programming by youth workers. My research highlighted that the more disengaged or disruptive young people were offered the least opportunities, which ran contrary to the democratic aims of youth arts programs to bring young people together with the arts on their own terms. While Arts Award was tasked with broadening access to the arts and culture for as wide a range of young people as possible, this chapter has demonstrated that youth arts programs can have an adverse effect on 'inclusion' from the experience of deficit pedagogies. Therefore, the argument is made that Arts Award's potential is not being reached.

The implications of Kuttner's (2015) typologies in relation to the design of future arts programs raises questions about what arts education does and can prepare young people to be. My research on Arts Award demonstrated affordances for developing young people as *informed cultural citizens*, whereas the program should have been aiming for *participatory cultural citizens* at least and *justice-oriented cultural citizens* at best. Cultural citizenship should be central to youth arts programs, as a way to strengthen programming and to work against the – often unacknowledged – disadvantages. In Part III of the book, I explore six international youth arts programs as a way of highlighting best practice, and revisit the themes of common culture, cultural democracy and cultural citizenship.

Part III

Accommodating common culture

Common culture is a process whereby young people draw on their available cultural resources as an input for their own cultural productivity, in the contexts of their everyday lives. This chapter develops arguments set out in Chapter 5, by exploring the kinds of arts practices that flourish within youth work settings. I present two international case studies, which demonstrate young people's take up of common culture. These include Dancehearts, based at Annantalo in Finland, which provides inclusive dance sessions; and Bolt FM (Scotland), which is a program that gives young people a voice using radio. These two programs exemplify, in particular, the value of informal education and kinaesthetic pedagogies. I argue that youth arts programs that accommodate common culture, for example those that engage with DIY and digital arts practices, are more likely to be responsive, engaging and ultimately impactful for the young people involved.

Focusing on an inclusive dance program, this chapter draws on the *pedagogy of collegiality* (Chávez and Soep, 2005) and DIY arts practice in the analysis of data from the two case study programs. Showcasing dance practice that is based on a social model of disability is designed to address our ability to read dance – our dance literacy – to be able to appreciate its manipulation of bodies, spaces and time (Kuppers, 2000). Participation in integrated dance programs has been shown to have a positive impact on young people's perceptions of dance ability and disability (Zitomer and Reid, 2011). In juxtaposition, the youth radio station draws on digital arts practices as a way of rooting youth arts firmly within the young people's experiences. Through being open access, dialogic and participatory, youth radio programs represent an 'asset-based' endeavour, which builds on young people's cultural funds of knowledge (Huesca, 2008; Green, 2013). Therefore these programs offer a space which can be used symbolically by young people, as a significant site of cultural production (Wilkinson, 2015).

Following an introduction to both case studies, I highlight key elements of Paul Willis' framework of common culture (Willis, 1990) including everyday and symbolic creativity and the continuum of expressive forms drawn on by young people. As explored in Chapter 1, Gaztambide-Fernández (2020) proposes the term 'cultural production' as opposed to 'the arts' as a way of privileging the practices, processes, and products of symbolic creativity situated in particular local contexts. This lens is taken up in this chapter in order to explore the case studies in relation to authentic modes of cultural production. In addition, common culture is also aligned to 'commoning' (Standing, 2019) and 'little publics' (Hickey-Moody, 2013b), so as to argue that while the arts offer young people a local and cultural embeddedness within society, making art and experiencing culture is a common right. First, I explore the positioning of common culture within youth arts programs.

Why common culture is important

> We are all invisible and unacknowledged creators of our own material culture.
>
> (Willis, 2005, p 75)

Culture is found in the everyday and everywhere around us. Young people have a clear and unfiltered consciousness of the culture in the world around them, and this is often misrecognised or not listened to. With youth arts programs, young people have the potential to shape what the arts mean to them from their everyday experiences. These programs draw on sources of everyday creativity and symbolic creativity (Willis, 1990), such as social media, cultural heritage and life stories. Common culture is key to understanding arts practice within youth arts settings, such as those explored in Chapters 5 and 6, which afford important opportunities for digital and DIY arts practices and identity work for young people today. Digital technologies and social media are key elements of common culture, not only as modes of production and consumption, but also as methods of communication that develop shared interests. Willis posits common culture as a process, whereby young people draw on their available cultural resources as an input for their own cultural productivity. Within a youth arts context, this acknowledges a wider diversity as 'meaning-making from below' (Willis, 1990). Willis argues for identification, recognition and support of existing creative experiences and activities not at present regarded as 'artistic' but which are now part of our common culture (Willis, 2005). For example, even though young people may be learning different string instruments and how to play in an orchestra, they are able to adapt and play music from their own cultural repertoires of pop music, YouTube or video games (see Chicago Arts and Music Project, Chapter 9).

My intention within this book has been to explore the new and different ways that young people experience culture and everyday forms of arts within youth settings. I hope to celebrate art marking in communities, rooted in young people's experiences and alternative spaces for engaging with this art (Burton et al, 2016). This is opposed to arts programs that are positioned as a quick fix and which are short term and offer inauthentic engagement (Belfiore, 2009). For young people who would not go to a gallery to see art but spend time learning new skills, teaching themselves and each other, digital arts practices are particularly enabling as they draw on DIY approaches. Often youth workers feel they are 'playing catch up' with the ideas young people bring with them and the things they have seen and want to emulate and do differently. The case studies in this chapter exemplify both of these approaches. Digital arts practices are also taken up in the next chapter through the case study on SWAN Youth Service, which employs an artist-in-residence, who specialises in digital media in order to be responsive and support young people's arts practice beyond the limits of the smartphone.

While common culture denotes a shared space of cultural consumption and production, a 'cultural commons' develops through our shared natural resources, which include not only natural forms such as parks and forests, but also our social and cultural institutions. Within public space the arts create a shared understanding and an evolving sense of culture. A true cultural commons draws on the arts to express our collective human culture, while supporting a multiplicity of cultural traditions (Standing, 2019). However, as Standing (2019) argues, this is being eroded by accelerated privatisation under the umbrella of austerity and a problematic reliance on corporate philanthropy. Therefore, youth arts programs are important opportunities to support shared attitudes, values and cultural resources, positioning young people as 'little publics' (Hickey-Moody, 2013b). Aligning with the values of commoning, youth arts programs with common culture at their heart draw upon expressive and intrinsic values of the arts and foreground a sense of community.

Annantalo

The Finnish Annantalo (translated as 'Anna's House') has been organising activities for children and young people in Helsinki since 1987. The aim of the organisation is to have a connection with every child and provide a place where children, young people and families can encounter art in an accessible way. The arts education offer of Annantalo extends to all elementary school pupils in Helsinki and is often their first encounter with art. Annantalo is financed by Helsinki City and organises 350 events each year. Art Testers[1] is a national scheme for 8th graders (14-year-olds), so that every young person can experience art in a child-oriented and participatory way. Every school in Helsinki provides classes for two hours per week, over a five-week period, where young people work with an arts educator. Pirjetta Mulari, Chief of Children's Culture and Director of Annantalo, noted the particular pedagogical position of the arts educators, which is akin to that of youth workers:

> 'They [arts educators] are so engaged in their work that they take more than the position of a teacher. They really care for the students

experience because there is a real interaction there. This keeps our kids engaged for years because they feel that it's a very important adult, it might be an artist, but it's also an adult, who they regularly see. So, this is really part of their growing up.' (Pirjetta Mulari, Chief of Children's Culture and Director of Annantalo)

Annantalo caters for a wide range of artistic activities that are designed from the viewpoint of the young person through collaborative making, experiencing and asking participants what they think. Recognising that young people are a minority, respect is given to participants' initiatives so that they can express their thoughts from a minority point of view. Arts educator Sanna Kuusisto believes that this approach benefits not only the individual, in that they are not pushed aside and forgotten, but also the whole community. Annantalo also advertises specialist arts groups for organisations working with or for children with disabilities. The program explored further in this chapter is Dancehearts, a dance group for every interested young person, whether they have a disability or not.

Dancehearts

Dancehearts is an art education group, based at Annantalo, for young people between the ages of nine and 18 years. The program has an intensified resource of facilitators working to ensure that everybody can influence and participate. Dancehearts makes possible participation in dance for young people with functional and movement variations. The premise for founding the group was that most young people have an unrestrained desire to dance and that dance should be encouraged to stimulate expression. In the activities of the group there is an unbridled desire to dance, folded into the joy of dancing, which can be boisterous and fun, but which also can be concentrated and emotive. The values of the program include a focus on art, creative process and improvisation. Arts educators engage with a kinaesthetic methodology, which encompasses multi-sensory perception, multi-artistic expression and dancing as practical processing. Sanna Kuusisto further explains:

'I think that it's so important for everybody to have the possibility to be together doing something that we feel that is meaningful, and that we also have a very practical thing to do together. It's clear we come here, we dance, we do exercises and we improvise together. It's no one's therapy, and we don't have be tailored to any external aims. Our activities with young people with disabilities are not political. It's not about getting them to "assimilate" in the normal society. So, we wanted this program to be a hobby, that the community themselves could bring things, that we could then have those as the aim and goals for our work. The most important is not what we are doing, if it's dancing or making visual arts or theatre or music, but it's that we are coming together and doing something that we all like to do.' (Sanna Kuusisto, Arts Educator)

This arts program is founded upon the belief that dance is an important and basic part of being a human, and the main focus of Dancehearts is the young people's bodies and dancing together with adults and arts educators, like a community dance team. The young people in the group always enjoy performing following a process of picking from all the different ideas that are generated, moulding together the overlapping ideas and making suggestions on the use of space or closeness to others, for example. Sanna explains that "We're trying to get the young people's voices as well as trying to be as sensitive as we can, and open and willing to give up our own thoughts." Despite the strong traditional rituals within dance as an artistic practice, Dancehearts is facilitated so that everybody is allowed to express themselves and explore how they would want to be in the sessions. Previous program participant Elina (30-year-old, white Finnish female) reflected that

> 'The dance day was always an expected and happy thing for me. In the group, we were improvising and practising dance movements together with others and a couple of times a year we had performance. In the dance group everyone could influence the making and the choreography. The music, sometimes live, was important in the group's work and created a supportive atmosphere.' (Elina, previous programme participant)

In the summer, the group hosts outdoor sessions that focus around open-air site-specific dance, including dancing with public statues in different public places outdoors (see Figure 7.1). Young people benefit not only from being outdoors for the whole day in the summertime, but also from having people passing by the group dancing in the park or the street. Sanna believes that it is good for the participants to have the courage to dance there in the middle of the streets where everybody can see them, where dancing together is formative and young people forget being there as performers. In response, participants reported enjoyment from active participation but also the commitment to an artistic practice, whereby developing a skill brings pleasure.

Kinaesthetic method

While Annantalo adopts a particular pedagogical position that is child centred, Dancehearts engages with the 'kinaesthetic method', which foregrounds

Figure 7.1: Dancing in response to public sculptures

Note: Photograph of *Dancehearts* open-air, site-specific summer dance program.

the importance of expression, being together and moving together. Sanna contends that in seeing and feeling other bodies and interaction, young people can learn things with their own bodies that they can start to do:

'Simply, it's dancing together so that we are different dancers. We are adults who are professional dancers or others who are not professional dancers, but still adults who like to move and have the courage to express themselves with movements. And then we have young people who have different abilities in moving themselves but in spite of the actual physical possibilities, we all share the same intelligence of recognising and noticing the kinaesthetic things which are happening in other people's bodies and that we are a part of the experience.' (Sanna Kuusisto, Arts Educator)

Working with young people with disabilities, the arts educators do exactly the same things which they would do with anybody they are artistically interested in, whereby they regard every group and every participant as special. In acknowledging that young people are different, the challenge for the facilitators is finding something in common, so that everybody in the group can feel good, can be heard and can be seen. Sanna further reflects that while they have participants who may not speak very much, they have reactions and interests and indicate those things which they feel are speaking to them more than others. The facilitators hear those responses, and can respect and react to them. Previous participant, and now volunteer with the program, Elina shared her experience of everyone being allowed to be their own self and that the movement reduction was not a barrier to dancing. She argued that the dance program gave the group the courage to realise themselves and to take others into account and that with the help of dance, it was possible to let out all kinds of emotions.

Further data will be drawn on from this program later in the chapter to explore the pedagogy of collegiality (Chávez and Soep, 2005) and dance as a DIY arts practice. Now I move on to describe the second case study, the youth radio program Bolt FM.

Bolt FM

Based in north-east Glasgow, the youth radio station offers young people the opportunity to develop skills in radio and train with professional-standard equipment, and gives them the chance to use these skills. As Scotland's longest-running youth radio station, Bolt FM's mobile program is able to connect small communities through visiting different locations: youth clubs, drop-ins at partner organisations and schools. Bolt FM is a community charity providing free meals and different programs for people in the community who are disadvantaged, but it is also a learning platform for young people who want to learn skills in radio technology and music production. Offering a mobile venue breaks down barriers to access and financial barriers as all activities are free. The program is funded 50 per cent through Glasgow City Council's communities fund and draws the remaining funding from charitable and arts funding sources such as Children in Need.[2] Young people are able to plan, present and record podcasts, radio dramas, documentaries and sound art, alongside an annual two-week takeover of the radio station for live transmission. They are supported by youth workers from a range of different backgrounds – radio, arts, and youth work – who each bring a different set of skills.

The organisation's main aim is to give young people a voice using radio. Young people can research the history of radio and then work on short scripts as if they were reporting historical events, alongside facilitating outdoor events and festivals where young people can get involved in live broadcasts. Helping young people to feel comfortable with themselves in their own voice is a key aim of the program, and then directing their issues and what their thoughts are on these for discussion with a wider audience. For those young people who say they 'hate' talking, some enjoy working with the technical aspects and particularly post production, where participants get to work with the same standard equipment as commercial radio programs: microphones, faders and computers that play music. The program also has links with other radio stations where young people can take up apprenticeships.

Youth workers who support the project view the art form of radio as a malleable blank canvas where young people can draw on their own artistic interests, but also as a tool for youth work:

> 'The program is about giving young people a place that every week they spend time with youth workers who they trust, who are going to be there for them and as much as, what we do is a youth radio project, we see radio as a tool to do youth work. Having that sort of trusted positive adult role model relationship is really important for us to have so young people can trust and look for support. It's not always a given for young people that they have that sort of relationships with adults, where they're being trusted and respected, and so I think it is a real benefit.' (Mark Chambers, Bolt FM Coordinator)

Every year, Bolt FM hosts a two-week FM broadcast where young people promote, prepare and present over 200 hours of live radio. Young people pick their 'slots', plan what they want to do either by themselves or with friends, talking, interviews, playing music and any other ideas they may have for their live show. As engineering a show takes a short amount of time, this also gives young people a huge amount of freedom, where they can direct what they want to do, and learn to become independent. Youth workers reflect that despite the equipment they work with being specialised, young people do not realise how much technical skill they already have and how transferable that is to a different type of kind of computer system. So that means that young people learn how to work things that look difficult at first, such as a mixing desk with faders, as shown in Figure 7.2, but actually within one session, they can do most of the things that would be expected of a radio presenter.

Youth radio has a power in terms of offering a 'safe space' for young people to chat and to socialise, while feeling listened to because they have a platform to talk about things that are important to them and to share their voice. This also has affordances for confidence and identity development, as described by Neil Young, Youth Team Leader for St Paul's Forum, where Bolt FM is based:

> 'One of the great things about the radio station is that young people can be who they want to be or be somebody completely different and take on a whole different persona. So, the judgement of what do you look like? What are you wearing? Is all gone. That can be a liberating thing, that lots of other people don't get that opportunity to have, and that's one of the things that I find special in that the young people can

Figure 7.2: Young person learns how to use a mixing desk

Note: Photograph taken at Bolt FM, during open access radio station session.

make themselves this big persona.' (Neil Young, Youth Team Leader for St Paul's Forum)

Having a radio station and microphones gives the program an opportunity to connect with a wide range of people in the community. Often this includes artists, musicians and bands but also local politicians. Young people set up the radio studio at Holyrood (Scottish Parliament) and interviewed several MSPs about the issues that they felt were important and genuinely affecting them. Responding to young people's requests to make more positive radio, participants have conducted interviews with charities that work locally for events such as Refugee Week[3] and the 'Off the Ball' campaign, led by three local women lobbying for free sanitary products at Celtic Park football ground. Young people have also been involved in working on scripted radio dramas and pitching their ideas at local community funding events.

Informal education approach

Like Annantalo, Bolt FM engages with arts practice as informal education, which is a key tenet of youth arts programs. Building upon a key youth work principle of voluntary participation, youth workers from Bolt FM argue for the value of 'meeting young people where they are at'. This involves informal education approaches based upon dialogical methods, where youth work practitioners engage young people in conversation about what they want to learn, using radio as a platform to give young people control. Program Coordinator, Mark Chambers, reflects on the informal education approach:

'Sometimes we "teach" young people radio skills resembling more like a school lesson, with particular skill they want to know, and then those are the types of learning that come up coincidentally, you know the kind of stealth learning. For example, let's say they picked that they want to talk about climate change on their radio show. So, then you can open up these conversations and very different things as well.' (Mark Chambers, Program Coordinator)

Participant and now volunteer with Bolt FM, Eilidh McMillan (21-year-old, white, British female) joined the program during what she called a "rough time in her life" and found that radio was a great outlet for her as a chance to connect, escape and be involved in things that she was passionate about, like music, talking to people and learning about other people's experiences. She reflects that being able to "hang out" with youth workers on the program afforded her an appreciation for informal education techniques that she now replicates in her own work:

'Seeing how Mark [Program Coordinator] interacted with us as young people and how he enabled us to do things was really inspiring to me. I thought that was something that I would love to be a part of and the radio that was an extra push for me as I love all things musical. And if I can do that for someone else. ... Just to be what the youth workers here have offered to me, I think that would be an amazing thing.' (Eilidh McMillan, Participant and Volunteer with Bolt FM)

Participant N (13-year-old, Asian British male) describes his experience on the radio as "like a duck taking to water". While he enjoys being a radio presenter and interviewing people, he has also developed confidence with the technical side, whereby he is now able to teach other young people how to create their own music. For young people who may be particularly averse to learning new things in front of peers, the affirmation of finding things they are good at builds confidence. Young people interviewed about this program eloquently described the power of confidence as self-assurance and belief in themselves, knowing that the time spent on the radio was a time for themselves, where they could get across what they wanted to say.

Accommodating common culture

The case studies of Dancehearts and Bolt FM are intended to demonstrate the value and benefits of accommodating common culture within youth arts programs. The arts practices involved draw on a continuum of expressive forms (Willis, 2005), as well as highlighting young people's everyday and symbolic creativity (Willis, 1990). The artistic mediums of dance and radio encompass both digital and DIY arts practice, which, I argued in Chapter 5, are vital elements of youth arts programs today. For example, the improvisation structures of dance as an arts practice and the individualised movement capabilities of young people are highly DIY, in conjunction with the affordances of working with digital technologies that radio offers as an art form. Further, both of these programs demonstrate a pedagogy of collegiality (Chávez and Soep, 2005), whereby the conventional structure of adult 'teacher' and young 'learners' is transcended, in favour of informal education approaches, typical of youth work practice. Both of these programs draw on a pedagogy of collegiality to enable young people to tell stories about their own lives and the conditions that surround them. Therefore, within common culture there is the opportunity for young people to offer alternative perspectives and more authentic narratives.

Authentic modes of cultural production

Within common culture, there is a change in demographics on who can become an artist, shifting the arts away from being a 'service' or a 'market' (Burton et al, 2016). When communities come together to create culture(s), they become a mode of social engagement and social justice work, whereby young people, traditionally without power in society, can make lots of provocative art. An example of this is the concept of 'Troublemaking', set out by Denmead (2019) in his ethnographic work in an urban youth arts studio, where young people challenged deficit-based identities through arts practice.

The analysis in this book has been inspired by Gaztambide-Fernández's (2020) contention that cultural production provides a framework through which the arts can be viewed in a productive and equity-based way, driven by relational encounters, rather than functioning as civilising instruments of institutional power. By recognising the arts at grassroots level and accommodating common culture, youth arts programs have the potential to enable authentic modes of cultural production. Participant N from Bolt FM argues for the value of radio as an authentic creative outlet, where "it constantly comes back to being about the young people and what they want to do". Mark Chambers supports this view, stating that

> 'Radio is in the eye of the beholder. It's about bringing out in the young person, what they're actually interested in and what they find entertaining. So, for some young people Bolt FM could be an outlet to try out some kind of journalistic type work. For some young people it's about a passion they have for music and trying to communicate

that. Or for some people it's just about having fun. We encourage young people to think about what it is that they like talking about, what they find interesting and engaging and try to bring that out. And also, that's kind of about validating to them, you know, that you think about the things that they care about are valuable and worthwhile.' (Mark Chambers, Program Coordinator for Bolt FM)

Both of these programs – Dancehearts and Bolt FM – position young people as artists and support arts practices that are rooted in young people's experiences, which are key affordances of common culture. Arts activities are designed from the point of view of the young person, as Chief of Children's Culture and Director of Annantalo argues: "We're really about making and experiencing. Of course, that's already participatory, but we do also ask them what they think or what kind of ways they would like to work or what themes they would like to bring in in the art, so I would say it's very child-oriented."

While common culture therefore offers opportunities for authentic modes of cultural production, the approach is also based on a child's rights perspective (UN) that nations have the responsibility to provide the possibilities for young people to encounter the arts.

Commoning

In his book *The Plunder of the Commons*, Standing (2019) argues for commoning, as public spaces that have been created for community activity. These include cultural commons, where the arts happen in the public domain, such as street art, busking and public performances. The Dancehearts program, as well as taking over public spaces for impromptu dance experiences (see Figure 7.3), focuses on young people experiencing cultural life outside of the institution of the school. Finland's curriculum is phenomenon based, where the requirement is that young people engage with organisations outside of school and in their cities. As I argued in Chapter 2, one of the key benefits of these programs is the wider reach and inclusivity beyond the school, as a form of commoning. Standing (2019) argues that if the cultural commons is eroded, learning, empathy and critical thinking are also eroded. Therefore, youth arts programs offer an opportunity for young people to take part in and create their own cultural commons, giving other commoners access to cultural activities that may be new to them, while also allowing room for experimentation and development. Mark Chambers eloquently describes how commoning manifests in the program:

'It's about young people bringing their own culture. You know they're bringing the music they're interested and they're bringing these stories in

Figure 7.3: Young person dances in public space

Note: Photograph of *Dancehearts* open-air, site-specific summer dance program.

the news or the things they want to talk about. But then also they have that direct engagement with a huge variety of different people placed at organisations around the city and get that experience of kind of different things that are going on.' (Mark Chambers, Bolt FM Coordinator)

The coming together of groups of young people around particular arts programs or practices is described by Hickey-Moody (2013b) as 'little publics'. In particular she refers to the materiality of their arts practices, which constitute a form of citizenship. Not only do young people become cultural producers, but they also become audiences for the arts, on their own terms. Eilidh McMillan describes the value of being both a radio presenter and listener, as pictured in Figure 7.4:

'It's a great way to share other people's stories as much as it's an amazing way for you to share, you know your own voice and things that you're passionate about. It's a great listening platform, you know, that's what radio essentially is. You listen to someone as a presenter or young person organising that and being involved. You get to hear about other people's lives, which, at least for me, I'm always so fascinated about. And it's so interesting to hear about other people's experiences and cultures.' (Eilidh McMillan, Participant and Volunteer with Bolt FM)

Figure 7.4: Young people devising a script for a radio show

Note: Photograph taken at Bolt FM, during open-access radio station session.

Commoning as part of common culture therefore represents a key affordance of youth arts programs to 'meet young people where they are at', to enable young people to create and celebrate their own culture in a collective and democratic way.

Conclusion

This chapter has presented one of the key themes of the book: common culture. Through the exemplar programs of Dancehearts (Finland) and Bolt FM (Scotland), the possibilities of common culture for affording authentic modes of cultural production and commoning have been explored. Throughout this chapter the alignment between the arts and youth work practice has been highlighted through informal education and inclusion approaches. Focusing in particular on the pedagogical approach of the kinaesthetic method, artistic practice is experienced collectively, yet celebrated differently. This, I have argued, enabled youth arts programs that accommodated common culture to be responsive, engaging and ultimately more likely to be impactful.

The two international case studies were selected because they are programs that are highly invested in young people's funds of cultural knowledge. No assumptions are made on behalf of the young people, no deficits are depicted and no prescribed ways of being are projected. Both programs also demonstrate the dedication, skills and compassion with which arts educators and youth workers alike engage with young people on the programs, as cultural producers rather than passive participants. Also, both programs have strongly signalled the importance of voice and identity development, whereby the arts are engaged with symbolically and expressively.

In viewing both of these programs as a focus on process rather than product, alternative spaces, such as the streets of Helsinki and the airwaves of Glasgow, offer an important way for young people to experience culture. Viewing culture as a shared natural resource, youth arts programs such as Dancehearts and Bolt FM uphold community values and commoning, where the arts are a fundamental part of being human, a basic right and a form of citizenship. Building upon this premise, the next two chapters showcase further international case studies which support cultural democracy (Chapter 8) and cultural citizenship (Chapter 9).

8

Celebrating cultural democracy

Cultural Democracy is a long-standing campaign that describes an approach to arts and culture that 'actively engages everyone in deciding what counts as culture, where it happens, who makes it, and who experiences it' (Arts Council England, 2018). This chapter contains two case studies which highlight best practice in supporting and celebrating cultural democracy and practical insights for arts programs with young people. The case studies include Propel Youth Arts WA (Western Australia), which is an arts-based youth advocacy organisation, and SWAN Youth Service (Ireland), which devises programs for young people to explore different artistic mediums and processes. SWAN places an importance on the arts as an opportunity for informal education, and its Reckless Arts program, which, hosts an artist-in-residence, is the focus of this case study. Through these exemplars, I demonstrate the value of youth-led arts programming and position young people as cultural experts as a way of celebrating cultural democracy within youth arts programs.

'Artist-Warriors' have been positioned as reclaimers of culture in relation to First Nations and Aboriginal arts (Kramer, 2004). One of the case studies in this chapter focuses on a particular youth arts festival – KickstART – which has been designed in order to celebrate and support Noongar[1] arts and culture in Perth, Western Australia. As well as breaking down stereotypes of cultural identity (McIntyre, 2012), youth-led arts programming is often antithetical to conventional norms and can reach wider into communities to find experiences and lived realities that better reflect and articulate youth culture (Brooks et al, 2015). In conjunction, the second youth arts program brings young people, youth workers and artists together through an artist-in-residence program funded in part by the National Youth Council of Ireland.[2] While the benefits of artist-in-residence programs are well known in the context of formal education as a more collaborative, meaningful and open learning relationship (Eckhoff, 2011), less is known about youth work and informal education settings. This chapter therefore explores how different forms of knowledge are mediated through youth arts programs, alongside the affordances of young people working with an artist-in-residence, in terms of laying claim to their position in the arts landscape.

In this chapter, data from interviews with young people, arts practitioners, festival coordinators, youth workers and project managers is presented in order to celebrate alternative cultural forms through youth-led arts programming. Key examples of shared cultural knowledge and resources are also given as ways in which the arts and culture are kept meaningful and vital. The programs featured in this chapter demonstrate the value of youth arts programs for encouragement, collaboration and experimentation, but also for understanding community. Finally, meaningful public engagement is explored from the perspective of supporting young people to enter spaces traditionally reserved for the cultural elites, ensuring that diverse perspectives are heard and contributing to a more diverse future landscape for the arts.

Is a cultural democracy possible?

Hadley and Belfiore (2018) argue that a re-envisioning and regeneration of what cultural democracy means within the present day is needed. Youth arts programs, which have a focus on artistic production rather than access to works of art, are a good vehicle through which young people can draw upon their own creative inspirations, which can include networks of youth workers, arts practitioners and other young people. This focus on young people as creative producers, alongside the open access provision of arts programs, ensures that everyone can participate, aligning with underpinning values of cultural democracy. Therefore, outcomes for the young people as artists become the focus, rather than outcomes for the arts by developing new audiences. This approach seeks to question hierarchies of cultural value, the power and authority society's elites have traditionally held over artistic production (Hadley and Belfiore, 2018). Youth arts programs hold value in their disruption of expected forms of participation and communication of culture (Jeffers and Moriarty, 2017) and acknowledgement of diverse cultural values within society. While voluntary participation is a key principle within youth work practice, there has been ongoing erosion of this democratic ideal through targeted approaches upheld by austerity policies, where the arts became tasked with combating social issues (Sim, 2019). Therefore, it is important to revisit cultural democracy through the lens of youth arts programs as a way of upholding democratic aims and community-responsive approaches.

Cultural democracy as a recognised global movement has flourished on some continents more than others. For example, in Norway, a four-year (2013–17) project funded by the Norwegian Research Council entitled *Reassembling Democracy: Ritual as Cultural Resource* (REDO) explored the ways in which communities mobilise cultural resources drawn from varied knowledge bases. These resources produced interactions between persons, communities and environments, as a way of enriching democratic processes (Houseman and Salomonsen, 2020). Of particular note within this project was the research at two cultural festivals which showcased indigenous arts and performances as a way of assembling and reassembling relations (Harvey,

2020). In contrast, exploring cultural democracy in America (Graves, 2010), a focus on everyday cultural transmission and informal arts practices aligns with the values of youth arts programs, explored in the previous chapter on common culture. In symbiosis, importance is attached to creating conditions which allow people to choose to be active participants rather than just passive receivers of culture and the sharing of values among various cultural groups. However, in his recent book *Audience Development and Cultural Policy*, Hadley (2021) draws on Foucault's theory of governmentality in order to critique the predominant UK model of cultural policy as top down and state led. In trying to produce 'model citizens', Hadley highlights the depiction of a deficit in relation to alternative cultural forms, which chimes with my arguments in Chapter 3 in relation to the deficit model of youth. Working with these global perspectives, the exemplars in this chapter demonstrate how cultural democracy can be enacted through youth arts programs.

This chapter focuses on two case studies that exemplify democratic modes of artistic production within youth arts programs. However, there are other case studies within this book that support these democratic ideals, such as Jugend- & Kulturprojekt e.V. (JKPeV), a European culture and education program that engages with the arts as a tool for sharing and openly expressing opinions with respect to young people from diverse heritages and backgrounds (see Chapter 9). The two case studies shared in this chapter include Propel Youth Arts WA (Perth, Australia), which supports a democratic model of programming for its annual KickstART festival, including employing a young person as creative coordinator and being led by a youth planning committee. In addition, SWAN Youth Service (Dublin, Ireland) offers a range of arts and media opportunities to young people via several programs and works with an artist-in-residence to support one particular program: Reckless Arts. Together these case studies exemplify how youth arts programs, which hold cultural democracy at their heart, are best positioned to support artistic practices and issues that have been identified by young people as culturally relevant to them and uphold mechanisms for youth-led decision making about the arts.

Propel Youth Arts WA

Founded in 2003, Propel Youth Arts WA aims to address a gap in the sector identified by young people in relation to pathways to employment within arts and cultural institutions, with a wider purpose to provide advocacy and a voice for young people in the arts sector. It is positioned as a 'service organisation'; young people are encouraged to become members, at no cost, and they are able to access a range of benefits. Working with young people between 12 and 26, the organisation provides opportunities for mentorships, connecting with different artists and supporting with grant writing as well as listening to young people's thoughts, wants and needs on bigger issues than the arts. For example, there is currently a strong focus on First Nations advocacy, as General Manager for Propel, Jamie Gleave, describes:

> 'That's resulted in us putting together an Aboriginal and Torres Strait Islander arts network. Young people have told us that there need for this. This needs to be established and the hope is that a group then becomes funded and then eventually becomes its own thing that's led by Aboriginal people. Rather than being something that's for Aboriginal people, it's actually led by them. For young people this is a very recent history. It's a history that's still happening, so it's an area that does need to be addressed in terms of representation of, not just people from different cultures and in our community, but particularly focusing on the most disadvantaged and marginalised, which in WA is Aboriginal people.' (Jamie Gleave, General Manager for Propel)

Propel is 90 per cent state government funded through the Department for Culture and the Arts and is reflective and responsive to what its members and partner organisations want, which culminates in public-facing programs. These include the 'Why Culture' program, which gives grants to young artists, and the annual KickstART festival, which is explored in further detail in the next section.

KickstART festival

Currently in its 11th year, the KickstART festival took place online in 2020 due to restrictions under COVID-19. An umbrella event taking place over a week in the Metro area of Perth, there are between 50 and 60 free events, workshops, talks, live performances and music gigs. Each year there is a different theme for the festival week that is selected by a youth-led planning committee and communicated to all the other local government bodies in the state. As well as reaching the broad community of young people in the Perth area, a lot of rural communities and towns like to participate in the week through initiatives such as the sketchbook gallery. A different young person is employed as the creative coordinator for the KickstART festival each year.

The KickstART festival is one of the main vehicles for Propel to engage with young people who are interested in the arts. Events are created and curated alongside young artists so that other young people can learn new skills and connect with each other. There is a focus on artistic development, personal growth and social development, as well as just enjoying the arts through some fun, hands-on activities during the school holidays. Each year the program responds to issues that are relevant to young people today, such as mental health, housing and unemployment. Young people are supported to apply for grants to be facilitators for events that happen within the KickstART festival. They can also be performers and stallholders, or volunteer during festival week. Participant Grace (24-year-old, white, Australian female) tells me that she was invited to be an assistant stage manager for one of the events where there was a large music line-up, which was a role she was interested in. Grace reflects:

'I think that the fact that it's an arts event and where the focus is on creating opportunities for young people, that's one of the biggest things that I love about KickstART. There are all these doorways for people to be involved and meet someone new and there's an opportunity here, or there's an opportunity there and that comes from opening up the planning committee to young people. Rather than a festival that's made to consume and then leave, it's a festival that's made for people to enjoy and then take away from and then grow themselves with that little opportunity or snippet that they've got. So those values and incentives of growth and invigoration and valuing the young person who's not a professional yet, that's definitely the most attractive part about it for me.' (Grace, Participant in KickstART)

The creative coordinator works with the Youth Planning Committee (YPC) to develop ideas and connect young people with other artists in Perth and support conversations and collaborations to develop a diverse program. The YPC also approaches different arts organisations in Perth to provide activities as part of the festival week. The key pedagogical approach of the creative coordinator is the one-to-one work with the young artists and the YPC in order to build strong connections, skill sharing, and learning. Kobi Arthur Morrison was creative coordinator for 2020, which was the 10th anniversary of the festival. Kobi is a musician and artist and leads a reconciliation (healing) choir, the Walyalup Kannajl community choir. The festival theme was 'Koorah Nitja Boordahwan', which means 'past, present, future'. Kobi's intention was to acknowledge past histories, collective paths and potential futures, with an emphasis on a wide range of individual understanding but within a community-oriented approach. Drawing on Kobi's Bibbulmun Noongar ethnicity,[3] the 2020 program was designed to inspire Aboriginal and Torres Strait Islander artists to celebrate their culture. Having worked on previous events with Propel, Kobi was keen to support the mentoring work the organisation does with young artists, not only in offering workshops as ways in to the creative industries, but for the value of trying new forms self-expression and their intrinsic values. He reports:

'I could have very easily made this just a music festival, but I decided against doing that because I didn't want to run the risk of losing somebody because they felt like they were not represented, especially when the festival was celebrating variety. So, I decided to see how many different iterations of art mediums we were willing to take on board without freaking ourselves out. So, what we decided to do was we would implement the ones that were easiest, like music, photography, visual arts and poetry. And then we decided that we were going to explore some more unconventional stuff that we're wanting to go forward with, like video games.' (Kobi Arthur Morrison, Creative Coordinator for 2020)

Youth-led arts programming

Within the role of creative coordinator for the festival, Kobi worked closely with the YPC, a group of around 20 young people who would meet once a month in the six months leading up to the festival and then weekly within the last month. The YPC is the key driver for festival programming, selecting the theme and the design of the festival and being part of the whole process to ensure that the content is relevant and engaging for young people. Recruitment for the YPC is done through social media and word of mouth and the young people who tend to get involved are those who are interested in leadership in the arts. These young people also spread the word among their friends and in their schools and communities. Peer-to-peer networks such as this facilitate a local grassroots pathway into knowing these communities and connecting through the arts. Based on his experience from 2020, Kobi argues for the value of this democratic and dialogic process, as pictured in Figure 8.1:

'Prior to the first committee meeting I had conversations with as many people as I could. I was trying to make sure that we're keeping it democratic, because that was definitely a priority. It was something really, in the forefront of my mind, that I didn't want to be calling a bunch of shots that just didn't reflect properly on the community and then end up being some kind of dictator. It was fantastic in the way that we are able to refer to each other and riff off each other to get to the point where it wasn't like, purposefully, not 100 per cent of way that I had envisaged it at the beginning. It was substantially better because we were able to track these vibes with everyone and it was really exciting to be able to understand people as individuals, but also seeing all these connective substance between everyone. It's been fantastic to have a chat with everybody on a more individual scale and having the possibility of picking their brains because we have some pretty inspiring young people out there. It's amazing to be able to have the time to just sit down and listen.' (Kobi Arthur Morrison, Creative Coordinator for 2020)

Figure 8.1: Artist talks to young people at KickstART festival

Note: Photograph taken by Tasha Tong.

Grace, who has been involved in the KickstART festival since 2017, describes the value of being part of the YPC as wider than being able to feature on a CV or resume. She focused on the importance of a co-mentoring space, where she could both "look up" to the creative coordinator, but also be "looked to" for artistic inspiration and influences. She reflected on the valuable learning experience through "opening each other's eyes" to different perspectives, and that if she were then to step away and be project facilitator, these were the elements that she would have to consider:

'It was a really great role to this step into because you're welcomed into this group and you have a voice. You're allowed to share your opinion on things and just express your likes and dislikes and what you'd hope to see happen for a festival that's for young people. But at the same time, there's no pressure on you to immediately contribute and prove your worth almost. It's just this safe space. It really helped me to find a sense of purpose. It gave me a real sense of fulfilment, so being able to look forward to these meetings every week, I think at the time that I joined, I was the youngest person on the committee. So that, like for me personally, that was a really cool experience to have all these older people to welcome me and also for me to look up to. But also, to be in that environment and be treated like I was just the same as everyone else had my ideas or opinions or whatever it was.' (Grace, Participant in KickstART)

Reflecting on the democratic process of being on the YPC, Grace felt aligned to the values that KickstART and Propel were promoting, such as compassion and community, with young people coming at the top of that list. Being part of something and making it happen was a fulfilling feeling for her. Grace reported that the fruition of many months' planning and the experience of being a valuable part of a large-scale, state-recognised event was a rewarding realisation after the festival. As well as developing her confidence in facilitating conversations in groups and teamwork, Grace was able to grow her networks and experience of understanding how the arts industry works. For her, the focus on event planning and management was a vehicle for solidifying her interest in being 'behind the scenes', rather than a performer or artist.

The second case study explores a program – Reckless Arts – which is designed to support young people's progression as artists within youth work settings.

SWAN Youth Service

SWAN Youth Service is based in the north-east of inner-city Dublin. The organisation works with young people aged 10–24 who are socio-economically marginalised, and aims to empower young people through informal education. Working with the arts is one way in which youth workers provide opportunities for the young people to learn about the inequalities impacting them and their local communities and encourage them to challenge these. SWAN provides small-group and issue-based youth work, summer programs and residentials, and youth leadership opportunities, as well as sports and arts activities. The organisation is funded by the Department of Children, Equality, Disability, Integration and Youth, the Department for Youth Justice, and the North East Inner-City task force, as well as smaller individual funding sources for specific programs.

The arts are engaged with as a vehicle of empowerment for the young people accessing SWAN in order for their voices to be heard in a meaningful way. A wider variety of art forms are offered either as taster sessions or when a young person requests to create something, but film and digital media such as podcasting and music production are currently the most popular. Eibhlín Harrington – SWAN Youth Service project leader – noted that the young people on the program already have creative ideas and artistic direction when they join:

'So, where they have an interest in something they can actually explore it themselves. They don't really need an exposure. Sometimes in informal settings and they can kind of seek things out and sometimes it's just about having the stuff physically there in front of them. So having cameras there or having the art supplies there and then just letting people just use them and try things. … The young people that I've seen involved in the programs are hugely creative and also have very high standards for themselves. They often have a picture in their own heads exactly what they want and how they want things to be, and that's where the partnership with the artist comes in. The young person will have a concept or a picture of what they want to achieve and they just need support from the artists to create that.' (Eibhlín Harrington, Youth Service Project Leader, SWAN)

SWAN has a historical and valuable relationship with artist–in–residence Shireen Shortt, which has contributed to a commitment to maintain ongoing opportunities with potential for progressing young artists' practice within a youth work space. Her role has been to provide a space where young people can explore their own artistic practice with support but also reflect critically on their lives, their environment and their community. As a result of her support, a group of young people emerged who wanted to progress their practice and started to self–identify as artists. This group created (and named) their own program – Reckless Arts – as a freer space where they could explore their own interests thematically, aesthetically and artistically, as well as having the opportunity to cross over into different artistic mediums.

Reckless Arts

Reckless Arts started in 2017, with a patchwork of funding, including the National Youth Council of Ireland (NYCI), with the intention of creating an arts program that is less defined for young people who are already working with an art form. A key aim of the program is to enable young people to have a voice and for that voice to be recognised. Artist–in–residence and participatory media practitioner Dr Shireen Shortt believes that part of the work of the program is to develop confidence and recognition of the participants' own capacity for self-representation and self-narration. Reckless Arts is not a fixed short-term program; there is no pressure of deadlines and spaces are held for young people if they need to spend time working on something else. An important objective for Reckless Arts is to look for spaces for young people to exhibit that are uniquely relevant to the artwork that has been produced, but also outside of youth work space specifically. The program aims to bring young people's work into a wider cultural sphere, for example 'Culture Night' (a free night of arts and culture across Ireland) and national film festivals.

The group frequently works with digital and visual art forms and Shireen's role is to support the formation of young people's ideas, give advice on the creation of artistic work and extend the production value of the work, so that the final outputs are higher quality. Shireen reflects that the participants have few barriers to creating work, always coming with digital content that has inspired them or with particular ideas on what they want to create. However, for the young people on the program, the notion of exhibiting their work in public seems the biggest challenge:

'We do get them to a point where they are happy to exhibit and even better, to discuss that work. Even to put their name on it – you'll see a stage when they won't even want to put their name on it, but by the end they've written the brochure and they're doing the introductory speech! I would see it as getting to a point of self-recognition and going through the steps of voice, listening, recognition ... all of those. So that they recognise the value of their own voice and the value of what they have to say and the value of their own narratives – or narratives that they might construct to represent themselves and their points of view.' (Shireen Shortt, Participatory Media Practitioner)

Youth workers and the artist-in-residence work together through a model of social education, whereby the arts are used as a medium and a tool to develop young people's critical thinking. Eibhlín reflects that a lot of the work created can be quite emotionally heavy, but it is also then powerful. Giving young people an opportunity to tell their own stories is particularly important within a community where they are often written *about* and spoken *about* but have few opportunities to say, "Well, this is actually my experience" or "This is what I think." Enabling young people's voice and respecting dialogue are key components of cultural democracy that enable youth arts practice to flourish.

Young people as cultural experts

Building upon this pedagogical approach of youth arts practice, which values relationships and being responsive, democratic principles of voluntary participation and open dialogue are upheld. The approach of SWAN Youth Service is to celebrate young people as the experts on their own lives. The program believes in the value of giving young people space to be creative producers, to analyse whatever it is that they are working on and to think more deeply, whether that be to reflect on their own experiences or simply to express themselves. Participant Tamzin Brogan (19-year-old, white, Irish female) did not see herself as a 'creative' young person, but on joining the program, started making films that were inspired by her life. After months of planning, storyboarding and scripting, Tamzin was able to cast her little sister in the lead role and film over a number of locations, including a school hall. The poster for her film 'Look Up' is shown in Figure 8.2. Describing herself as 'her most harsh critic', she would often comment on something she was

Figure 8.2: 'Look Up' by Tamzin Brogan

Note: Poster for a short film by Tamzin Brogan.

not happy with in the work. However, having the opportunity to exhibit and get feedback on her work was the most important part of the process:

> 'It was really good because I felt like people who were important to me got to see my work and got to see how I felt. People from SWAN have done a lot for me throughout my life. I wanted to show them how they felt to me. But the exhibition was just amazing as there were so many important people there recognising work that young people did from Dublin. There were journalists there. ... Loads of people came to see our work and left comments. Having people talking about my video was so emotional as they actually see it from a different perspective and what it represented to them.' (Tamzin Brogan, Participant in SWAN Youth Service)

Tamzin reflected on presenting her film at an exhibition and doing "a little speech", but overwhelmingly reported the value of the comments book, which she read a few times, enjoying the comments about both the artistic qualities and the honest realism of her work. Another young person who also worked with film was Darragh Flood (18-year-old, white, Irish male), who joined the program with his brother after SWAN Youth Service had visited his school. During his time at Reckless Arts, he made four short films, two of which were selected for the Cork Film Festival and Fresh Film

Figure 8.3: 'The Crying War II' by Darragh Flood

Note: Film poster created by Darragh Flood.

Festival. The film poster for 'The Crying War' is pictured in Figure 8.3. Moving from his home-based practice of making film clips for YouTube, Darragh was supported through Reckless Arts in learning how to use the equipment, create a storyboard, and access locations and props; in post production and film editing; and then in the promotion of his work. He reported that the support was invaluable at pushing him forward to make his ideas a reality, promoting his work to get it "out there" and bringing him into the professional world:

> 'When I started, I was a "know it all" person, who thought they knew want they were doing. But then when it came to doing it, I was actually clueless. SWAN supported me with the equipment and the people to help. So, I knew from that point that if I ever needed help, I could easily go to SWAN. So, from where I started to where I am now, I'm starting on my own production company, photography business and videography business. I would never have been able to do that if I hadn't had that support there.' (Darragh Flood, Participant in SWAN Youth Service)

Darragh reported that one of his proudest achievements was being asked to be a young mentor, to support other young people from the program. He was overwhelmingly enthusiastic about the value of youth arts groups to help young people achieve "anything that they can put their minds to", "to never put your ideas down" and "to take you off your feet and really push you to where you want to be in life":

> 'The thing I enjoyed the most was the involvement. If I had an idea that was really big and really hard to do, Shireen would be like "yeah, let's do it". She never puts an idea down. Sometimes the ideas might be unreachable, but they will always encourage us to be brave and to reach them.' (Darragh Flood, Participant in SWAN Youth Service)

These participant reflections demonstrate the impact of youth arts programs, but also highlight the pedagogical approach within spaces of informal education: being involved in a democratic process where culture is shaped and created by young people and then promoted by an artist-in-residence to achieve wider recognition, aligned to cultural democracy practised in youth arts settings.

Celebrating cultural democracy

> The reclamation and reinforcement of shared identities, especially those rooted in shared culture, serve as a significant means through which historically maltreated and socially marginalized populations might combat adversity. (Brooks et al, 2015, p 720)

Informal education and critical pedagogies inherent in youth work and arts practice work well with democratic processes, such as youth-led arts programming, explored in this chapter. Brooks et al (2015) argue that young people are characterised as unreachable due to a lack of interest in the culture, which begs two questions: whose culture? And who is reaching? Arts institutions have typically sought to draw young people into their buildings with an offer of canonical art, yet what is happening with young people's common cultures is rarely acknowledged. Du Bois' (1943) concept of cultural democracy represents a sharing of values among various cultural groups signalling not only one culture but many. By recognising young people as cultural experts, we accommodate and celebrate alternative cultural forms.

Alternative cultural forms

One of the aims of Propel is to connect young people with the arts and cultural institutions within Perth. As the organisation is funded by the state government, they recognise that they are a small player in a kind of older western-world thinking, which challenges them to find ways in which they can support those more grassroots initiatives without stifling them. As a result,

Propel works against the much critiqued 'outreach model' (Sotomayor and Kim, 2009; Belfiore, 2010; Sagan et al, 2010) in order to support artistic practice at the level of local communities. Jamie, General Manager, reports a change in the perception of culture:

> 'What the institutions, like museums and galleries, struggle with in terms of older art forms or older western art forms, is in terms of who they're reaching. And yet they receive disproportionately larger amounts of funding for their work, which is a whole other conversation with its own merits. The thing for me, that I've noticed is that there's a move in the kind of perception of what our culture is. It's shifting more and more away from what you would see in a theatre or what you would see on the wall in the Gallery, or what you'd watch on TV or whatever, to what we do. It doesn't have to be excellent and it doesn't have to be even seen by anyone else. Maybe it's something that maybe it's just between me and you. Or maybe it's between our immediate friends or family. Or maybe it is between like a group of migrants or a group of people who are bonded by the age they are. It's more of like a collective sharing.' (Jamie, General Manager, Propel)

Within the KickstART festival, there are many examples of collective culture, led by diverse groups of young people. Creative coordinator for 2020, Kobi Arthur Morrison, drew on his own cultural heritage – Noongar mother and English father – in order to encourage more understanding by acknowledging everyone as a unique cacophony of cultures. This philosophy underpinned the approach of the festival in supporting young people's alternative cultural forms, as a part of both their cultural heritage and common culture, which is unique to them. Kobi further explains:

> 'I think that being able to help everybody understand their own culture, by utilising Noongar culture, as my example, I wanted to be able to try and express, in some way, that they are unique and that they are unique in their specificity with understanding things. I think that it's very much increased tenfold when it comes to the arts, because that is a means of expression that everybody has. It's one thing to be a part of the culture of the artist, it's another thing to be a part of the culture of the musician, and it's another culture to be part of the visual artists. You've got cultures and then subcultures within those and so on.' (Kobi Arthur Morrison, Creative Coordinator for 2020)

Another motivation for the KickstART festival to support alternative cultural forms is the celebration of a vibrant and growing art scene within Perth. While fears are expressed by older generations that the arts are dying,

Figure 8.4: Young artist presents their work

Note: Photograph taken by Tasha Tong.

youth-led arts programming offers a vehicle for young people to make independent decisions because they are passionate about their art or the arts community and share an understanding about the arts world around them. For example, Figure 8.4 shows a young Artist introducing an exhibition. Being the creative coordinator, and in the upper end of the demographic 12 to 26, Kobi felt the significance of his role in terms of promoting youth arts, while not seeking to restrict the possibilities or reproduce social hierarchies:

'I wanted to emphasise that I'm not a leader as much as I'm facilitator in the way that we are wanting to bundle up everything that everybody wants into the right kind of package that taps into exactly what we're all collectively wanting to achieve. I wanted to make sure that we strive together as a community and help everybody understanding each other as equals.' (Kobi Arthur Morrison, Creative Coordinator for 2020)

The YPC was a key mechanism for sharing cultural knowledge and developing resources, events and experiences through the festival program. This model will be explored further in Chapter 10.

Shared cultural knowledge and resources

Graves (2010) asks an important question: what does your community need to keep its culture vital and meaningful? The two case studies in this chapter exemplify the development of shared cultural knowledge and resources as an integral element of youth arts programs. For example, Propel works with a planning committee for the KickstART festival, however representation and discussion are not limited to one committee. As an organisation, they recognise the importance of engaging with young people in a deeper way by having regular opportunities for discussion, which could be in an informal setting or at a roundtable meeting. Having that kind of representation and longer conversations with young people is vital to making sure that Propel is on the right track. Cecile Vuaillat, Project Manager for Propel, describes the process of generating shared cultural knowledge:

> 'We identify exactly what is important to young people and what needs to be addressed and these days it's a lot about youth representation, like representing people who are culturally, linguistically diverse, indigenous young people and people from lower socio-economic backgrounds, giving them that platform and the opportunities to really share their stories. Once we have discussed these key themes and these are the important things to start and then myself or other staff members might suggest some groups or people we might know and we say, "We've heard that they've done this kind of event and they might be really interesting." And then the young people suggest some people they know or who they've interacted with. So, it's kind of pitching things both ways.' (Cecile Vuaillat, Project Manager for Propel)

Youth arts programs encompass two elements which are key to cultural democracy and the generation of shared cultural knowledge. First, as shown earlier, arts practice mediates across different forms of knowledge, and secondly, open access spaces for knowledge exchange are vital (Gkartzios and Crawshaw, 2019). SWAN upholds a similar democratic process to Propel in supporting youth-led programming with the identification of issues that are important or relevant to young people and the encouragement of critical thinking through discussion. In addition, SWAN regularly and successfully applies for funding to engage artists-in-residence in order to facilitate this process alongside youth workers. The role of the artist-in-residence is to ensure that young people get exposure to the different art forms, as participants have not always had these opportunities. This may be as simple as providing arts supplies or cameras but could extend to dialogue about the young person's creative idea and how it can come to fruition and get out there in the world. For example, the organisation now has a recording studio operating in the basement, which was suggested by the young people, who then sought and eventually got funding. Another example of democratic practice is described in the following excerpt by artist-in-residence Shireen Shortt:

'We try and build on the skills of young people who have been involved in arts programs and to encourage them as peer arts mentors for other young people because as much as it is about democracy and young people identifying what they want, it's also about opportunity and exposure because sometimes young people don't know what's possible or what they are capable of, or what might actually interest them. So, it's about creating those opportunities for exposure as well, and that's something that we really prioritise, that when art is created in the project that it's very visible to other young people, so that they can see what's possible as well.' (Shireen Shortt, Artist-in-Residence, SWAN)

Shireen describes a delicate balance between leaving young people to explore and knowing when to "push them". Her motivation for being an artist-in-residence at SWAN stems from her own personal dissatisfaction with the way the creative industries and the arts landscape operate. Like many cultural critics (Brook et al, 2020; Friedman and Laurison, 2020) she argues that there is a lack of diversity, which obscures a plurality of perspectives and voices. The position of SWAN and Propel is that young people should be contributing to that landscape, so that they can inform wider arts practice and also get to have the chance to communicate their perspectives.

Meaningful public engagement

As explored earlier in this chapter, the benefits of artist-in-residence programs include encouragement, collaboration and experimentation through 'artist–student interaction' (Eckhoff, 2011). In a departure from researching artists-in-residence through mainstream formal schooling, the case study explored in this chapter investigates an informal arts setting. Affordances previously noted include how artists-in-residence support young people with envisioning, developing a craft, and stretching and exploring ideas, as well as understanding community (Hunter-Doniger and Berlinsky, 2017). These elements were clearly reported in the data from the young people who were part of the Reckless Arts group. Darragh, for example, reflected on his ideas "never being put down", his exposure to film competitions and constant encouragement to develop his ideas and to promote his work. He recognises the importance of "being as invested in your local community as well as being invested in your own career and artistic progression". Describing the exhibition of her artwork, Tamzin reflects on the value of being able to "share [her] story and have people listen" and being put in "situations you wouldn't see yourself in". Both these participants reflect on the importance of meaningful public engagement with their work.

Further exploring the role of the artist-in-residence in facilitating a youth arts program that holds cultural democracy at its heart, Shireen argues that

'Cultural Democracy … not that we name it all the time … is a key driving force in Reckless, that the young people, who are at that stage of wanting to be emerging artists, that we help them gain access to those spaces, to those platforms where they are going to be listened to, where they are going to be heard and recognised for the value of what they have to say about who they are as individuals. These young emerging artists have access to create their chosen artworks and having publics engage with those in meaningful ways. These young people who are seldom heard. They are misrepresented and they are denied a voice in their own narration when they are represented. So, widening access is a key objective, not only to being looked at, but creating within that landscape so that other people can understand and learn about people from their own point of view, rather than misrepresentations of who they are.' (Shireen Shortt, Artist-in-Residence, SWAN)

This approach leads to important questions within youth arts programs about how young people can be supported to expand their artwork so that it becomes a catalyst for discussion. The aspiration within Reckless Arts is that young people can occupy and lay claim to their place within the arts landscape through developing their own artistic confidence and getting exposure to public spaces so that they can get 'comfortable':

'The young people can feel a bit out of place at first, which I think can happen in any workplace, that you don't feel like you are equipped to operate within. So, in arming them with the confidence to get comfortable in those spaces and knowing that they belong there, takes a different set of negotiations than just chucking someone into an environment. That environment must be ready to engage meaningfully and make these industry links in terms of mentorship or at least guidance for their learning. To be able to engage in professional artistic guidance and support, is a really healthy experience, to respond to different people's processes. Getting young people into a new space with the confidence to feel that they belong there, means that they can lay claim to their position there in terms of cultural democracy. It means that they can play their part in the whole landscape of producing artwork and producing artists.' (Shireen Shortt, Artist-in-Residence, SWAN)

Culturally democratic principles, within youth arts programs, are twofold. First, they represent an opportunity for a wide and diverse range of cultures to be recognised, as a 'cacophony' as described by Kobi. Young people as cultural experts and producers are at the forefront and are able to draw on a range of cultural and artistic influences and to celebrate a lived experience of culture that is present in the here-and-now. Secondly, cultural democracy aims to redress a balance, displacing long-standing cultural hierarchies. Youth arts programs and practitioners, therefore, have a responsibility to ensure that young people's voices are heard and that their cultural products are seen as a way of widening the artistic landscape for future artists.

Conclusion

In this chapter, I have drawn on two international case studies in order to celebrate young people as generators and reclaimers of culture. The youth arts programs highlighted – Propel Youth Arts WA and SWAN Youth Service – exemplify a wider reach for the arts, different forms of knowledge and alternatives to normative hierarchical culture. Through these exemplars, I have sought to celebrate the value of cultural democracy for youth arts programs, which support young people to lay claim to their position within the arts landscape. I have shown that youth arts programs offer a spectrum of democratic processes from youth-led programming to committee planning, from collaboration to consultation. For young people to have the opportunity to tell their own narrative and assert their own identities through meaningful public engagement is vitally important. Therefore, both case studies supported a multiplicity of perspectives and voices, which are so easily afforded by the arts, in addition to questioning hierarchies of power within the arts and beyond. Therefore, youth arts programs that embed cultural democracy support the wider critical pedagogical aims of youth work. From this perspective, youth arts are more than simply a 'service' for young people, they are a democratic entitlement.

Although cultural democracy is a global movement, it is unevenly supported and understood across the world, due to differing government regimes and political positions that frequently depict deficit models in relation to both youth policy and the arts. Both case studies worked against this by presenting truly collaborative approaches when working democratically in groups or with key individuals such as artists-in-residence, highlighting the importance of peer-to-peer networks. Key to a democratic model of youth arts programs is the platforming and profiling of diverse cultures coming from grassroots level, either through festivals, exhibitions or events. This emphasises the importance of making connections for young people to be able to bring their creative work outside of the youth club walls, so that youth arts is not pigeonholed. In terms of cultural democracy, youth arts programs offer both a shared cultural knowledge, and also an important space for knowledge exchange. Finally, I explored whether a cultural democracy is possible and how young people can be supported to generate cultural knowledge and shared resources. Both programs engaged with the arts as ways for young people to understand their community/ies and further understand the world and their place within it. This leaves one more important question: what kinds of 'citizens' do youth arts programs develop? This will be taken up in the next chapter.

9

Cultivating cultural citizenship

One of the key questions of this book is: what types of citizens do arts programs develop young people to be? This chapter argues for the value of the arts in supporting participatory democracy and social change and explores youth arts programs which hold cultural citizenship at their heart. Two case studies are presented, which demonstrate the value of arts programs for the development of cultural citizenship. These are Chicago Arts and Music Project (CAMP), as an example of an arts program which responds to the needs of local communities and empowers young people towards social action; and a European program from Jugend- & Kulturprojekt e.V. [Youth and Culture] (JKPeV) in Germany, which uses the arts as a tool for social inclusion and the celebration of cultural difference. I argue that youth arts programs should be supporting and cultivating young people as cultural citizens, emphasising the importance of dialogue on 'otherness' and the value of building community relations.

CAMP is an El Sistema program, which promotes the transformative value of music as life changing. While the Venezuelan origins of El Sistema were devoted to the pedagogical 'salvation' of children and young people through collective music instruction, more recently El Sistema programs have been underpinned by social action through music (Baker, 2016). Music tutors and program leaders are referred to as 'Citizen Artists' and there is a belief that learning to make music together can enable young people to overcome difficult circumstances, becoming productive, empathetic citizens (Booth and Tunstall, 2016). For example, El Sistema in Sweden focuses on intercultural dialogue, breaking segregation patterns and connecting people from diverse backgrounds (Bergman and Lindgren, 2014), alongside affordances for young people's musical agency from a collective dimension (Lindgren et al, 2016).

Intercultural learning, stemming from youth arts programs, is exemplified within the second case study of JKPeV. This international youth program supports young people in learning about their own culture and origins, while challenging their own personal identity. Opportunities for intercultural dialogue enrich cooperation and communication with people from other cultures (Šinkūnienė and Skuolytė, 2013). International youth programs have been shown to support young people's experiential and cultural knowledge as critics and agents of resistance in the face of growing global socio-spatial inequality (Gallagher et al, 2017). JKPeV's exemplar program 'You Are Welcome' draws on theatre-based pedagogy, whereby theatre becomes a lens through which young people engage with their world and wrestle with representations of themselves (Gallagher and Wessels, 2013). Programs such as these frequently culminate in an interactive, audience-led performance as a way of bringing art, education and citizenship together (Silva and Menezes, 2016).

This chapter engages with a variety of concepts and examples in order to demonstrate how the case study programs cultivate cultural citizenship. First, the affordances of arts practices as civic education are explored in conjunction with the relational practices of youth work through 'connected civics' (Ito et al, 2015). In addition, the analysis of data highlights the value of art forms, such as music and theatre, as 'third spaces of encounter' (Thomson and Hall, 2020), alongside the importance of building platforms for young people's expression. Finally, the chapter explores youth arts programs as a space of new possibilities, in particular in relation to identities, imagined futures and temporary communities.

Cultural citizenship

Youth arts programs have the potential to explore and celebrate diverse cultural identities and support democracy and social change. The principles of cultural citizenship can be applied to young people's artistic practice as a mechanism for promoting civic responsibility and addressing inequalities within society (Kuttner, 2015). Youth arts programs that support young people to be 'cultural citizens' also support them to be active decision makers and develop a symbolic presence (Pakulski, 1997; Stevenson, 2010). Engaging with the arts can afford a process of critical learning and resistance. Therefore, a cultural understanding of citizenship encompasses young people working with the arts in their communities, identifying social needs and taking up leadership roles. This approach can have a significant impact on the less visible and more marginalised groups in society.

As the arts offer us a shared understanding of the world and a shared understanding of each other, youth arts programs that engage with cultural citizenship offer a learning experience in diverse cultures for young people. This can be from both a local and global perspective. For example, Propel Youth Arts WA (see Chapter 8) has a focus on supporting Indigenous populations, as the issue of decolonisation was central for young people accessing their program. As well as using artistic practice to learn about the world in which young people are growing up, youth arts programs offer the opportunities for participants to be critical about the conditions which they face. With SWAN Youth Service (see Chapter 8), for example, the arts are used as a vehicle to give young people a voice and redress power imbalances as a way of retaining agency within their own lives. Engaging with Kuttner's (2015) typology of cultural citizenship, we can see the potential for youth arts programs to develop 'justice-orientated citizens'. Justice-orientated cultural citizens feel a responsibility to use their art to improve their community, directly confront injustice and promote diverse cultural perspectives (Kuttner, 2015). This theoretical framework is mobilised within this chapter.

Gaztambide-Fernández' work on cultural production defines youth arts programs as a space for engagement with participatory politics, which can become central to how young people form their ideas and build political identities (Gaztambide-Fernández and Arráiz Matute, 2015). The term 'connected civics' is proposed to understand the connection between youth expressive cultural practices and civic culture, through a form of learning that is deeply connected to young people's interests and identities (Ito et al, 2015). Recent research has highlighted a 'relational citizenship for all', whereby the arts create transformative spaces in which to challenge dominant assumptions, foster critical reflection, and envision new possibilities for mutual support, caring and relating (Dupuis et al, 2016). As explored in Chapter 6, these values align with youth work pedagogies. Thomson and Hall (2020) argue for the value of intercultural art practices in bringing diverse communities together to create a 'third space' for conversations. These arts practices, much like the ones that are the focus of this chapter, are often multi-model and multi-media in artistic form and can serve to decentre conventional genres and practices. Shared artistic practices, through spontaneous 'moments of encounter' (Goessling and Wager, 2020), represent important opportunities for power shifting and sharing, as a key affordance of cultural citizenship.

Youth arts programs framed around cultural citizenship can provide a structured, supportive process for young people to contribute their viewpoints, expertise and ideas, and actively engage in community change work towards social justice goals (Wright, 2020). As explored in Chapter 3, dominant deficit youth discourses can impact what kinds of arts programs young people are offered. Cultural citizenship connects the arts with social justice as a way to disrupt these negative perceptions and expectations. Art making for social justice can promote young people's knowledge production and celebrate them as cultural agents (Wright, 2020). Goessling (2020) offers the concept of 'Youthspaces' as a framework that positions young people as experts and cultural producers to envision an alternative and more socially just future world. Drawing on Freire's praxis for critical consciousness (Freire, 1996), Goessling explores arts engagement as a transformative collective inquiry, whereby young people become aware of the structures that have influenced their lives and develop the agency required to take social action. The two case studies offered in this chapter align with these approaches of connecting communities through culture, social justice arts education and investigating alternative perspectives of the world around us. Together these case studies embody what a cultural citizenship approach within youth arts programs might look like and the values they bestow.

Chicago Arts and Music Project

CAMP aims to develop musical excellence and nurture young musicians. The program also focuses on social activism, where music is used as a tool for positive change within the community. CAMP is based in the Breakthrough FamilyPlex,[1] where, in conjunction with local schools, the program recruits young people aged between eight and 14. Young people are brought together from different schools, areas and backgrounds, sharing the specific issues within their neighbourhoods. Classical music activities within the sessions include individual tuition, small group work, large orchestral ensembles, composition and conducting. Typically, young people enter the program with no instrumental background and little musical experience from school. The organisation was set up by founder and lead music educator Lindsay Fredrickson in 2017 through initial funding from inheritance and then continued funding from government, foundation funders and individual contributions.

As well as musical activities, young people engage with visual arts and writing, however classical music is the main music genre, with a range of orchestral instruments being provided to each participant. Lindsay prioritises diversity within the classical music genre, including a range of pop, rap, jazz and Broadway pieces alongside traditional classical pieces. These preferences are articulated by the participants as the interests and lived experiences of the young people are central to the program. Lindsay argues that

> 'You can bring classical music to young people, and you can tell them that it's a really important thing and you can tell them why it matters. But unless they see that it matters in their own life or how it's relevant to their family or their community, they don't invest in the same way. They're uniquely tied to issues that matter to them.' (Lindsay Fredrickson, Founder and Lead Music Educator of CAMP)

Every concert also includes a young person's composition, which tends to be rap or pop. Lindsay hopes that nurturing a diversity of genres within classical instruments will lead to a diversity of classical musicians and composers, which she recognises is sorely lacking. Nayelli Duran, one of the music educators on the program, noted that

> 'In the classical music world, it is very heavily dominated by white musicians. As a Hispanic musician, that's something that I was very aware of once I got to the University level, that I was one of the only people who was brown. So, the project wants to give that opportunity, to these students because the vast majority of our students are black.' (Nayelli Duran, CAMP Music Educator)

Figure 9.1: Music matters

Note: Photograph of student-led composition and conducting.

As well as composing music, each young person has the opportunity to conduct a concert (see Figure 9.1). Lindsay strongly believes that the orchestra belongs to the young people and tells them it is their orchestra. Particularly when it comes to the responsibility of conducting, the power and glory of conducting remains in the young people's hands. In addition, a key aim of the program is responding to the local community and the issues that matter to the participants within their neighbourhoods. Each new school year starts with a discussion with young people about what they want to see change in their community. The subjects have included bullying, gun violence and racial injustice. Music educators have noted the importance of language in these discussions and the risk that with issue-based work negative stereotypes may be reproduced. As explored in Chapter 3, these deficit identities conversely impact arts programs not only through labelling participants, but also through working to make young people think they live in 'bad' communities.

Building community relations

The dual aim of CAMP is to develop young people's musical capabilities, but also to effect a change in society. In relation to cultural citizenship, Lindsay Fredrickson believes that musicians are good citizens who have a responsibility to do good things in their community: "I explain that we have a unique role because people give us a platform and people would give us a stage where they come see us perform. We're really lucky that we have a captive audience, where we can say whatever we want to up there, so we might as well take that opportunity."

In the second year of the program, young people started working with the Chicago Police Department to explore the impact of gun violence on their community. The first session started with a 'peace circle' led by the Breakthrough Violence Prevention Initiative,[2] where three police officers were invited to come in and answer questions. The program culminated in the officers composing music with the young people, as Lindsay describes:

'The questions were good because our kids did not hold back at all and I think that was healthy. They asked a lot of questions. There were some that were funny and some that were really heavy. We've had a lot of students who have lost family members to gun violence and I think it was really enlightening. The police officers would stay to help the young people compose music, but they didn't have any idea what they were supposed to do! But at the end the young people played what they had come up with together. The thing that we all came away with and we talked about was, we realised that police are just people too. We're all individual humans and it was a helpful thing to realise the humanity of everyone there.' (Lindsay Fredrickson, Founder and Lead Music Educator of CAMP)

Through the program, music educators engage young participants in discussion about what issues they want to focus on, for example, see Figure 9.2 'peace circle'. At the time of collecting data for this case study, Chicago had seen a lot of rioting and looting. It had been a difficult time for the young people and their communities, with the lives lost in the Black community, including George Floyd, Breonna Taylor and Elijah McClain.[3] On the first day of Breonna Taylor's court case, there was a moment of silence across the city of Chicago at 7:00 o'clock, which was in the middle of a rehearsal. This sparked a discussion within the group on the Black Lives Matter movement. Nayelli Duran wanted to use that opportunity to encourage the young people to start thinking about what kind of community they actually wanted. She reports the reflective value of citizenship dialogue with the young people: "And one of the young people said something like: 'We deserve a safe and clean community because our lives matter and because our community matters.' It was really intense when it happened and that made me want to cry. I still see that as a very powerful moment."

At the end of the program, the vision was to have a big community concert, where other musicians would join and each song would be dedicated to a black life. Elijah McLean, who was a violinist, would have a classical piece played for him; and for Ahmad Arbery, who was a man killed while out for a run, the

Figure 9.2: Young people take part in a peace circle

Note: Photograph of activity led by the Breakthrough Violence Prevention Initiative.

young people would play an arrangement of a song called Run Boy Run. The event would culminate in a collective composition of a piece commissioned from a black composer, in which the young people would participate alongside some guest artists and the police. However, with the restrictions of the COVID-19 pandemic, this live element did not come to fruition.

Empathy, compassion and goodness

Music Educators Nayelli Duran and Ana Marroquin strongly believe in music as a catalyst, an approach to help young people with social learning and social change. Both draw on a particular pedagogical approach within youth arts which is integral to its practice. Ana, drawing on her professional background in social emotional learning (SEL)[4] notes changes in empathy, compassion and understanding of the opinions of others: "Children first start off not knowing how to respond to emotion, not knowing how to express their emotions and know how they feel. Through the music and arts on the program, they see a way of how to communicate better, and be honest with each other, not holding back."

Nayelli's underlying pedagogy is based upon education in human values (EHV),[5] where educators have a responsibility to let young people know they are good and to "bring out goodness":

'Obviously, I want them to know how to play Twinkle Twinkle Little Star on an instrument. That's what I'm being paid for. But what is more important to me is that my students know that they're capable of being good, and so I tell them no matter what anybody tells you or no matter what people have led you to believe, or what teachers have told you or your siblings have told you, you are good.' (Nayelli Duran, CAMP Music Educator)

Young participant AD (11-year-old African American male) reflected on what he enjoys the most about being part of an orchestra, namely the relationships with different people: "So, you pretty much know everybody in the orchestra, maybe not everybody, but you're pretty close to everybody in our orchestra and we get to have fun in our breaks and we get to play a lot."

Another young person, R (11-year-old Indonesian female), values the program as her "own space" where she can work one-to-one with a music educator, but also make music with her friends. She reflected on how the program helped to build her confidence, particularly with public performances, and helped to develop her creativity and criticality: "I liked it when I got to conduct the whole orchestra. It was pretty cool that I was in control. CAMP has definitely shaped me into being a more creative and open-minded person."

Having explored how CAMP supports the building of community relations and the values of empathy, compassion and goodness, as part of cultural citizenship, I now move on to the second case study as an exemplar of 'otherness' dialogue.

Jugend- & Kulturprojekt e.V.

Jugend- & Kulturprojekt e.V. located in Dresden, Germany, was founded in 2004 with the aim of promoting EU citizenship and active participation. Translated as 'Youth and Culture' the association is dedicated to equipping young people with certain competencies so that they are active citizens, whether that be within the arts or using creativity in their own lives. The organisation aims not only to enrich the cultural scene of Dresden, but also to promote cultural diversity and cultural understanding in a locality that currently faces the challenge of right-wing extremism. Working with young people aged 18–30 on collaborative projects across Europe, JKPeV organise volunteering opportunities, strategic partnership projects, trainings and education programs. Young people work together with arts practitioners on workshops for other young people, training for trainers, and devising educational materials, including visual arts, filmmaking and storytelling. Often culminating in the hosting and organisation of large-scale arts and cultural events, young people support the projects through undertaking their own research, promoting workshops and supporting JKPeV in the implementation of cultural and art events.

Program Manager of JKPeV, Myrto-Helena Pertsinidi, describes the benefits for young people taking part in these international programs:

'We give young people the voice to express their feelings, and to unleash their creativity because these are important tools to have a say in our community and our society. The most important thing that we do, in order to connect people, is to use art as a tool because it is inclusive.' (Myrto-Helena Pertsinidi, Manager, 'You Are Welcome' program)

Funded by both regional funding and European funding (Erasmus Plus), arts and cultural activity allows participants, local and foreign, to better understand the cultural diversity present within the European Union. At the same time, programs offer a fresh outlook on familiar problems through the sense of belonging to a greater group. This includes setting up dialogue between young people and policy makers in Dresden and other cities involved in the programs in discussing the challenges of living together and possible future solutions.

Within JKPeV programs, the arts play an important role as an informal learning method which promotes values such as democracy, human rights, solidarity, cultural diversity, acceptance and inclusion. Participant Alvaro Sanz Lamperez (24-year-old, white, Spanish male), explains the benefits of this approach in terms of appealing to his interests and making new connections through art:

'One of the really good things about JKPeV is that they are flexible. You can choose the programs you want to get involved in, and I'm really interested in migration, social integration and so on. And I was also really interested in this idea of communicating through art. So, I got to know people in this arty environment, who I would have never met, because we don't share the same places, friends, connections, etc. So, for me it was a totally new experience because I got to know more in depth the films, street art, visual and performing arts and learned how to communicate and what you communicate to the people if you really want to have a social impact.' (Alvaro Sanz Lamperez, Participant in JKPeV)

JKPeV runs a range of longer-term programs lasting between one and three years, with multiple activities taking place at any one time. This case study focuses on the 'You Are Welcome' project, which ran from April 2017 to February 2019, co-funded by the Europe for Citizens program of the European Union. The project brought together eight countries and 11 partners, all committed to supporting migrant and refugee integration, community development and promoting evidence-based migration policy making.

'You Are Welcome'

The 'You Are Welcome' program aimed to tackle the stigmatisation of immigrants and refugees and to support the integration of third-country nationals into the local communities of the countries involved in the program. In addition, the program worked with young people as volunteers and participants in arts events in order to promote mutual understanding, solidarity, human rights and diversity in the societies of the participating countries. These partner countries included Greece, Denmark, the United Kingdom, Hungary, Czech Republic, Slovakia and the former Yugoslav Republic of Macedonia.[6]

The program started with a phase of youth-led research around how refugees and immigrants are received and integrated. Young people conducted a survey titled *How we view each other* in each of the partner locations and then, based on the results of the research, organised local campaigns. The young people with JKPeV focused their campaign on hate speech and worked with a Syrian artist to design postcards with short messages on, which were distributed around the city of Dresden. An installation was created with the postcards so that people could find them and interact. Myrto-Helena Pertsinidi reflected on this creative process as a way of awakening awareness and promoting the tolerance of difference through young people's ideas:

> 'I think opportunities, as such, given to young people to reflect, create and discuss with us, enable them to organise together activities, workshops and campaigns, which consequently make them feel more responsible and develop a sense of initiative. This motivates them to be active citizens. This sense of initiative and belonging encourages them to see that they have the world in their hands and they can change things. I have been very grateful for all these young people that supported us so much, who contributed through their ideas, through their knowledge and were so dedicated.' (Myrto-Helena Pertsinidi, Manager, 'You Are Welcome' program)

The 'You Are Welcome' program worked with a range of artistic practices, and in particular with theatre and film. Short videos were created that set out acceptance, mutual understanding, respect of common values and promoted diversity for counter-narratives as a more accurate perception of third-country nationals.[7] These creative outputs were intended to assist the audience in understanding cultural differences and were shared with partner countries and culminated in the 'No Hate Film Festival'. The festival included a range of workshops for young people: zine making, storytelling and theatre methods. As part of this process young people learned how to set the program, how to think about what kind of activities could be implemented and for what reason, how to manage an event, how to run a workshop and how to promote an event. Because young people were part of the program from beginning to the end, the evaluation phase was important to capture their experiences, their opinions and the challenges that they faced. Alongside these organisational skills, young people appreciated the opportunity to address particular issues of citizenship. Volunteer Alvaro valued the program for the opportunity to think through, discuss and take action on issues that were important to him:

'I have been particularly interested in the topic of migration and third-country nationals, and what I found especially innovative about this project was that it works towards the goal to develop some counter-narratives against racism, xenophobia, and so on, and the way it tries to connect with the people through art.' (Alvaro Sanz Lamperez, Participant in JKPeV)

Otherness dialogue

Another element of the 'You Are Welcome' program was hosted in Copenhagen, Denmark and developed a series of theatre workshops, which culminated in an immersive theatre performance. Led by Dr Rita Sebestyén, this element brought the representatives of the international partners together to speak about their childhood experiences (see Figure 9.3). Young people were encouraged to write about a lullaby they remembered from their childhood and to bring an object to which they are connected that tells a story about their lives. Activities such as these were designed within the program to explore commonalities and otherness. Rita describes the value of questioning 'real-life' perceptions:

'When we enter a space, both real and metaphysical, when it is an international project, you have to build a communication system from scratch. Nothing is taken for granted and nobody is majority and this is such an incredibly beautiful experience. It's very difficult actually to go back to real life after this new journey. So, nothing is monolithic anymore and we set the rules up together. In an international project, everybody gives their bit and it's like a puzzle. It's a totally new cultural space.' (Rita Sebestyén, Theatre Workshops Leader)

The action-installation/installation-performance took place in the heart of Copenhagen on a boat which is used as a theatre. Using the boat like a

Figure 9.3: Young people work with a range of artistic mediums in envisioning alternative communities

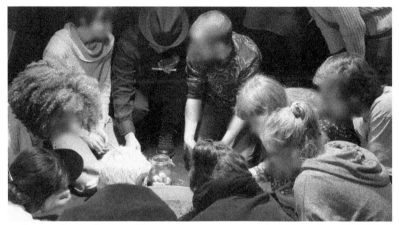

Note: Photograph taken by Stine Ebbesen.

huge stage, four zones were created that represented four different stages of human life, including community building and conflict solving. The audience would enter the boat with a young performer-facilitator who led people throughout, orientating the audience through the zones. The performer-facilitator would react and respond to the audience's actions, as well as acting out defined roles in each of the four stages of the installation. The audience were provided with a set of rules at each stage to build a parallel identity, community, society, and their own interwoven narratives. The unpredictability of the responses and reaction of the audience were designed to empower the participants and give voice to underrepresented and marginalised layers of society (Sebestyén, 2019). Rita explains that

'We now share with this experience, and this is called existence, which means that we are the agents of these temporary communities. And at the same time if you are not active, you won't represent yourself, so you have to be active. I think this is very important and you have to communicate your part and you have to find your own piece in the puzzle. And if you're not active, if you're not taking responsibility, then the others will figure it out.' (Rita Sebestyén, Theatre Workshops Facilitator)

The idea of constructing an alternative world presents a heterotopia[8] as a way of privileging the imaginations of young people over current societal constructions. The parallel worlds built by the young performers and audiences of this performance offered a small and shifting temporary community by which to articulate ideas and notions of change in relation to European citizenship and migration.

Cultivating cultural citizenship

> The process of uncovering, owning, distilling and deepening an analysis through critical arts pedagogies can serve as a call to action that encourages young people to put their convictions into practice through collective action to transform unjust conditions and work with others towards social justice aims. (Wright, 2020, p 44)

Drawing on the field of civic education, cultural citizenship is an approach whereby a plurality of cultural perspectives and practices are recognised as a way of developing participatory citizens for a democratic society. Kuttner (2015) conceptualises as 'justice-orientated citizens' those who feel a responsibility to use their art to improve their community and directly confront injustice, while understanding that social change must be a collective effort utilising multiple forms of cultural and social action. JKPeV's European volunteer (EVS – European Voluntary Service), Alvaro, articulates this collective sensibility and value of youth arts programs for envisioning and contributing to social change:

> 'I do know that what we do by participating in this sort of project is that we put in our grain of sand. It's going to take a long time and a lot of effort until we reach our ultimate goal. However, I like the idea of participating in this social change and I definitely think that "You Are Welcome", in particular, because of the topics we're talking about – racism, xenophobia – allows people to put in their grain of sand towards the goal of tackling racism, xenophobia and Hate Speech.' (Alvaro Sanz Lamperez, Participant in JKPeV)

Both of the case studies in this chapter support young people to 'put in their grain of sand' and communicate social issues through the arts, with program aims of social as well as artistic impact. Both programs are situated in cities and regions where tension exists between diverse populations and therefore the arts are used as a vehicle to work through issues of race and immigration. CAMP Music Educator Nayelli Duran argues that

> 'This isn't a program just to teach the students how to play an instrument. We have students going out and cleaning up a park in their community or going to different events or rallies to play music and talking with the police officers, knowing that there's a lot of

tension between police officers and the people in their community. I think that having those experiences going out into your community, but understanding that you're cleaning your community because you deserve good things is valuable. I think even if they don't fully understand it now, when they get older, I really do believe that those are going to be the formative experiences that they take with them. … So, we want to make sure that our students are aware of their value and fight for the respect and dignity that they deserve, that quite frankly, our country hasn't really been giving them. I am really looking forward to seeing that years from now.' (Nayelli Duran, CAMP Music Educator)

Connected civics

Connected civics (Ito et al, 2015) refers to a form of learning that is mobilised by young people's deeply felt interests and identities, as a form of civic voice. CAMP Music Educator Ana Marroquin reflects on the importance of youth arts programs as safe environments for young people to be able to discuss and become aware of social issues:

'With the projects that we do, they wake us up! They really bring the issues to a safe place to talk in. Sometimes I feel like the young people don't have a safe place to talk about these issues. So, we get to discuss these issues with no judgement. Everyone is able to have their own opinion and we are able to talk to each other in that way. That's important for us that the young people can feel part of a safe environment and that they can feel part of the change as well.' (Ana Marroquin, CAMP Music Educator)

The value of this connection to their communities and space to focus on any areas young people want to explore is echoed by CAMP participant AD:

'So, every year we pick something. Like this year, we're focusing on Black Lives Matter. Last year we were doing gun violence and the year before that, I think we were doing bullying. And so, every year we have a focus that we will talk about, usually on Fridays and we'll just talk about it and do maybe a few activities about why are those kind of things important. They're important because it's what's happening in the community and we all come from our community and we all play, and so it is good to talk about what's happening around us.' (AD, Participant, CAMP)

Community-based youth arts programs offer a transformative space in which critical reflection can happen, assumptions can be challenged and new possibilities for mutual caring can be born. Dupuis et al (2016) term this as a 'relational citizenship of all', which is eloquently described by CAMP Founder, Lindsay Fredrickson:

> 'I think there's something unique about the arts, and I assume it's like this with other arts programs too, but it's just very intense. There is a strong connection among the group. It's very family like. You know you're forced into something that's very difficult with each other, and so you just bond very quickly, and so it's really awesome to see how much they care about each other.' (Lindsay Fredrickson, Founder and Lead Music Educator of CAMP)

Gaztambide-Fernández and Arráiz Matute, 2015 argue that youth cultural production can promote and support new modes of political engagement. The arts offer an outlet for exchanging ideas and producing 'cultural artefacts', which are a means of addressing social and political oppression. Therefore, as demonstrated through these programs, it is not only the development of young people's artistic practice as a vehicle for social change that is important, but also the implementation, performance and presence within the public sphere.

Third spaces of encounter

Arts programs that support cultural citizenship are viewed as inclusive because they bring diverse communities together to create a 'third space' for conversations, where young people learn democratic art-making practices and have opportunities for 'epistemic justice' in questioning power within social and political life (Thomson and Hall, 2020). Within JKPeV's programs, intercultural dialogue is the most important element, in order to forefront the convergence of young people from different cultures. Program Manager Myrto-Helena Pertsinidi believes that

> 'We need to bring young people together to exchange their opinions, but to know and to understand that whenever they express their opinion and share their inputs, they should be respected and whenever somebody else speaks, he/she should be respected. So, they value being active listeners and do not judge somebody immediately because of having a different culture.' (Myrto-Helena Pertsinidi, Program Manager for JKPeV)

Theatre workshops and performances, such as the ones included in the 'You Are Welcome' program (see Figure 9.4) offer 'moments of encounter' that are embodied, productive, moving, telling, comforting, messy, continuous,

Figure 9.4: Theatre as a space of intercultural encounter

Note: Photograph taken by Stine Ebbesen.

playful, frustrating, changing, struggling and bonding in terms of explaining transformational learning (Goessling and Wager, 2020). Workshop facilitator Rita Sebestyén asks important questions about how we create communities and who decides the rules on how we live together. She further explains:

'I'm really fascinated by temporary communities because you have to reflect when you enter in a space again, physically or metaphysically, where there are patterns. It's just like entering a family or entering a country, where you wouldn't question the patterns. But when you have to build from scratch, you build on common cultural norms, so that actually helps you, and then you reflect on what you have and inevitably reflect on stereotypes.' (Rita Sebestyén, Theatre Workshops Facilitator)

These moments of encounter, not only with diverse populations, but with our own thinking about how society is formed and the maintained socially constructed boundaries, reflect the process of engaging young people in cultural citizenship.

New possibilities for identities

Youth arts programs become places of possibility, where young people are afforded the tools and resources necessary to imagine multiple identities. Goessling (2020) posits 'Youthspaces' as a framework that centres those with direct experiences of oppression as cultural producers to envision a more socially just future-world. Young participant Alvaro further explains that

'Absolutely every single experience you go through during your lifetime changes you. So, in regard to this project, I've been learning about many different new things. I discovered a more in-depth view of issues or topics like art. I consider that I've been open minded before, but in this way, I could say that it's widened my perspective. It gave me the opportunity to learn more about things I have already known and to learn new things. I think this sort of experience enhances your ability to thrive in multicultural contexts. It makes you more aware about things like how to consider how other people think and feel. It gave me this opportunity to grow in a personal way in this direction.' (Alvaro Sanz Lamperez, Participant in JKPeV)

Arts programs supported by experienced youth workers, artists, researchers and activists provide a structured, supportive process for young people to develop critical pedagogies through contributing their viewpoints and ideas and actively work towards social justice goals (Goessling, 2020; Wright, 2020). Youth arts programs that aim to cultivate cultural citizenship position young people as cultural producers and can serve to promote their diverse perspectives and understandings. Arts practices offer an analytical tool that opens up a multi-modal, reflective space and supports a platform for youth to reimagine new possibilities for their intersectional identities, encounters, systems, and present and future worlds (Wright, 2020). JKPeV's EVS volunteer, Alvaro, explains the dilemma in relation to 'reaching' all young people:

'We have to focus on the idea of having a positive impact on society because I think there are many people willing to put their efforts in this direction. I think it's important first of all, to reach out to these people, because these people's motivations are going to lead them to projects like these. At the same time, I think this is the easy part, to reach out to the people that would be willing to work with you and to share your goals. The more difficult part is to have an impact on people who think differently or are not aware of these kinds of topics.' (Alvaro Sanz Lamperez, Participant in JKPeV)

Reflecting the cultural and civic values of those who think differently is one of the challenges for cultural citizenship. In response, rather than being defined by deficit identities, youthspaces are strength based, where young people are considered co-researchers, valued experts and knowledge generators.

Conclusion

Within this chapter, two case study programs – CAMP and 'You are Welcome' from JKPeV – were purposely selected within two global locations that are facing challenges to democracy and citizenship. For CAMP in Chicago, this is in terms of race relations and for the 'You are Welcome' program in Dresden the action is against Hate Speech. These exemplars have explored the value of youth arts programs in relation to social issues in order to show how the arts can make a difference. Focusing, in particular, on the concept of cultural citizenship, this lens has avoided previous criticisms of claims of 'child-saving' (Belfiore, 2006; Davies, 2010) and deficit identities (Te Riele, 2006; Turnbull and Spence, 2011) and focused instead on empathy, collective experience and intercultural learning.

I argued that youth arts programs should be supporting and cultivating young people as justice-orientated cultural citizens (Kuttner, 2015) and demonstrated how the arts can build community relations, dialogues of otherness and 'connected civics' (Ito et al, 2015). The two programs in this chapter highlighted the affordances of youth arts programs for carving out important spaces for participatory politics. A cultural citizenship approach to youth arts programs adds social aims to already existing artistic ones, but this is rooted within young people's worlds and draws on their lived experiences. In alignment with youth work pedagogies, this approach forefronts dialogue, relationship building and mutual respect.

Cultural citizenship is an underpinning framework that can support critical dialogue, social action and speak back to real-life situations. In addition, the framework facilitates a shift away from issue-based work that can reproduce stereotypes (Beswick, 2018) towards acknowledgement of the value of youth arts in envisioning future worlds and new identities. Examples given in this chapter have drawn attention to the affordances of youth arts programs for conflict resolution at local and national level and the importance of playful and messy moments of encounter. To return to the words of JKPeV's EVS volunteer, Alvaro, these programs have enabled young people to feel as though they are putting in 'their grain of sand'.

The last three chapters of this book (Part III) have focused on three key questions:

- What kind of arts/culture happens in youth spaces?
- Who decides on arts/culture and how do youth work and the arts work together?
- What kind of citizens do youth arts programs develop young people to be?

The next chapter moves on from the conceptual exploration of common culture (Chapter 7), cultural democracy (Chapter 8) and cultural citizenship (Chapter 9), to return to the data gleaned from youth workers and young people on practical advice for future youth arts programs. Throughout the book, I have argued that youth arts practitioners and youth workers have an ethical responsibility to offer the best possible arts programs. In Chapter 10, I collate guidance from practice, in conjunction with previously successful models from global youth programs, to show how the arts can make a difference.

Enabling youth arts programs to flourish

This book started by grappling with a series of conceptual tensions within youth arts programs. These included cultural hierarchies, assumptions of social impact and the classed take-up of youth work. Looking globally, I explored three diverse approaches – creative arts youth work, the arts as intervention, and positive youth development – in order to critique the range of programs on offer to young people today. This was followed up with the introduction of three alternative perspectives – common culture, cultural citizenship and cultural democracy – which were taken up in the analysis of data within Part III. The final conceptual tension that I challenged was the deficit discourse of youth and how problematic labelling of young people leads to poorer-quality, more restricted arts programs. The negative implications of these tensions are issues of social justice, of which youth arts practitioners should be aware and are well placed to address.

In Part II, I presented my own research on an arts program – Arts Award – which is offered within youth settings in England. I considered, in particular, the arts practices and pedagogies on offer and concluded that while this program has clear synergy with youth work settings in relation to 'subcultural' arts practices and informal education pedagogies, social hierarchies continue to be reproduced. I argued that within the English context, arts programs that focus on 'increasing access' and 'measurement' put youth arts in risky terrain. The instrumental shift of programs within England is the result of many years of austerity youth and arts policy. In response, Part III took up a global lens, to explore best practice and inspirational case studies of youth arts programming. This final chapter returns to those programs in order to investigate implications for practice and how these can be made reality. I focus, in particular, on maintaining youth work principles, artistic quality, partnerships, planning and evaluation. Two models are drawn from the case studies – the youth arts festival and working with an artist-in-residence – as exemplars of how the arts and young people can be at the centre of every program.

Global perspectives

Collating six international case studies was designed not only to celebrate best practice in youth arts programs, but also to explore valuable perspectives in developing future programs. In Chapter 7, I demonstrated why youth arts programs effectively accommodate common culture. Frequently manifesting in DIY and digital arts practices, a common cultural framework represented a way of firmly rooting youth arts programs within young people's interests, while building on their cultural funds of knowledge. Dancehearts (Finland) was exemplary as an 'asset-based' perspective, which drew on kinaesthetic methods within dance. The informal education approach of Bolt FM (Scotland) highlighted the value of open-access, dialogic and participatory youth programs that embrace the pedagogy of collegiality (Chávez and Soep, 2005). Young people's symbolic creativity (Willis, 1990) is key to a common cultural approach, which develops 'commoning' (Standing, 2019) and cultural responsivity, and privileges these perspectives.

Young people's right to make art and experience culture was explored in Chapter 8 through celebrating cultural democracy. The two case studies within this chapter – Propel Youth Arts WA (Australia) and SWAN Youth Service (Ireland) – demonstrated the value of youth-led arts programming as a way of positioning young people as cultural experts. Not only can youth-led arts programming better articulate youth culture, but it can also challenge conventional hierarchies and cultural stereotypes, which may help young people lay claim to their position in the arts landscape. Celebrating cultural democracy within youth arts programs enables alternative cultural forms to emerge, alongside the development of shared cultural resources and knowledge. The two democratic approaches taken by these programs through a youth arts festival and an artist-in-residence scheme were effective vehicles for meaningful public engagement, whereby young people are supported to enter spaces more traditionally reserved for the cultural elites. These two approaches will be further developed in this chapter through a focus on implications for practice.

Cultivating cultural citizenship was the focus of Chapter 9, which sought to explore the value of youth arts programs in supporting participatory democracy and social change. The two case studies presented – CAMP and JKPeV – effectively positioned young people as 'justice-orientated cultural citizens' (Kuttner, 2015) through arts activities which enabled the development of empathy, compassion and 'goodness', the building of community relations and valuable dialogue around 'otherness'. Various theoretical concepts were drawn upon, such as 'connected civics' (Ito et al, 2015) and 'third spaces of encounter' (Thomson and Hall, 2020), which demonstrated the value of youth arts programs as a space of new possibilities, in particular in relation to identities, imagined futures and temporary communities.

As noted in the Introduction, the claims of 'global' in the book title may be challenging to substantiate. To be inclusive of non-westernised societies, further research should be undertaken into cultural practices and youth work in developing countries. For example, youth work in sub-Saharan Africa is being used as pedagogic tool to provoke consciousness (Sallah, 2018), developing the rural communities (Baloyi, 2014) and supporting the reintegration of young ex-offenders (Chauke and Malatji, 2021). On the Indian continent, a shift has been noted away from deficit-based models of 'youth for development' towards an assets-based approach (Mishra, 2014) and further refocusing on the holistic development of a young person (Padhan and Mishra, 2015). This new research has been effective in highlighting new and emerging practice, which moves beyond the white, western salvation rhetoric of colonial times.

The real-life envisioning of these theoretical approaches through the six international case studies demonstrated *why* youth arts programs are beneficial and impactful. This chapter completes our deep exploration into youth arts practice and pedagogies by setting out the key elements of *how* youth arts programs can flourish.

Maintaining youth work principles

A key message from this book is the effective synergy between youth work and arts practice. The youth workers and arts educators interviewed reflected on the value of the arts as a vehicle for expression, but also as a springboard for discussion about what might be going on in the lives of young people. Within youth arts programs, the building of respectful relationships is important, alongside collaborative approaches to informal education. One example, given by CAMP, is the setting of 'ground rules' together, when starting to work with a new group. Young people are invited to contribute suggestions on how they would expect others to behave so that they feel ownership over an informal code of conduct for the whole group. Building relationships, so that young people feel supported and in a safe, non-judgemental environment, are important principles of youth work, as Myrto-Helena Pertsinidi explains:

> 'Always be by their sides. They need support. They need your opinion. You know they need your advice, and that's important. We should not criticise their work, but we should find ways in order to tell them, how we would advise them to do certain things, maybe in a different way, so that the next time they could achieve their goal better. Because we're also not gurus. We're not experts in everything. We also make mistakes and we need to show this human side of ourselves. We are not perfect and that we do not judge them.' (Myrto-Helena Pertsinidi, Program Manager for JKPeV)

As well as reflecting on the joys of their work, youth workers were also clear about the challenges and emotional labour of working in these roles.

In building safe spaces and enabling expression through artistic forms and dialogue, practitioners had to be prepared to work in socially therapeutic ways. This often includes working on the self, as Nayelli Duran describes:

'It can be very very emotional. I really don't believe that it's possible to detach yourself from the issues that the young people are going through. I really think that you have to be willing to have those hard conversations with them and to be willing to open yourself up and to be real with them. Because young people know when you're not being real and that's going to involve doing a lot of personal work also on yourself. So, it's going to be really emotional. But I think that you have to be prepared for that if you want to work in a program where the young people honestly just have really tough lives.' (Nayelli Duran, CAMP Music Educator)

This 'ethics-of-care' approach (Banks, 1999) to being a youth arts practitioner stems not from instrumentalist perspectives of 'child-saving' (Davies, 2013) or 'education for the poor' (Seebach, 2008) but from core youth work principles which uphold voluntary participation.

Voluntary participation and dialogue

The set-up of youth arts programs within community centres, rather than schools, was reported to increase participation and reduce barriers to access. Through voluntary participation in open access programs, young people are choosing to be there. Youth workers reported young people's responsibility and commitment to programs which they found empowering. Shireen Shortt argued:

'I try to commit to those democratic principles through voluntary participation, taking time to make sure that I'm having conversations and really listening, to what young people have to say and want to express. And give them the space to explore that themselves without trying to impose your plans on them. Having said that, I think that people can get quite scared of having a dialogue with young people as they don't really want to influence or "contaminate" their ideas. I would reject that, in the sense that, I think young people are perfectly capable of taking on your point of view, reflecting on it and either rejecting it or taking your perspective on board and maybe using that to shape and inform their own point of view. Young people are equally as capable of critical thinking and engaging in conversation as we are.' (Shireen Shortt, Artist-in-Residence, SWAN)

This pedagogical approach, shared across each of the case studies, is founded upon a dialogic process, which youth workers viewed as key to working with young people. Embarking on a 'shared journey' through arts programs enabled young people's interests, perspectives and own life experiences to be captured and respected. Being responsive in this way was reported as an important element of building relationships and trust with different groups of young people.

Trust and time

While the open access nature of youth arts programs was deemed beneficial in relation to principles of voluntary participation, the transient nature of young people in youth settings can represent a challenge. Youth workers reflected on the degrees of patience and commitment to building and maintaining relationships that were required. Communication was deemed as important, whether between youth workers and artists or young people and youth workers. Keeping lines of communication open at all times and keeping doors open for young people to re-engage with programs and continue with the creative work they had started were recommended. Eibhlín Harrington encouraged trust in the process, which, she argued, often yields higher-quality work:

> 'With the arts and with young people, the final piece will come together. It will happen; however it happens. But it's the process that's so important. That slowing down. I think the conversations with young people, that just being open to exploring ideas of art, whether they take a U-turn on something that they've been working on for months, or they decide to go in a different direction, I think that's the biggest challenge for practitioners and funders. Being able to relax and let the young people lead us and let them guide us and it will go somewhere. It might not go where you originally planned, but it will go somewhere and it will only be a quality piece at the end if you allow that to happen.' (Eibhlín Harrington, Youth Service Project Leader, SWAN)

As explained by Eibhlín, trusting the process and trusting young people to lead facilitated the slowing down of time. This may be challenging for shorter-term arts programs or those who are working to funders' deadlines. Previous research on youth arts programs has shown that time is one of the most important things to consider when working with young people, an example being the Creative Margins network, which sought to bring a radical democratic youth and community work perspective to socially engaged arts practice.[1] Within this program, young people reported the value of being given time, but also maintaining a sense of momentum and progression through splitting programs into smaller diverse tasks. This included administration, time management and human resources tasks, which will be considered later in this chapter.

The giving of time by youth workers is highly valued by young people facing chaotic and fast-paced lives. Shireen Shortt reflects on the value of making, remaking and grappling with ideas:

'You need time without the pressure of creating something, but also time and space for a young person to grapple with a particular theme. Young people have their own logics and aesthetic values that they bring to the project that you can't give them. Nor would you want to. They can learn a lot in terms of the formal techniques but they need time and space to grapple with the ideas. Yes, you can ask them their opinions, but they're not going to have it formed and ready to go. They've got to develop their own perspective through making things, playing with things and grappling with them. Undoing it, re-doing it, chucking it out and starting again.[2] It takes time and putting a time limit or tight time frame on it, is counterproductive. Then it's in danger of becoming ventriloquism or something that is just being done to get done. Rather than young people doing something to explore their understanding of the world and trying to communicate it. That's going to take a little bit of reflection, time and space.' (Shireen Shortt, Artist-in-Residence, SWAN)

There was a clear argument from the youth workers that maintaining youth work principles led to a better experience for the young people and a higher-quality arts program.

Artistic quality

In Part II of this book, I shared my findings on the Arts Award program and argued that within youth settings artistic quality and process can be overshadowed by other factors such as measurement, 'hard outcomes' and behaviour modification. In Chapter 4, I recommended an emphasis on process over product, experience over outcome and valuing of creative expression and artistic development. I demonstrated that access to quality arts practice was unfortunately restricted for some young people, but the way that programs could avoid this was by offering access to arts professionals, industry-standard equipment and challenging pedagogies. My research highlighted varieties in pedagogical practice which depended on young people's perceived behaviour and impacted assumptions made about their artistic ability. In drawing attention to this form of disadvantage, exemplary pedagogies, which synergise the arts and youth work, can be forefronted through collaboration, informal education and border pedagogy (Coburn, 2011b). I argued that the arts should remain at the heart of all youth arts programs and that young people's artistic development should always be a core aim. Ensuring the highest-quality artistic practice for a youth arts program offers a pathway through the rhetorical and structural constraints that young people taking up the arts in youth settings often face.

Youth workers interviewed as part of the case studies uniformly expressed that the quality of the program remains more important than the number of young people they serve. Being stretched beyond what a program is able to do risks reducing artistic quality for participants. Often pressure is applied from funding bodies to do more and to 'squeeze the dollars', however program managers advised pushing back on this and sustaining high-quality artistic work. Length of program was also related to artistic quality, in particular in terms of the time required to build relationships. Shireen Shortt reflected:

'I'm really lucky in the length of time that we have for programs. You don't necessarily get that if you are operating as "the artist" or "the filmmaker", where you can be parachuted in. That time at the start, where you are building relationships can be quite an extended time period and it's necessary if you are really going to commit to participatory practice that is significantly underpinned by democratic principles and sensibilities. But the particular situation that I'm in with SWAN Youth Service is longitudinal and I recognise that not every Artist gets to experience that. It's a real commitment on SWAN's part organisationally putting funding bids in together, getting young people involved and working in partnership.' (Shireen Shortt, Artist-in-Residence, SWAN)

This quote demonstrates the importance of participatory and democratic arts programs for artistic quality. In addition, partnerships and organisational commitment to hosting an arts program within a youth setting, and supporting young people to be involved and take ownership, are further factors which contribute to artistic quality. These themes will be taken up later in this chapter, with a discussion on the varying degrees of partnership.

SWAN Youth Service, in particular, has a focus on gaining exposure and meaningful public engagement for the artistic work created by the young people on their arts program, Reckless Arts. As explored in Chapter 8, this is designed to enable young people to lay claim to their position within the arts landscape. In preparation for this, young people are involved in exhibition applications, planning and media training so they are able to speak about their artwork. For young people, being able to see their work outside of the youth setting raises not only their understanding of themselves as artists, but also gets their work seen so that people can engage with it. Mechanisms of gleaning feedback such as Q&A sessions and exhibition comments books are important opportunities for young people to reflect upon the quality of their own artistic practice.

Partnerships

All programs featured as case studies reported on the value of working in partnership. For CAMP, this was both a partnership with the Breakthrough FamilyPlex, where the program was based, as well as local community partners. For Annantalo, partnerships with the network of Helsinki elementary school culture coordinators were vital. For JKPeV, working with international partners was important so that young people could benefit from cultural mixing and diverse perspectives, but also engaging with local and national government so that programs were more visible. Bolt FM reported the value of working in partnership and collaborating with other organisations as a way of trying to work with a wide variety of young people. Shared resources were reported, in terms of funding, space and materials, alongside shared learning. Lindsay Fredrickson argues for the value of new youth programs partnering with organisations that have a previous track record:

> 'Make sure you partner with somebody who already has success doing youth programming and learn from them. Lean on them and make sure that they are supportive of what you do. Breakthrough are really supportive of our mission. They don't try to step in. They allow us autonomy, which is really, really important. They never have given us any instructions and things we have to do. They just let us be, which is really nice. They never undermine us and they always want to show us off.' (Lindsay Fredrickson, Founder and Lead Music Educator of CAMP)

Nicola Sim's recent book *Youth Work, Galleries and the Politics of Partnership* (2019) explores the benefits of partnership work between youth and arts organisations as expanding practice, exchanging knowledge and seeding organisational change. She also highlights the tensions that lie behind the rhetoric of partnership, including demands on time, wasting resources and exacerbating inequality. However, Sim remains optimistic that the youth and arts sectors can work together in meaningful, inclusive and significant ways, mainly due to the commitment and passion practitioners convey for working with young people in creative and democratic ways (Sim, 2019).

Sim (2019) sets out three typologies of partnership, which are useful ways to think about configuring a youth arts program:

- *Temporary 'co-ordinated' field*: most typically workshop-based and artist-led programs over a few weeks leading to a final outcome.
- *Temporary 'co-operative' field:* a 'joined-up' approach where creative activity takes place in community or youth spaces, using the skills of practitioners trained to work in those spaces.
- *Temporary 'collaborative' field*: an experimental, open access space where both youth and arts practitioners come together with young people. This approach is more likely to draw on pedagogies from detached youth work.

These typologies help to conceptualise the partnership work in working with artists through the international examples in this book.

Working with artists

What is interesting to note from the case studies is the differing ways that each of the programs works with artists and arts practitioners. By exploring a range of approaches, I hope to demonstrate that there is no one-size-fits-all approach to youth arts programs and that these approaches differ based on the program aims, the cohort of young people and, of course, the funding. For example, Dancehearts and CAMP employ art/music educators to work on their programs. While these art/music educators recognise the pastoral side to their work with young people, their training comes principally from arts education rather than youth work. With Bolt FM, the practitioners working on the program are youth work trained, but also have creative skills from previous education or hobby interests that they bring to the program. This approach, most aligned with CAYW (Beggan and Coburn, 2018), is becoming more common in youth work settings and would be defined as a temporary 'co-operative' field. The third model, which is most aligned with Sim's typology of temporary 'collaborative' field, is represented through Propel's KickstART festival creative coordinator and SWAN's artist-in-residence program. The SWAN Youth Service has engaged an artist-in-residence across a number of programs, and the artist's regular presence at the setting means she works in collaboration with youth workers and young people in an open and experimental way.

As a way of visualising these varieties in partnership, I have adapted Hart's Ladder of Participation (Hart, 1992) (see Figure 10.1). This ladder is a well-used resource in youth work training designed to encourage authentic participation of young people in youth programs, and I now incorporate the tripartite relationship between youth workers, artists and young people in youth arts programs.

Figure 10.1: Ladder of youth participation within arts programmes

> *8. Youth-initiated, shared decision with adults:* tripartite relationship between young people, youth workers and artist.
>
> *7. Youth-initiated and directed:* young people have set the program aims and worked with youth workers to recruit an artist. Young people feel ownership through regular input to planning, development and evaluation
>
> *6. Adult-initiated, shared decisions with young people:* youth workers and artist have decided the 'need' for the program, however young people have contributed to the planning of the program
>
> *5. Consulted and informed:* an artist has consulted with youth people and youth workers on the aims and outcome of the program, however young people have been informed of what they must do in order to take part
>
> *4. Assigned but informed:* an artist has been employed by a youth program and has set the aims, artistic medium and outcome for young people to follow
>
> *3. Tokenism:* an artist has been asked to lead just one workshop in a youth setting and is 'parachuted in'
>
> *2. Decoration:* young people have been asked to add surface details to creative work produced solely by an artist
>
> *1. Manipulation:* no artists or young people have taken part in creative activities

Source: Adapted from Roger Hart's Ladder of Participation (1992).

Working up the ladder in order to exemplify different levels of collaboration, rather than hierarchical positioning, I categorise the bottom three levels: Manipulation, Decoration and Tokenism, as Hart did as 'non-participation'. This means that the arts program is unlikely to have any beneficial impact upon the young people due to one-off and non-exploratory artistic experiences, where participants are unsure they have developed artistic skills at all. Levels 4 and 5 denote an artist-led program with varying levels of consultation, whereby young people are likely to feel informed, but not empowered or included in the decision-making process. At Level 6, the 'need' for an arts program has been decided by government policy, funders or arts organisations, which is most aligned to the AI approach explored in Chapter 2. This particular approach is more likely to involve young people in planning, however it may be positioned as child-salvation or solving a social problem. Level 7, which represents the majority of case studies within this book, demonstrates young people's involvement in program planning and evaluation, with the core objective of supporting participants' artistic development. Youth workers, arts educators and practitioners have reported young people's sense of ownership in this process but also the importance of 'adult direction' to support skills development, self-efficacy and social networking. Finally, level 8 – the tripartite relationship between young person, youth worker and artist – is a scenario which calls for a radical and democratic shift in power sharing, not only within youth and arts organisations, but within society as a whole. This approach is most aligned to cultural democracy, as explored in Chapter 8.

While adapting this ladder framework may serve as inspiration for those planning new arts programs for young people, the limitations of each level of the framework should also be acknowledged. During the interviews for the international case studies, practitioners reported restrictions in both timescale and funding. We know that longer-term arts programs are more likely to have the most significant impacts on young people (Catterall, 2002; 2009), however these also come at a significant cost. While always striving to offer a high-quality youth arts program, there was a sense that it was more effective to work with smaller numbers of young people over an extended time frame, which appears to run contrary to many 'bums on seats' and 'value for money' youth-funding policies (Lynch et al, 2015; de St Croix, 2018). In addition, the quality of and commitment to youth arts programs is often dependent on staff capacity, prior cultural knowledge and confidence. Under austerity measures and funding cuts, not all youth organisations enjoy a 'safe space' to develop new ways of working. Many are simply trying to survive. The restrictions of differing national youth and arts policies frequently shape the offer of youth arts programs, despite youth workers' best interests and efforts. In recognition of these limitations, the adapted Ladder of Participation offers a way forward in supporting the best possible quality of youth arts programs.

Artist-in-residence case study

SWAN Youth Service is a youth organisation that has hosted a number of artist-in-residence programs. Many of these programs have been funded by the Artist and Youth Work Residency Scheme, which is managed by the National Youth Arts Programme of the NYCI to develop youth arts in Ireland, and co-funded by the Arts Council of Ireland and the Department of Children, Equality, Disability, Integration and Youth. The National Youth Arts program aims to realise the potential of young people through good-quality youth arts practice within youth work organisations, with the vision that every young person in Ireland gets to experience the arts. Saoirse Reynolds, Youth Arts Program Officer for NYCI, explains that

> 'It's about the young person. It's about developing the best possible outcomes for them, and that's by supporting the youth sector to deliver high-quality youth arts programs. We obviously believe in the power of youth arts and what it can do, and what we keep hearing time after time is that we can support them, we can train them, we can kind of empower them and we can get them the confidence that they need through funding and recognition of the skills of the artists. For the young people, the opportunity of having the artists come into their organisation, is just brilliant.' (Saoirse Reynolds, Youth Arts Program Officer, NYCI)

The Artist and Youth Work Residency Scheme has annual funding rounds and includes 'Explorer Grants' for projects, services and organisations that are beginning to explore youth arts as well as 'Full Grants' for larger-scale residencies. Running since 2005, the scheme looks to support youth organisations that really value the work of artists and arts practitioners and want to partner with professional artists in order to extend and enhance the opportunities for young people to experience and participate in the arts. Funding is applied for following call-outs, mail-outs and local radio promotion, and a panel, made up of different representatives each year, decides on the successful applicants. The panel is facilitated by NYCI staff and is comprised of youth work specialists, arts professionals, and a young person with experience of youth arts, each of whom are paid the same amount to attend. Saoirse was passionate about the involvement of a young person on the selection panel:

> 'It's important that young people are involved, as they can call it if an application has young people involved in the process or not. They're also looking for if this proposal is something that young people would want to be involved in. You find that they have a different perspective and that's what makes the panel so unique. I think that's what gives the process strength because each application is viewed through different lenses, so a youth worker might be saying "no, this doesn't work", whereas the young person can disagree. I think the young people enjoy that and that conversation is just powerful.' (Saoirse Reynolds, Youth Arts Program Officer, NYCI)

As well as managing the Artist and Youth Work Residency scheme, NYCI hosts networks, training events and other projects which bring artists and youth workers together, so that they can share their learning and collaborate. These 'hubs' and training events are spaces where different skill sets and knowledges are recognised, and training is facilitated so that different levels of confidence can be shared. If successful in the Artist and Youth Work Residency scheme, both youth worker and artist are invited to attend a training day which supports partnership working. As Saoirse describes:

> 'The focus of the training is how they're going to work together, because you find in some cases they've never worked together. They haven't properly sat down and chatted to each other. So, just giving them space to consider all the different things before they go meet a group of young people properly. Things like the artist's contract to make sure they are paid properly, but also what they will deliver. They do a project plan and framework on how that might work to deliver on that. We also flag common things that go wrong each year, like the young people haven't engaged or the relationship has broken down. So, it's highly supportive.' (Saoirse Reynolds, Youth Arts Program Officer, NYCI)

The supportive scaffolding offered by NYCI in supporting artist residencies in youth organisations throughout Ireland has been shown as beneficial not only for organisational change within the youth sector, but also for working with young people in creative ways.[3]

Connecting young people

Some of the key affordances of the Artist and Youth Work Residency scheme include connecting young people with local artists' networks, raising awareness of how young people's work can be shared and platformed, and making connections within the arts sector that extend beyond the life of the program. For Propel, their partnerships and professional relationships with arts organisations and government institutions were important for connecting young people to the arts sector. Organising large-scale events, such as the KickstART festival, offered opportunities for making connections by working with a wide range of different partners. Kobi Arthur Morrison reported that

> 'It's been really exciting to be able to introduce young people to the "next" people and trying to connect them and connect again. I would say, just don't be afraid to have the conversation "hey I'm searching for such and such, and I like your work because of such and such". That has become one of my favourite things to be able to do, so that if I bump into somebody under the particular context of the arts, I'm usually able to come up with a reason as to why I admire this person and connect a young person through that. ... We're very much a community that's wanting to band together and help each other, to lift each other up and reaffirm each other, to see that young artist get that thing out of their head and onto the page, onto the stage or onto the screen. I absolutely love the notion of being able to live the rest of my life being able to help support people to get their thing out there, get their idea out there.' (Kobi Arthur Morrison, Creative Coordinator for 2020)

It is important that youth arts programs think about the connections they can make for young people. These informal arts networks can sustain artistic practice and engagement beyond the life of the program.

Planning and evaluation

Every one of the international case study programs involved young people in planning. Youth workers often referred to this as 'giving power away' and acknowledged that a collaborative approach to program planning not only gave young people a sense of ownership, but made the final 'product', whether that be a radio show or a theatre performance or an exhibition, higher quality. Shared decision making and the freedom to raise whatever issues young people wanted to were deemed key to this process. Rita Sebestyén further explains program design as a two-way process:

> 'I was thinking that we have a program, these are the objectives. If you're curious then come tell me your ideas, let's discuss it and I give you as much freedom as possible. So, from my perspective it was more about what can I learn from the youth? And if they want me to give them something, if they are interested, these are my skills, my ideas. But what are your things? Teach me.' (Rita Sebestyén, Theatre Workshops Facilitator)

Youth-led planning approaches from the case studies included initial research, funding applications, artist recruitment, program planning, controlling finances and setting budgets, board management and program evaluation. It was acknowledged that involving young people in decision making at these stages was not an 'easy option', that building relationships and taking time were important approaches to ensuring that young people felt ownership of the program. There was also a sense that young people could be included in more tokenistic ways, which should be avoided. Myrto-Helena Pertsinidi talks about weighing the 'giving of power' more heavily than the completion of a successful program:

> 'And if I want to involve young people, then I need to inspire them, because if I just tell them "this is your task, to do", they might not be much engaged. But by giving them this sense of initiative and talking to them about your passion because this is our passion, we do it because we love doing, we love implementing some such programs, I think they understand the intentions. Young people are clever enough to understand the intentions, and you always need to give them space to express their creativity. But if you just assign them quite limited tasks, you know, some do administrative work or they distribute flyers to promote the program and its events, this is not engaging enough. You need to give space to create something by themselves. It might not be the most successful program, but that's not the point.' (Myrto-Helena Pertsinidi, Program Manager for JKPeV)

A dialogical approach to program planning was echoed by many of the other case studies. Often this started with a focus on youth culture itself and youth workers' skill in finding ways to 'meet the young people where they are at' and 'on their level', while recognising this may look different to different people. Jamie Gleave believes that:

'If you want information on what young people want and how to reach them, and what projects would be best for young people, well, obviously the experts in that field are young people. If you want do something in your area, talk to the young people. I mean, it sounds really obvious, but a lot of people don't do this. If you're just doing it to tick-a-box, then maybe think a bit harder of a better reason. You've got to know why you want to engage with young people and you've got to engage with them on that level.' (Jamie Gleave, General Manager, Propel)

In Chapter 8, the case study on Propel included the KickstART festival as an example of youth-led programming and cultural democracy. I return to this festival as a way of drawing upon a particular model, a particular way of working around events and festivals, that can involve young people in every aspect.

The festival model

The Propel Youth Arts WA case study focused on an annual youth arts festival. Festivals and events are a regular feature of many youth arts programs – such as Bolt FM's two-week radio takeover and SWAN's exhibitions – and there are many opportunities within these events for young people to take a lead. In this section, I draw on the festival as a model for youth arts programs, with a particular focus on planning. As explored in Chapter 8, Propel employs a young person as creative coordinator for the KickstART festival. The young person in the role changes each year as they help develop a specific theme, connect with other artists across Perth and build a program with the support of the YPC. Kobi Arthur Morrison reflects on the process of working with the YPC:

'Naturally the festival does change every single year. Change is always a good thing. You can't just stay with the same thing every single time because trends change, young people, opinions change. You have to focus on new issues to respond to, like responding to the political climate as well. Young people are super opinionated, super in touch with what's going on in the world and I think to ignore that is really naive and you really have to just continue to follow, just go with the change every single time.' (Kobi Arthur Morrison, Creative Coordinator for 2020)

Programming and planning a youth arts festival is a busy time for young people. Cecile Vuaillat supports this process by assisting with logistical planning, for example putting together artists' contracts and following up with venues. Being part of the YPC, young people get the experience of being young leaders and attending formal meetings, but they also get the opportunity to facilitate workshops and have exhibitions. This is often with the guidance of a professional mentor from the industry, who can support their learning experience. Cecile explains further:

'I think our practice of having a youth committee and having them be like a holistic part of how we do things is really important. I'm a young person, most of my colleagues are young people, but we do have to make sure that the vessel does remain relevant to young people. So, you do need those young people to be leading it, to come up with the ideas and to be able to approve the theme, the programming and the venues ... basically every aspect of it as well. You really need to have young people working at every level, including the volunteers. All of our artists are young people and I think the only place where we have adults is if there are mentors or if we have a keynote speaker, where someone is able to share their professional knowledge and skills. So, in terms of the KickstART festival, young people are at the forefront of every single element, so it makes it makes it really unique and lovely.' (Cecile Vuaillat, Project Manager for Propel)

Drawing on the expertise of the team at Propel, who have been running the KickstART festival for over 10 years, having a range of supportive partners was recommended. This support may not always be financial, it may be in the form of free venues or goodwill to get events up and running. From their experience, running a youth arts festival is always supported, even by people who would not otherwise have anything to do with the arts, such as people in the community, local businesses or local councils. However, Jamie Gleave recommends not growing too large. He reflects that "Festivals are stressful and there's a lot of expectation behind that word 'festival'. ... At one point, KickstART went for a whole month, it was awful. So, we pared it back to being just a week." Therefore, there is a delicate balance between programming ambitiously versus the realisation of what is possible within your boundaries. The festival model, therefore, hosts opportunities for collaborative, youth-led planning, being responsive to and appealing to young people's artistic interests, as well as effectively platforming local and global youth culture.

Evaluation

The importance of evaluation of youth arts programs was also stressed by several of the case study programs. Approaches to evaluation ranged from bespoke digital evaluation applications (apps) to celebration events attended by program funders. For example, Annantalo uses an evaluation app called *Art Testers* (see Figure 10.2) that works on mobile devices, funded by the

Figure 10.2: Screenshots from the Art Testers app

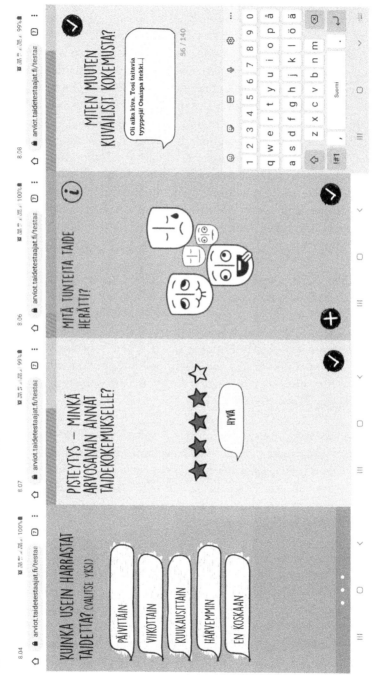

Note: Young people have the opportunity to share their thoughts, insights and opinions about art through a browser app where they can review and make comments on their experience. https://taidetestaajat.fi/en

Union of Children's' Cultural Centres, Finnish Cultural Foundation, Swedish Cultural Foundation and the Ministry of Education and Culture. This has been designed with interesting visuals and simple questions that encompass different ways of talking about the arts that are most understandable to young people. Based on ratings data, young people can respond to what they liked best and can also offer answers to what young people feel is important in the arts activities they are doing. Pirjetta Mulari, Chief of Children's Culture and Director of Annantalo, finds this method of evaluation valuable as the structure was set up from the beginning and followed consistently.

Bolt FM's approach is to capture the value of their program through celebration. Neil Young supports a celebratory culture within Bolt FM, which enables young people to capture the change that has happened. The organisation engages with regular evaluation methods, such as forms given by funders and quotes from young people, but strives to connect all these elements through a live experience. The encouragement of Neil is to celebrate youth arts programs more:

'So, when they've done the broadcast and they can see the difference. … Yes, we've got forms, we've got little bits that we'll get some quotes from, but if I could find a way of just capturing the "Wow, I can do stuff moments" then that would be the one thing that I would want to do because it's just so beautiful to watch. There's nothing beats that. I love putting a funder in a room with a young person who's doing that and they just watch it happen. And you can't write it in a report.' (Neil Young, Youth Team Leader for St Paul's Forum)

In addition to evaluation for the purposes of future program development and reporting to funders, the feedback element for young people's artistic and personal progression was also noted as valuable. Feedback for the young people involved in arts programs can also be achieved with meaningful public engagement with their artistic work. Eibhlín Harrington argues for the value of audience engagement work:

'Because they're sick of us telling them how amazing their work is and how powerful and they're so critical of themselves as well. So, I think having that positive feedback and people connecting with their art, gives that feedback to them, because I don't think they see it often themselves. The young people that have come through the arts program, they're hugely critical of themselves, so I think when they get that feedback it's fantastic. That's what I love about the exhibition space, because it's real. It's face to face, it's right there in the moment. People are seeing it and people are able to talk to the young people straight away. It's fantastic when you can see people seeing your art, you get that kind of feedback you get that response from other people and that can be quite surprising sometimes for young people.' (Eibhlín Harrington, Youth Service Project Leader, SWAN)

For many youth workers and arts educators interviewed for the case studies, ways of evaluating youth arts programs were much more aligned to the positive and beneficial experiences of the young people. Shireen Shortt argues that "If you are talking about a practice that is responsive and it is exploratory, once you have invested that time and space for that to emerge on its own, without having to try and impose it, it's destined to be somewhat successful – depending on how you measure success." This quote opens up a wider discussion on how the arts and youth work are measured and evaluated (Matarasso, 1997; Belfiore, 2012; Doherty, 2019), a debate that shows a disconnect between experience and the expectations of policy. The 'Rethinking Impact, Evaluation and Accountability in Youth Work' project (Doherty and de St Croix, 2022) produced further valuable research-informed practical resources for youth workers. However, the guidance from practitioners is clear: evaluation is important, but a written report can never tell the whole story. This is a call to think differently about what matters and to draw upon the expressive means of the arts themselves to tell more holistic stories.

Following the completion of my PhD study, a resource was created by Upstart Projects, commissioned by Arts Award and Trinity College London. This resource outlines the benefits of involving young people in the design and development of programs and how programs can be planned in collaboration with young people, encouraging agency and reflection. Games for planning and evaluation are included, alongside a five-step process:

1. Planning with young people
2. Connecting young people and artists
3. Developing ownership
4. Making the program count
5. Evaluating with young people.

This resource, created by Upstart Projects CIO for Trinity College London, may be found in the Appendix.

Recommendations

What this book has tried to do is to ask questions: questions that youth workers and practitioners should be asking when working with the arts and young people; questions of which we may not be aware, as was the case for me at the beginning of my PhD journey; questions that may challenge our assumptions, perspectives and positions; questions that seek to improve practice and strengthen the field. It is important to ask questions, but also to acknowledge that there is no 'correct answer'. There is no one-size-fits-all approach. However, there is valuable learning that can be recognised and built upon. Every cohort of young people is diverse, therefore every youth arts program should be different. The case studies in this book have demonstrated this diversity and highlighted the need for cultural, social and political responsivity.

Therefore, I close this book by giving a summation of these questions, which not only revisit the subtitles in this chapter, but draw upon the key themes of common culture, cultural democracy and cultural citizenship.

Your position

- What do you think the arts can do? And why do you think this?
- How do you view young people? What experience do you have to support this?
- Why are you organising this program?

Program aims

- What is the aim of your program?
- Which particular group of young people will benefit? And how?
- How do you know what your program aims to do is in the best interests of the young people?
- What kind of 'cultural citizens' does your program support young people to be? (see Chapter 9)
- How can your program encourage diverse perspectives, cultural awareness, community building and critical pedagogy?

Youth involvement

- How are young people involved in the planning, running and evaluation of your program?
- How much 'power' are you comfortable in giving up within your program?
- What are the opportunities for young people to lead, but also to be seen and heard? (see Chapter 8 on cultural democracy)
- What level of partnership will you work at with respect to (1) other organisations, (2) artists, (3) young people?

Artistic practice and quality

• What arts practices will your program involve?
• How do you know these will be of interest to your young people?
• How will your program accommodate 'common culture'? (see Chapter 7)
• How does the artistic quality reflect the demography and democratic approaches of your program?

Youth work principles

• What pedagogical approach will youth workers and arts educators apply on your program?
• Does your program offer opportunities for voluntary participation and dialogue?
• Will your program support young people through relationship building, trust and the giving of time?

Impact

• What would 'success' look like for your program? And whose vision of 'success' is this?
• How would you 'measure' and celebrate it?
• Have you outlined a consistent evaluation approach from the start that can both speak young people's language and appeal to funders?

Appendix

Planning and running an arts project with young people

- This short resource for Arts Award advisers outlines how you can plan a project in collaboration with young people
- If you involve young people in designing and developing a project, they are more likely to be motivated and gain greater benefit
- Arts Award is the perfect vehicle for supporting this process because it encourages learner agency and reflection within real projects
- You may find that some artists have less experience of collaborating with young people in this way, but if you explain the principles they are likely to embrace the approach

- The resource is designed as a five-step process but the steps will probably overlap
- The resource is based on research by Dr Frances Howard into the experiences of young people undertaking Arts Award as part of informal education, youth work and alternative education programmes. This resource has been developed for Arts Award by Upstart Projects who offer training in developing youth voice and co-producing with young people at **upstartprojects.uk/training**

TRINITY COLLEGE LONDON

ARTS COUNCIL ENGLAND

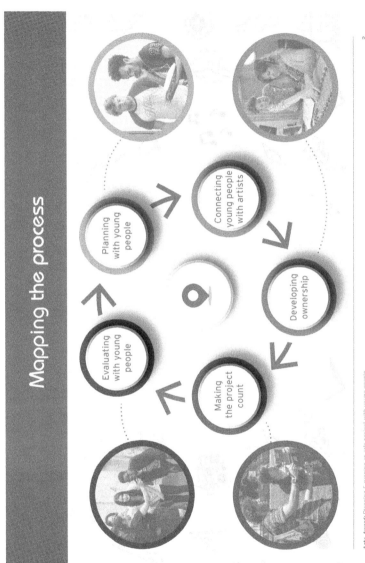

Mapping the process

- Planning with young people
- Connecting young people with artists
- Developing ownership
- Making the project count
- Evaluating with young people

1 Planning with young people

Discuss these questions

What cultural experience do these young people bring?

Use arts games to explore ideas

What do they want from the project?

What are their arts interests and aspirations?

Questions to ask yourself & your group

Are they open to new experiences?

STARTING POINT

Arts Award: Planning & running an arts project with young people

3

Games for planning

Hot air balloon

This simple activity can help young people think about a new project. Take a piece of flip-chart paper, draw a hot-air balloon with a basket. Ask the group to use post-it notes to add the following ideas:

Balloon

What will make the project fly? What do young people think will make this project work well? (eg the right professional artist, pay travel expenses to attend, location of venue etc). These are things you should try to address.

Basket

What might challenge the project (pull it down)? What do young people think you should avoid doing? (eg not have meetings during school time, not use a 'posh' venue, not take too long). How can you overcome these?

The Sky

If the sky was the limit, what would young people want to do or experience? (eg a performance by a Top 10 artist? Have limos pick everyone up?) Maybe you can find a way of organising this? Maybe a local celebrity or someone with ties to the area would be interested?

Create the story

Generating ideas for the project

Take a piece of paper (one per group member) and pass it around the group with each person writing the answer to a preset question. Assume there's five people, these questions could include:

▶ What do we want to do?
▶ Who do we want to work with?
▶ Where should the project take place?
▶ What is the key attraction?

Now you have five stories to discuss.

'Why?' Game

Participants work in pairs. Person A asks "What do you want to achieve through this project?" Person B responds and this is noted. Person A asks "Why?", and Person B needs to answer, again this is noted and the "Why?" is asked again. Repeat the "Why?" around six times. The end result should have distilled the reason why that participant wants the project to happen.

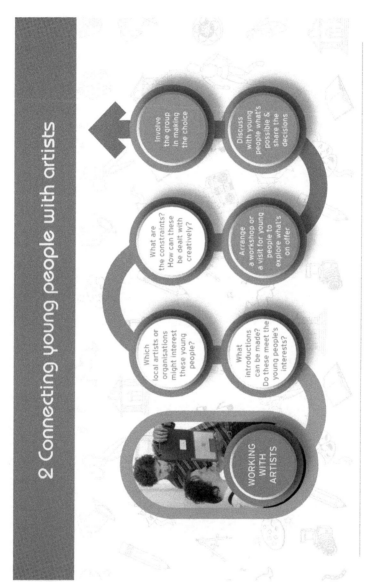

2 Connecting young people with artists

Involve the group in making the choice

Discuss with young people what's possible & share the decisions

What are the constraints? How can these be dealt with creatively?

Arrange a workshop or a visit for young people to explore what's on offer

Which local artists or organisations might interest these young people?

What introductions can be made? Do these meet the young people's interests?

WORKING WITH ARTISTS

3 Developing ownership

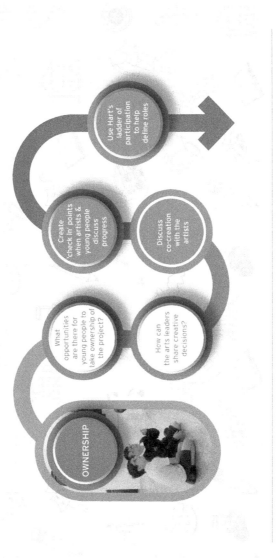

OWNERSHIP

What opportunities are there for young people to take ownership of the project?

How can the arts leaders share creative decisions?

Create check in' points when artists & young people discuss progress

Discuss co-creation with the artists

Use Hart's ladder of participation to help define roles

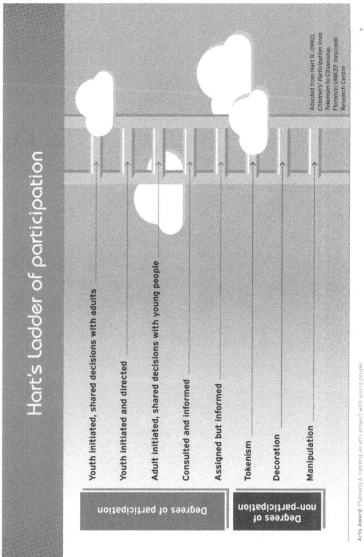

Hart's Ladder of participation

Degrees of participation

- Youth initiated, shared decisions with adults
- Youth initiated and directed
- Adult initiated, shared decisions with young people
- Consulted and informed
- Assigned but informed

Degrees of non-participation

- Tokenism
- Decoration
- Manipulation

Adapted from Hart R. (1992). Children's Participation from Tokenism to Citizenship. Florence: UNICEF Innocenti Research Centre

Arts Award: Planning & running an arts project with young people

176

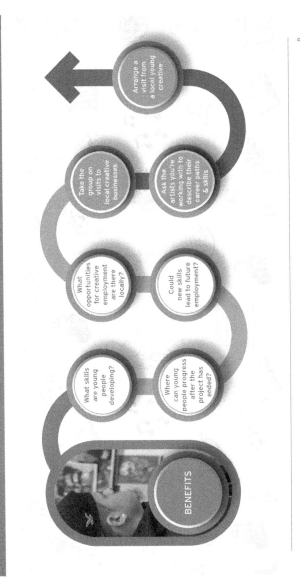

4 Making the project count

Arrange a visit from a local young creative

Take the group on visits to local creative businesses

Ask the artists you're working with to describe their career paths & skills

What opportunities for creative employment are there locally?

Could new skills lead to future employment?

What skills are young people developing?

Where can young people progress after the project has ended?

BENEFITS

5 evaluating with young people

Use evaluation games

Discuss the project with the group

Make time to support next steps for individuals

What does the individual or group want to do next?

How could the project be improved?

What did young people enjoy and why?

What skills do they feel they developed?

WHAT WORKED?

Arts Award: Planning & running an arts project with young people

9

Games for evaluation

Did we hit the target?

► Draw three concentric circles on flipchart paper, like a target. Label the centre 'Great', second circle 'Good', third 'OK' and outside the target 'Needs improvement'

► Draw a cross through the target to make four segments, like quarters of a cake, and label them with some of the aims of the project, such as Learning skills, Working with artists, Creating art work, Influencing the project

► Give participants and the project team a set of sticker dots. Each person then sticks a dot in the relevant circle in each segment - allowing the group to see everyone's ratings as one image. Discuss where the dots coincide and where there are differences

Statue Responses

► Ask the group to walk gently around the space reflecting on the project/meeting/day

► Facilitator can vary the walking pace between one (really slow) and five (fast walk)

► Facilitator asks "What is one thing you will take away from today?", count down from three, repeat your question after one and call "Freeze". Participants then create a statue/frozen image representing their response to the question

► Facilitator can ask individuals to explain their response

► Repeat the process with different questions etc

► You can develop this to asking people to work in pairs or threes, with 30 seconds to agree a scene that represents their feedback

VoxPops

► Give participants two or three questions. Ask them to work in pairs to film simple VoxPops in response - shooting selfie style or interview style. Ensure both partners give responses

► Bring the group together and review the responses

► Alternatively young people record audio clips, or you could film a live interview with a panel of two or three young people responding to the questions, TV interview sofa style

Arts Award: Planning & running an arts project with young people

10

Source: Created by Upstart Projects CIO for Trinity College London.

179

Notes

Chapter 1

1. Gallery 37 is a not-for-profit organisation in Chicago. Its purpose is to attract artistically inclined city youth to work as apprentice artists at a vacant downtown lot known as Block 37.
2. Sim draws on Bourdieu's concept of field to demonstrate symbolic violence between youth work and gallery education.
3. Every Child Matters is a UK government initiative for England and Wales that was launched in 2003, at least partly in response to the death of Victoria Climbié. It is one of the most important policy initiatives to be introduced in relation to children and children's services in the last decade, and has been described as a 'sea change' to the children and families agenda. Every Child Matters covers children and young adults up to the age of 19, or 24 for those with disabilities, and has five key aims: stay safe, be healthy, enjoy and achieve, make a positive contribution and achieve economic well-being.
4. Arts Award can be achieved at five levels, four qualifications (Explore, Bronze, Silver and Gold) and an introductory award (Discover). www.artsaward.org.uk

Chapter 4

1. Cost as of 16 January 2021. Source: www.artsaward.org.uk
2. Figure as of 20 September 2020. Source: www.artsaward.org.uk
3. Data from 2018/19 participation report. Source: https://www.artsaward.org.uk/site/?id=2055
4. The research sites have been given pseudonyms.
5. Youth Music is a national charity (England) funded by the National Lottery via Arts Council England, which supports investment in grassroots music organisations and young people themselves in order to make, learn and earn in music.
6. Names of the young people have been changed.

Chapter 5

1. An EP is a music recording that contains more tracks than a single but which does not qualify as a full album.

Chapter 6

1. NOCN is a regulated awarding organisation, offering hundreds of qualifications including Skills for Life and employability qualifications, which young people attending the programs were encouraged to take up.
2. The 'arts skills share' is part D of the Bronze Arts Award, where young people are required to pass on a skill to others. This could be through a workshop, demonstration or presentation of that skill.

Chapter 7

1. Art testers is a national scheme funded by private foundations and public bodies; the Helsinki part is coordinated from Annantalo.
2. BBC Children in Need is a charity whose vision is that children and young people in the UK have a safe, happy and secure childhood and the chance to reach their potential. They fund programs that make differences in children's lives and help prevent or overcome the effects of the disadvantages they face.

3   Refugee Week is a UK-wide festival celebrating the contributions, creativity and resilience of refugees and people seeking sanctuary. Founded in 1998 and held every year around World Refugee Day on 20 June, Refugee Week is also a growing global movement. Through a program of arts, cultural, sports and educational events alongside media and creative campaigns, Refugee Week enables people from different backgrounds to connect beyond labels, as well as encouraging understanding of why people are displaced, and the challenges they face when seeking safety. Refugee Week is a platform for people who have sought safety in the UK to share their experiences, perspectives and creative work on their own terms: www.refugeeweek.org

Chapter 8

1   The Noongar (/ˈnʊŋɑː/, also spelt Noongah, Nyungar, Nyoongar, Nyoongah, Nyungah, Nyugah, Yunga) are Aboriginal Australian peoples who live in the south-west corner of Western Australia.
2   The National Youth Council of Ireland funded the first year of the program (2017/18) and then SWAN Youth Service kept it up and running with other funding. NYCI partially funded the Reckless group again two years later (2019/20). Other funding for the program was received from Dublin City Council and the Arts Council.
3   The Bibulman tribe are the traditional owners of the south-western region of Western Australia. Noongar are Indigenous Australians from the Perth (Western Australia) area are also known as Bibbulmun.

Chapter 9

1   The Breakthrough FamilyPlex is a multifunctional community facility designed to support East Garfield Park, Chicago, by empowering people to live fuller, healthier lives.
2   The Breakthrough Violence Prevention Team partners with local residents to interrupt violence, create safe spaces, and provide opportunities and resources for those being restored to community. Convened by Metropolitan Family Services, the framework provides a comprehensive approach to reducing violence. Its work is rooted in non-violence, trauma-informed care, hyper-local collaboration and restorative justice practices.
3   George Floyd was an African American man murdered by a police officer during an arrest on 25 May 2020. Breonna Taylor was a black medical worker who was shot and killed by Louisville police officers in March 2020. Elijah McClain was a 23-year-old black American massage therapist from Colorado, who died after being placed in a chokehold by police in August 2019.
4   SEL helps children work on things like coping with feelings and setting goals. It also helps with interpersonal skills such as working in teams and resolving conflicts. SEL can help young people who learn and think differently talk about their challenges and build self-esteem. https://www.understood.org/articles/en/social-emotional-learning-what-you-need-to-know
5   EHV is suitable for children aged 4–11 years. EHV is a series of empowering lesson plans based on five universal core values, which transcend religious and cultural differences. Cross-curricular in its approach, some elements of the EHV program focus on tranquillity, encouraging children to develop calmness, whereas other aspects help them build up assertiveness and self-esteem. It leads children to discover, explore, practise and imbibe lasting values, which they can readily apply in school, at home and in the wider community, all the while enabling them to grow and flourish. https://humanvaluesfoundation.com/our-history
6   The program partners included: Jugend- & Kulturprojekt e.V., Dresden, Germany; Coordinator, Municipality of Dresden, Germany; Memorare Pacem e.V., Dresden,

Germany; Aristotle University of Thessaloniki, Thessaloniki, Greece; AddArt NGO, Thessaloniki, Greece; Otherness project, Denmark; Oldham Council, Oldham, United Kingdom; Glaser Jakab Foundation, Budapest, Hungary; Institute pro regionalni rozvoj, Prague, Czech Republic; ADEL, Stropkov, Slovakia; Association Center for Intercultural Dialogue, Kumanovo, former Yugoslav Republic of Macedonia.

[7] A country that is not a member of the European Union as well as a country or territory whose citizens do not enjoy the EU right to free movement, as defined in Article 2(5) of Regulation (EU) 2016/399 (Schengen Borders Code).

[8] Heterotopia is a concept elaborated by philosopher Michel Foucault to describe certain cultural, institutional and discursive spaces that are somehow 'other': disturbing, intense, incompatible, contradictory or transforming.

Chapter 10

[1] http://www.creativemargins.net/2019/02/14/creative-margins-bringing-a-radical-democratic-youth-and-community-work-perspective-to-socially-engaged-arts-practice/

[2] Shortt draws on David Gauntlett's book - *Making is connecting: The social power of creativity, from craft and knitting to digital everything* (2018) in this description.

[3] NYCI, Artist in Residency Scheme 2017/18 Report.

References

Ahn, J. (2012). Teenagers' experiences with social network sites: Relationships to bridging and bonding social capital. *The Information Society, 28*(2), 99–109.

Alliance, A. (2013). *Re-imagining futures: exploring arts interventions and the process of desistance.* https://www.artsincriminaljustice.org.uk/wp-content/uploads/2016/07/Re-imagining_Futures_Research_Report_Final.pdf

Altman, R. and De, M. (2010). Expanding possibilities for underserved and marginalised youth using Freire's critical pedagogy of active and reflective arts practice: Three case studies from Bronx (USA), Coventry (UK) and New Delhi (India). *The University of Melbourne Refereed, 1*(5), 1–20.

Anwar McHenry, J. (2009). A place for the arts in rural revitalisation and the social wellbeing of Australian rural communities. *Rural Society, 19*(1), 60–70.

Anyon, J. (1980). Social class and the hidden curriculum of work. *Journal of Education*, 67–92.

Archer, L. and Hutchings, M. (2010). 'Bettering yourself'? Discourses of risk, cost and benefit in ethnically diverse, young working-class non-participants' constructions of higher education. *British Journal of Sociology of Education, 21*(4), 555–74. doi:10.1080/713655373

Arts Award (2014). *Adviser Toolkit.*

Arts Council England (2004). *The impact of the arts: Some research evidence*: Arts Council England.

Arts Council England (2018). *Cultural democracy in practice.* https://64million artists.com/wp-content/uploads/2018/09/culturaldemocracy.pdf

Atkins, L. (2013). Researching 'with', not 'on': Engaging marginalised learners in the research process. *Research in Post-Compulsory Education, 18*(1–2), 143–58.

Baker, A. M. (2015). Constructing citizenship at the margins: The case of young graffiti writers in Melbourne. *Journal of Youth Studies, 18*(8), 997–1014.

Baker, G. (2016). Editorial introduction: El Sistema in critical perspective. Action, Criticism, and Theory for *Music Education, 15*(1), 10–32.

Baker, S. and Homan, S. (2007). Rap, recidivism and the creative self: A popular music programme for young offenders in detention. *Journal of Youth Studies, 10*(4), 459–76.

Baloyi, G. (2014). The promotion of youth work through policies in the context of South Africa. *Mediterranean Journal of Social Sciences, 5*(20), 1063–67.

Banks, S. (1999). *Ethical issues in youth work*: Psychology Press.

Bansel, P. (2015). The subject of policy. *Critical Studies in Education, 56*(1), 5–20.

Barrett, M. S. and Smigiel, H. M. (2007). Children's perspectives of participation in music youth arts settings: Meaning, value and participation. *Research Studies in Music Education, 28*(1), 39–50.

Batsleer, J. (2008). *Informal learning in youth work*: SAGE.

Batsleer, J. (2011). Voices from an edge. Unsettling the practices of youth voice and participation: Arts-based practice in The Blue Room, Manchester. *Pedagogy, Culture & Society, 19*(3), 419–34.

Batsleer, J. (2021). Re-assembling anti-oppressive practice (1): The personal, the political, the professional. *Education Sciences, 11*(10), 645.

Batsleer, J. and Davies, B. (2010). *What is youth work?*: SAGE.

Batsleer, J., Beever, E., de St Croix, T., Jones, K., McVeigh, G., Smith, C. and Amin, H. (2020). A citizen enquiry into the lives of youth workers in the time of Covid-19. *Youth and Policy*. https://www.youthandpolicy.org/articles/citizen-enquiry-into-the-lives-of-youth-workers-in-covid-19/

Baudrillard, J. (1994). *Simulacra and simulation*: University of Michigan Press.

Beggan, E. and Coburn, A. (2018). Creating 'one big masterpiece'– synthesis in creative arts youth work. *Concept, 9*(2), 15–30.

Belfiore, E. (2006). *The social impacts of the arts – myth or reality?*: Policy Exchange Limited.

Belfiore, E. (2009). On bullshit in cultural policy practice and research: Notes from the British case. *International Journal of Cultural Policy, 15*(3), 343–59.

Belfiore, E. (2010). Art as a means of alleviating social exclusion: Does it really work? A critique of instrumental cultural policies and social impact studies in the UK. *International Journal of Cultural Policy, 8*(1), 91–106.

Belfiore, E. (2012). 'Defensive instrumentalism' and the legacy of New Labour's cultural policies. *Cultural Trends, 21*(2), 103–11.

Bennett, A. (2018). Conceptualising the relationship between youth, music and DIY careers: A critical overview. *Cultural Sociology, 12*(2), 140–55.

Bergman, Å. and Lindgren, M. (2014). Social change through Babumba and Beethoven – musical educational ideals of El Sistema. *Swedish Journal of Music Research/Svensk Tidskrift för Musikforskning, 96*(2), 43–58.

Bertacchini, E., Bravo, G., Marrelli, M. and Santagata, W. (2012). *Cultural commons: A new perspective on the production and evolution of cultures*: Edward Elgar Publishing.

Beswick, K. (2018). Playing to type: Industry and invisible training in the National Youth Theatre's 'Playing Up 2'. *Theatre, Dance and Performance Training, 9*(1), 4–18.

Bianchini, F. and Parkinson, M. (1994). *Cultural policy and urban regeneration: The West European experience*: Manchester University Press.

Biesta, G. (2014). Learning in public places: Civic learning for the twenty-first century. In G. Biesta, M. De Bie and D. Wildemeersch (eds), *Civic learning, democratic citizenship and the public sphere* (pp 1–11): Springer.

Boele van Hensbroek, P. (2010). Cultural citizenship as a normative notion for activist practices. *Citizenship Studies, 14*(3), 317–30.

Booth, E. and Tunstall, T. (2016). *Playing for their lives: The global El Sistema movement for social change through music*: WW Norton & Company.

Bottrell, D. (2009). Dealing with disadvantage: Resilience and the social capital of young people's networks. *Youth & Society, 40*(4), 476–501.

Bourdieu, P. and Passeron, J.-C. (1977). *Reproduction in education, culture and society*: SAGE.

Bowler, R., Green, S., Smith, C. and Woolley, L. (2021). (Re) assembling anti-oppressive practice teachings in youth and community work through collective biography (2). *Education Sciences, 11*(9), 497.

Brackertz, N. (2007). *Who is hard to reach and why?* Institute of Social Research Working Paper, Swinburne University of Technology Institute of Social Research, Victoria.

Bradbury, A., McGimpsey, I. and Santori, D. (2013). Revising rationality: The use of 'Nudge' approaches in neoliberal education policy. *Journal of Education Policy, 28*(2), 247–67.

Bradford, S. and Cullen, F. (2014). Positive for youth work? Contested terrains of professional youth work in austerity England. *International Journal of Adolescence and Youth*, 19(sup1), 93–106.

Brocken, S. (2015). The fight for identity: Arts and youth work in collaboration. *BERA, Youth work, informal learning and the arts: Exploring the research and practice agenda, Nottingham, 18.*

Brook, O., O'Brien, D. and Taylor, M. (2018). Panic! It's an arts emergency. Social class, taste and inequalities in the creative industries. http://create london.org/event/panic2018/

Brook, O., Taylor, M. and O'Brien, D. (2020). *Culture is bad for you: Inequality and the Cultural and Creative Industries*: Manchester University Press.

Brooks, C. M., Daschuk, M. D., Poudrier, J. and Almond, N. (2015). First Nations youth redefine resilience: Listening to artistic productions of 'Thug Life' and hip-hop. *Journal of Youth Studies, 18*(6), 706–25.

Brown, R. and Jeanneret, N. (2015). Re-engaging at-risk youth through art – The evolution program. *International Journal of Education & the Arts, 16*(14–32).

Bryderup, I., et al (2011). *Social Pedagogy and Working with Children and Young People: Where Care and Education Meet*: Jessica Kingsley Publishers.

Buckingham, D. (ed.) (2008). *Youth, identity, and digital media*: MIT Press.

Buckingham, D. and Jones, K. (2001). New Labour's cultural turn: Some tensions in contemporary educational and cultural policy. *Journal of Education Policy, 16*(1), 1–14.

Bull, A. and Scharff, C. (2017). 'McDonald's music' versus 'Serious music': How production and consumption practices help to reproduce class inequality in the classical music profession. *Cultural Sociology*, 11(3), 283–301.

Bungay, H. and Vella-Burrows, T. (2013). The effects of participating in creative activities on the health and well-being of children and young people: A rapid review of the literature. *Perspectives in Public Health*, *133*(1), 44–52.

Burgess, J., Foth, M. and Klaebe, H. (2006). *Everyday creativity as civic engagement: A cultural citizenship view of new media*. In *Proceedings 2006 Communications Policy & Research Forum* (pp. 1–16). Network Insight Institute.

Burnard, P. and Dragovic, T. (2015). Collaborative creativity in instrumental group music learning as a site for enhancing pupil wellbeing. *Cambridge Journal of Education*, *45*(3), 371–92.

Burton, J., Jackson, S. and Willsdon, D. (2016). *Public servants: Art and crisis of the common good*: MIT Press.

Candlin, C. and Crichton, J. (2010). *Discourses of deficit*: Springer.

Catterall, J. S. (2002). The arts and the transfer of learning. In Deasy, R. J. (ed) *Critical links: Learning in the arts and student academic and social development*: Arts Education Partnership.

Catterall, J. S. (2009). *Doing well and doing good by doing art: The effects of education in the visual and performing arts on the achievements and value of young adults*: I-Group Book.

Catterall, J. S. (2012). The arts and achievement in at-risk youth: Findings from four longitudinal studies. Research Report# 55. National Endowment for the Arts.

Charmaz, K. (2014). *Constructing grounded theory*: SAGE.

Chauke, T. A. and Malatji, K. S. (2021). An exploration of violent behaviour of young ex-offenders on the Cape Flats, South Africa: Suggestions for youth work practice. *Southern African Journal of Social Work and Social Development*, *33*(2), 17–34.

Chávez, V. and Soep, E. (2005). Youth radio and the pedagogy of collegiality. *Harvard Educational Review*, *75*(4), 409–34.

Coburn, A. (2011a). Building social and cultural capital through learning about equality in youth work. *Journal of Youth Studies*, *14*(4), 475–91.

Coburn, A. (2011b). Liberation or containment: Paradoxes in youth work as a catalyst for powerful learning. *Youth and Policy*, *106*, 60–77.

Coburn, A. and Gormally, S. (2019). Creating educational synergies. *Youth and Policy*. https://www.youthandpolicy.org/articles/creating-educational-synergies/

Cohlmeyer, D. (2014). Developing a technology philosophy for digital youth work. *Concept*, *5*(1), 7–14.

Coles, R. and Howard, F. (2018). Filmmaking education and enterprise culture: An ethnographic exploration of two filmmaking education contexts and their relation to bedroom culture and the creative workplace. *Ethnography and Education, 13*(3), 273–85.

Curtis, K., Roberts, H., Copperman, J., Downie, A. and Liabo, K. (2004). 'How come I don't get asked no questions?' Researching 'hard to reach' children and teenagers. *Child & Family Social Work, 9*(2), 167–75.

Daniels, H. and Cole, T. (2010). Exclusion from school: Short-term setback or a long term of difficulties? *European Journal of Special Needs Education, 25*(2), 115–30.

Davies, B. (2010). Straws in the wind: The state of youth work in a changing policy environment. *Youth & Policy, 105,* 9–36.

Davies, B. (2011). This is youth work: Stories from practice. *Defence of youth work. Unison and Unite.* http://www.indefenceofyouthwork.org.uk/wordpress/wp-content/uploads/2011/10/20252-Youth-stories-report-2011_4th-11.pdf

Davies, B. (2013). Youth work in a changing policy landscape: The view from England. *Youth & Policy, 110*(6–32).

Davies, I., Evans, M. and Reid, A. (2005). Globalising citizenship education? A critique of 'global education' and 'citizenship education'. *British Journal of Educational Studies, 53*(1), 66–89.

De Certeau, M. and Mayol, P. (1998). *The practice of everyday life: Living and cooking* (Vol. 2): University of Minnesota Press.

de Roeper, J. and Savelsberg, H. J. (2009). Challenging the youth policy imperative: Engaging young people through the arts. *Journal of Youth Studies, 12*(2), 209–25.

de St Croix, T. (2016). *Grassroots youth work: Policy, passion and resistance in practice*: Policy Press.

de St Croix, T. (2018). Youth work, performativity and the new youth impact agenda: Getting paid for numbers? *Journal of Education Policy, 33*(3), 414–38.

Delanty, G. (2003). Citizenship as a learning process: Disciplinary citizenship versus cultural citizenship. *International Journal of Lifelong Education, 22*(6), 597–605.

Delgado, M. (2018). *Music, song, dance, and theatre: Broadway meets social justice youth community practice*: Oxford University Press.

Denmead, T. (2019). *The creative underclass: Youth, race, and the gentrifying city*: Duke University Press.

Department for Education and Skills (2003). *Every Child Matters: Change for Children in Schools*: DES Publications.

Doherty, L. and de St Croix, T. (2019). The everyday and the remarkable: Valuing and evaluating youth work. *Youth & Policy.* https://www.youthandpolicy.org/articles/valuing-and-evaluating-youth-work/

Doherty, L. and de St Croix, T. (2022). Valuing Youth Work – Reflecting on the value and evaluation of youth work. Centre for Public Policy Research, King's College London. https://www.kcl.ac.uk/ecs/assets/rethinking-impact/valuing-youth-work-research-informed-practical-resources-for-youth-workers.pdf

Du Bois, W. (1943). A chronicle of race relations. *Phylon (1940–1956), 4*(4), 362–87.

Dupuis, S. L., Kontos, P., Mitchell, G., Jonas-Simpson, C. and Gray, J. (2016). Re-claiming citizenship through the arts. *Dementia, 15*(3), 358–80.

Eckhoff, A. (2011). Art experiments: Introducing an artist-in-residence programme in early childhood education. *Early Child Development and Care, 181*(3), 371–85.

Edwards, K. (2009). Disenfranchised not 'deficient ': How the (neoliberal) state disenfranchises young people. *Australian Journal of Social Issues, 44*(1), 23–37.

Eisner, E. W. (2002). *The arts and the creation of mind*: Yale University Press.

Ennis, G. M. and Tonkin, J. (2018). 'It's like exercise for your soul': How participation in youth arts activities contributes to young people's wellbeing. *Journal of Youth Studies, 21*(3), 340–59.

Fahmy, E. (2008). Tackling youth exclusion in the UK: Challenges for current policy and practice. *Social Work & Society, 6*(2), 279–88.

Fernández-de-Castro, P., Aranda, D., Moyano, S. and Sampedro, V. (2021). Digital youth work: A systematic review with a proposal. *Social Work Education*, 1–19.

Finlay, I., Sheridan, M., McKay, J. and Nudzor, H. (2010). Young people on the margins: In need of more choices and more chances in twenty-first century Scotland. *British Educational Research Journal, 36*(5), 851–67.

Finney, J. and Burnard, P. (2010). *Music education with digital technology*: Bloomsbury Publishing.

Fleming, M. (2008). *Arts in education and creativity: A review of the literature*. Arts Council: Creative Partnerships.

Foucoult, M. (1975). *Discipline and punish*: Gallimard.

Fransberg, M. (2019). Performing gendered distinctions: Young women painting illicit street art and graffiti in Helsinki. *Journal of Youth Studies, 22*(4), 489–504.

Freire, P. (1996). *Pedagogy of the oppressed* (revised): Continuum.

Friedman, S. and Laurison, D. (2020). *The class ceiling: Why it pays to be privileged*: Policy Press.

Friedman, S., Laurison, D. and Miles, A. (2015). Breaking the 'class' ceiling? Social mobility into Britain's elite occupations. *The Sociological Review, 63*(2), 259–89.

Gadsden, V. L. (2008). The arts and education: Knowledge generation, pedagogy, and the discourse of learning. *Review of Research in Education, 32*(1), 29–61. doi:10.3102/0091732x07309691

Gallagher, K. and Wessels, A. (2013). Between the frames: Youth spectatorship and theatre as curated, 'unruly' pedagogical space. *Research in Drama Education: The Journal of Applied Theatre and Performance, 18*(1), 25–43.

Gallagher, K., Starkman, R. and Rhoades, R. (2017). Performing counter-narratives and mining creative resilience: Using applied theatre to theorize notions of youth resilience. *Journal of Youth Studies, 20*(2), 216–33.

García, B. (2004). Urban regeneration, arts programming and major events: Glasgow 1990, Sydney 2000 and Barcelona 2004. *International Journal of Cultural Policy, 10*(1), 103–18.

Gauntlett, D. 2018. *Making is Connecting: The Social Power of Creativity, From Craft and Knitting to Digital Everything*: John Wiley & Sons.

Gaztambide-Fernández, R. (2013). Why the arts don't do anything: Toward a new vision for cultural production in education. *Harvard Educational Review, 83*(1), 211–37.

Gaztambide-Fernández, R. (2020). The orders of cultural production. *Journal of Curriculum Theorizing, 35*(3).

Gaztambide-Fernández, R. and Arráiz Matute, A. (2015). Creation as participation/participation as creation: Cultural production, participatory politics, and the intersecting lines of identification and activism. *Curriculum Inquiry, 45*(1), 1–9.

Gkartzios, M. and Crawshaw, J. (2019). Researching rural housing: With an artist in residence. *Sociologia Ruralis, 59*(4), 589–611.

Goessling, K. P. (2020). Youth participatory action research, trauma, and the arts: Designing youthspaces for equity and healing. *International Journal of Qualitative Studies in Education, 33*(1), 12–31.

Goessling, K. P. and Wager, A. C. (2020). Places of possibility: Youth research as creative liberatory praxis. *Journal of Youth Studies, 24*(6), 746–64.

Goffman, E. (2003). *Stigma*: Sociologické nakladatelství (SLON).

Gormally, S. and Coburn, A. (2014). Finding nexus: Connecting youth work and research practices. *British Educational Research Journal, 40*(5), 869–85.

Gosine, K. and Tabi, E. (2016). Disrupting neoliberalism and bridging the multiple worlds of marginalized youth via Hip-Hop pedagogy: Contemplating possibilities. *Review of Education, Pedagogy, and Cultural Studies, 38*(5), 445–67.

Graves, J. B. (2010). *Cultural democracy: The arts, community, and the public purpose*: University of Illinois Press.

Green, K. L. (2013). 'The way we hear ourselves is different from the way others hear us': Exploring the literate identities of a Black radio youth collective. *Equity & Excellence in Education, 46*(3), 315–26.

Green, N. (2003). Outwardly mobile: Young people and mobile technologies. In Katz, J. (eds) *Machines that become us: The social context of personal communication technology*, 201–218: Transaction Publishers.

Grenfell, M. (2011). Bourdieu: A theory of practice. In *Bourdieu, language and linguistics* (pp 7–34): A&C Black.

Gripsrud, J. (2000). Learning from experience: Cultural policies and cultural democracy in the 20th century. *International Journal of Cultural Policy, 7*(2), 197–209.

Gross, J. and Wilson, N. (2020). Cultural democracy: An ecological and capabilities approach. *International Journal of Cultural Policy, 26*(3), 328–43.

Haberman, M. (2010). The pedagogy of poverty versus good teaching. *Phi Delta Kappan, 92*(2): 81–7.

Hadley, S. (2021). *Audience development and cultural policy*: Palgrave Macmillan.

Hadley, S. and Belfiore, E. (2018). Cultural democracy and cultural policy. *Cultural Trends, 27*(3), 218–23.

Hager, L. L. (2010). Youth arts residencies: Implications for policy and education. *Youth Theatre Journal, 24*(2), 111–24.

Hämäläinen, J. (2003). The concept of social pedagogy in the field of social work. *Journal of Social Work, 3*(1), 69–80.

Hammersley, M. and Atkinson, P. (2007). *Ethnography: Principles in practice*: Routledge.

Harris, A. and Lemon, A. (2012). Bodies that shatter: Creativity, culture and the new pedagogical imaginary. *Pedagogy, Culture & Society, 20*(3), 413–33.

Hart, R. (1992). Ladder of participation. In *Children's participation: From tokenism to citizenship*: UNICEF.

Hart, R. (2013). *Children's participation: The theory and practice of involving young citizens in community development and environmental care*: Routledge.

Hart, S. (2009). The 'problem' with youth: Young people, citizenship and the community. *Citizenship studies, 13*(6), 641–57.

Harvey, G. (2020). Indigenous rituals re-make the larger than human community. *Reassembling Democracy: Ritual and Cultural Resource*, 69–85.

Hayes, D., Hattam, R., Comber, B., Kerkham, L., Lupton, R. and Thomson, P. (2017). *Literacy, leading and learning: Beyond pedagogies of poverty*: Taylor & Francis.

Heath, S. and Robinson, K. (2004). Making a way: Youth arts and learning in international perspective. In N. Rabkin and R. Redmond (eds), *Putting the arts in the picture* (pp 107–26): Columbia College Chicago.

Heath, S., Fuller, A. and Johnston, B. (2010). Young people, social capital and network-based educational decision-making. *British Journal of Sociology of Education, 31*(4), 395–411.

Henley, D. (2012). Cultural Education in England: An independent review. https://www.gov.uk/government/publications/cultural-education-in-england

Hickey-Moody, A. (2013a). Affect as method: Feelings, aesthetics and affective pedagogy. In *Deleuze and research methodologies* (pp 79–95): Edinburgh University Press.

Hickey-Moody, A. (2013b). *Youth, arts, and education: Reassembling subjectivity through affect*: Routledge.

Hickey-Moody, A., Savage, G. C. and Windle, J. (2010). Pedagogy writ large: Public, popular and cultural pedagogies in motion. *Critical Studies in Education, 51*(3), 227–36.

Hillman, M. (2018). The Resistant Artist: Street Art as Radical Youth Work. *CYC-Online. September*, 86. https://www.cyc-net.org/cyc-online/sep 2018.pdf#page=86

Hollingworth, S., Robinson, Y., Chalgianni, E. and Mansaray, A. (2016). Arts Award impact study 2012–2016: A report for Trinity College London. www.artsaward.org.uk/resource/?id=4294

Houseman, M. and Salomonsen, J. (2020). *Reassembling democracy: Ritual as cultural resource*: Bloomsbury Academic.

Howard, F. (2017). The arts in youth work: A spectrum of instrumentality. *Youth & Policy*. https://www.youthandpolicy.org/articles/the-arts-in-youth-work/

Howard, F. (2020). Pedagogies for the 'dis-engaged': Diverse experiences of the Young People's Arts Award Programme. *International Journal of Art & Design Education, 39*(3), 672–85.

Howard, F. (2021a). 'It's like being back in GCSE art' – Engaging with music, film-making and boardgames. Creative pedagogies within youth work education. *Education Sciences, 11*(8), 374.

Howard, F. (2021b). Researching event-centred projects: Showcasing grounded aesthetics. *Qualitative Research.* https://journals.sagepub.com/doi/10.1177/1468794121990973

Howard, F. (2022a). Artistic production and (re) production: Youth arts programmes as enablers of common cultural dispositions. *Cultural Sociology.* 17499755211066371.

Howard, F. (2022b). Using and abusing the arts with 'at-risk' youth. *Journal of Applied Youth Studies*, 1–16.

Howard, F., Brocken, S. and Sim, N. (2018). Youth work, arts practice and transdisciplinary space. In P. Alldred, F. Cullen, K. Edwards and D. Fusco (eds), *The SAGE handbook of youth work practice* (pp 271–83): SAGE.

Huesca, R. (2008). Youth-produced radio and its impacts: From personal empowerment to political action. In Carpentier, N. and De Cleen, B. (eds), *Participation and media production: critical reflections on content creation* (pp 97–111): Cambridge Scholars Publishing.

Hughes, J., Miles, A. and McLewin, A. (2005). Doing the arts justice: A review of research literature, practice and theory. http://www.artsevidence.org.uk/media/uploads/evaluation-downloads/doing-the-arts-justice-2005.pdf

Hull, G. A., Stornaiuolo, A. and Sahni, U. (2010). Cultural citizenship and cosmopolitan practice: Global youth communicate online. *English Education, 42*(4), 331–67.

Hunter-Doniger, T. and Berlinsky, R. (2017). The power of the arts: Evaluating a community artist-in-residence program through the lens of studio thinking. *Arts Education Policy Review, 118*(1), 19–26.

Ito, M., Soep, E., Kligler-Vilenchik, N., Shresthova, S., Gamber-Thompson, L. and Zimmerman, A. (2015). Learning connected civics: Narratives, practices, infrastructures. *Curriculum Inquiry, 45*(1), 10–29.

Jancovich, L. (2011). Great art for everyone? Engagement and participation policy in the arts. *Cultural Trends, 20*(3–4), 271–9.

Jeffers, A. and Moriarty, G. (2017). *Culture, democracy and the right to make art: The British community arts movement*: Bloomsbury Publishing.

Jeffs, T. and Smith, M. (2002). Individualism and youth work. *Youth and policy, 76,* 39–65.

Jermyn, H. (2001). The arts and social exclusion: A review prepared for the Arts Council of England. http://webarchive.nationalarchives.gov.uk/20160204124308/http://www.artscouncil.org.uk/advice-and-guidance/browse-advice-and-guidance/arts-and-social-exclusion-a-review-prepared-for-the-arts-council-of-england

Jermyn, H. (2004). The art of inclusion. http://thamesvalleypartnership.org.uk/somethingbrilliant/wp-content/uploads/art-of-inclusion-jermyn.pdf

Jones, I. D. and Brady, G. (2022). Informal education pedagogy transcendence from the 'academy' to society in the current and post COVID environment. *Education Sciences, 12*(1), 37.

Jones, S. (2014). How people read and write and they don't even notice: everyday lives and literacies on a Midlands council estate. *Literacy,* 48(2): 59–65.

Kane, K. M. (2014). Transformative performing arts and mentorship pedagogy: Nurturing developmental relationships in a multidisciplinary dance theatre program for youth. *Journal of Education and Training Studies,* 2(2), 224–32.

Karkou, V. and Glasman, J. (2004). Arts, education and society: The role of the arts in promoting the emotional wellbeing and social inclusion of young people. *Support for Learning, 19*(2), 57–65.

Kelly, P. (2006). The entrepreneurial self and 'youth at-risk': Exploring the horizons of identity in the twenty-first century. *Journal of Youth Studies,* 9(1), 17–32.

Kelly, P. (2011). Breath and the truths of youth at-risk: Allegory and the social scientific imagination. *Journal of Youth Studies, 14*(4), 431–47.

Kiilakoski, T. and Kivijärvi, A. (2015). Youth clubs as spaces of non-formal learning: Professional idealism meets the spatiality experienced by young people in Finland. *Studies in Continuing Education, 37*(1), 47–61.

Kinder, K. and Harland, J. (2004). The arts and social inclusion: what's the evidence? *Support for Learning, 19*(2), 52–66.

Kivijärvi, A., Aaltonen, S. and Välimäki, V. (2019). The feasibility of an online discussion group as a component of targeted youth work in Finland. *Children and Youth Services Review, 105*, 104411, 1-9.

Kramer, J. (2004). Figurative repatriation: First nations 'artist-warriors' recover, reclaim, and return cultural property through self-definition. *Journal of Material Culture, 9*(2), 161–82.

Kuppers, P. (2000). Accessible education: Aesthetics, bodies and disability. *Research in Dance Education, 1*(2), 119–31.

Kuttner, P. J. (2015). Educating for cultural citizenship: Reframing the goals of arts education. *Curriculum Inquiry, 45*(1), 69–92.

Laermans, R. (1993). Bringing the consumer back in. *Theory, Culture & Society, 10*(1), 153–61: SAGE.

Lauha, H. (2019). Why do we need digital youth work? In (eds), *Digitalisation and youth work* (pp 15–19) Estonian Youth Work Centre (EYWC) – Government Agency for Youth Policy and Youth Work Development.

Lawy, R. and Biesta, G. (2006). Citizenship-as-practice: The educational implications of an inclusive and relational understanding of citizenship. *British Journal of Educational Studies, 54*(1), 34–50.

Leccardi, C. (2016). Youth cultures in the new century: Cultural citizenship and cosmopolitanism. In (eds), *Youth, Space and Time* (pp 115–130): Brill

Lee, J.-A. and Finney, S. D. (2005). Using popular theatre for engaging racialized minority girls in exploring questions of identity and belonging. *Child & Youth Services, 26*(2), 95–118.

Lin, C.-C. and Bruce, B. C. (2013). Engaging youth in underserved communities through digital-mediated arts learning experiences for community inquiry. *Studies in Art Education, 54*(4), 335–48.

Lindgren, M., Bergman, Å. and Sæther, E. (2016). The construction of social inclusion through music education: Two Swedish ethnographic studies of the El Sistema programme. *Nordic Research in Music Education Yearbook, 17*, 65–81.

Livingstone, S. (2007). From family television to bedroom culture: Young people's media at home. In Devereux, E. ed., *Media studies: Key issues and debates*, 302–21: SAGE.

Lombard, K.-J. (2013). Art crimes: The governance of hip hop graffiti. *Journal for Cultural Research, 17*(3), 255–78.

Long, J., Welch, M., Bramham, P., Hylton, K., Butterfield, J. and Lloyd, E. (2002). Count me in: The dimensions of social inclusion through culture and sport. http://citeseerx.ist.psu.edu/viewdoc/download?doi= 10.1.1.466.2996&rep=rep1&type=pdf

Lynch, J., Walker-Gibbs, B. and Herbert, S. (2015). Moving beyond a 'bums-on-seats' analysis of progress towards widening participation: Reflections on the context, design and evaluation of an Australian government-funded mentoring programme. *Journal of Higher Education Policy and Management, 37*(2), 144–58.

MacDonald, G. B. and Valdivieso, R. (2001). Measuring deficits and assets: How we track youth development now, and how we should track it. In: Benson, P. L. and Pittman, K. J. (eds) *Trends in Youth Development. Outreach Scholarship*, vol 6: Springer.

MacDonald, R. (2008). Disconnected youth? Social exclusion, the 'underclass' & economic marginality. *Social Work & Society, 6*(2), 236–48.

Machin, S. (2006). Social disadvantage and education experiences. *OECD Social, Employment and Migration working papers.* http://www.oecd.org/social/soc/36165298.pdf

Mai, L. and Gibson, R. (2011). The rights of the putti: A review of the literature on children as cultural citizens in art museums. *Museum Management and Curatorship, 26*(4), 355–71.

Manchester, H. and Pett, E. (2015). Teenage kicks: Exploring cultural value from a youth perspective. *Cultural Trends, 24*(3), 223–31. doi:10.1080/09548963.2015.1066078

Mantie, R. (2008). Getting unstuck: The One World Youth Arts Project, the music education paradigm, and youth without advantage. *Music Education Research, 10*(4), 473–83.

Martin, G. and Hickey, A. (2016). Cultural studies, DIY pedagogies and storytelling. In A. Hickey (ed.), *The pedagogies of cultural studies* (pp 149–64): Routledge.

Matarasso, F. (1997). *Use or ornament? The social impact of participation in the arts*: Comedia.

McDonnell, J. (2014). Reimagining the role of art in the relationship between democracy and education. *Educational Philosophy and Theory, 46*(1), 46–58.

McGimpsey, I. (2018). The new youth sector assemblage: Reforming youth provision through a finance capital imaginary. *Journal of Education Policy, 33*(2), 226–42.

McIntyre, A. (2012). Making the invisible visible: First Nations music in the classroom. *Canadian Music Educator, 54*(1), 24–6.

Melvin, J. (2019). The future of online youth work. In G. Bright and C. Pugh (eds), *Youth Work* (pp 184–203): Brill.

Merli, P. (2002). Evaluating the social impact of participation in arts activities. *International Journal of Cultural Policy, 8*(1), 107–18.

Miller, J., McAuliffe, L., Riaz, N. and Deuchar, R. (2015). Exploring youths' perceptions of the hidden practice of youth work in increasing social capital with young people considered NEET in Scotland. *Journal of Youth Studies, 18*(4), 468–84.

Miller, T. (2007). *Cultural citizenship: Cosmopolitanism, consumerism, and television in a neoliberal age*: Temple University Press.

Mills, M. and McGregor, G. (2013). *Re-engaging young people in education: Learning from alternative schools*: Routledge.

Mishra, R. (2014). Rethinking youth work in India: Does youth development approach make sense? In *Social entrepreneurship: A livelihood option with social transformation*. https://www.academia.edu/17107432/Rethinking_youth_work_in_India_Does_Youth_Development_Approach_Make_Sense

Morrow, V. (2001). Young people's explanations and experiences of social exclusion: Retrieving Bourdieu's concept of social capital. *International Journal of Sociology and Social Policy, 21*(4/5/6), 37–63.

Myers, O. (2016). *Breaking the binary: Reclaiming space for youth arts in the 21st century*. Dissertation. Manchester Metropolitan University.

National Youth Agency. (2009). Artswork with socially excluded young people. https://s3.eu-west-1.amazonaws.com/assets.nya2.joltrouter.net/wp-content/uploads/20210421110111/artswork-with-socially-excluded-young-people.pdf

Noddings, N. (2013). *Caring: A relational approach to ethics and moral education*: University of California Press.

Nolas, S.-M. (2014). Exploring young people's and youth workers' experiences of spaces for 'youth development': Creating cultures of participation. *Journal of Youth Studies, 17*(1), 26–41.

Nols, Z., Haudenhuyse, R. and Theeboom, M. (2017). Urban sport-for-development initiatives and young people in socially vulnerable situations: Investigating the 'deficit model'. *Social Inclusion, 5*(2), 210–22.

O'Brien, A. and Donelan, K. (2009). *The arts and youth at risk: Global and local challenges*: Cambridge Scholars Publishing.

O'Brien, D. (2010). Measuring the value of culture: A report to the Department for Culture, Media and Sport. https://assets.publishing.service.gov.uk/government/uploads/system/uploads/attachment_data/file/77933/measuring-the-value-culture-report.pdf

Ord, J. (2014). Aristotle's phronesis and youth work: Beyond instrumentality. *Youth & Policy, 112*, 56–73.

Osler, A. and Starkey, H. (2005). *Changing citizenship*: McGraw-Hill Education.

Padhan, M. and Mishra, R. (2015). Youth programmes in India: A critical review. In (eds), *Youth development: Emerging perspectives* (pp 821–9): Shipra Publications.

Pakulski, J. (1997). Cultural citizenship. *Citizenship studies, 1*(1), 73–86.

Parker, A., Marturano, N., O'Connor, G. and Meek, R. (2018). Marginalised youth, criminal justice and performing arts: Young people's experiences of music-making. *Journal of Youth Studies, 21*(8), 1061–76.

Pawluczuk, A., Webster, G., Smith, C. and Hall, H. (2019). The social impact of digital youth work: What are we looking for? *Media and Communication, 7*(2), 59–68.

Peppler, K. A. and Y. B. Kafai (2007). From SuperGoo to Scratch: Exploring creative digital media production in informal learning. *Learning, Media and Technology, 32*(2): 149–66.

Peterson, R. A. and Kern, R. M. (1996). Changing highbrow taste: From snob to omnivore. *American Sociological Review,* Vol 61, October: 900–7.

Petracovschi, S., Costas, C. and Voicu, S. (2011). Street dance: Form of expressing identity in adolescents and youth. *Timisoara Physical Education & Rehabilitation Journal, 3*(6).

Poyntz, S. R., Coles, R., Fitzsimmons-Frey, H., Bains, A., Sefton-Green, J. and Hoechsmann, M. (2019). The non-formal arts learning sector, youth provision, and paradox in the learning city. *Oxford Review of Education, 45*(2), 258–78.

Putnam, R. D. (2001). *Bowling alone: The collapse and revival of American community*: Simon and Schuster.

Rapp-Paglicci, L. A., Ersing, R. and Rowe, W. (2007). The effects of cultural arts programs on at-risk youth: Are there more than anecdotes and promises? *Journal of Social Service Research, 33*(2), 51–6.

Reay, D. (2017). *Miseducation: Inequality, education and the working classes*: Policy Press.

Rhodes, A. M. and Schechter, R. (2014). Fostering resilience among youth in inner city community arts centers: The case of the artists collective. *Education and Urban Society, 46*(7), 826–48.

Rimmer, M. (2010). Listening to the monkey: Class, youth and the formation of a musical habitus. *Ethnography, 11*(2), 255–83.

Rimmer, M. (2012). The participation and decision making of 'at risk' youth in community music projects: An exploration of three case studies. *Journal of Youth Studies, 15*(3), 329–50.

Robinson, Y., Paraskevopoulou, A. and Hollingworth, S. (2019). Developing 'active citizens': Arts Award, creativity and impact. *British Educational Research Journal, 45*(6), 1203–19.

Rogers, T. (2016). Youth arts, media, and critical literacies as forms of public engagement in the local/global interface. *Literacy Research: Theory, Method, and Practice, 65*(1), 268–82.

Rosaldo, R. (1994). Cultural citizenship and educational democracy. *Cultural Anthropology, 9*(3), 402–11.

Ruiz, J. (2004). *A Literature Review of the Evidence Base for Culture, the Arts and Sport Policy*. http://www.gov.scot/Publications/2004/08/19784/41507

Russell, L. (2013). Researching marginalised young people. *Ethnography and Education, 8*(1), 46–60.

Sagan, O., Candela, E. and Frimodig, B. (2010). Insight on OutReach: Towards a critical practice. *International Journal of Education through Art, 6*(2), 145–61.

Sallah, M. (2018). # Backwaysolutions# Candleofhope: Global Youth Works approaches to challenging irregular migration in Sub-Saharan Africa. In. Del Felice, C. and Peters, O. (eds) *Youth in Africa: Agents of Change*: Casa África – La Catarata.

Savage, M., Devine, F., Cunningham, N., Taylor, M., Li, Y., Hjellbrekke, J., Le Roux, B., Friedman, S. and Miles, A. (2013). A new model of social class? Findings from the BBC's Great British Class Survey experiment. *Sociology, 47*(2), 219–50.

Schnorr, D. and Ware, H. W. (2001). Moving beyond a deficit model to describe and promote the career development of at-risk youth. *Journal of Career Development, 27*(4), 247–63.

Sebestyén, R. (2019). 'IF': Planning, research and co-creation of an existential installation-performance. *Hungarian Studies Yearbook, 1*(1), 52–66.

Seebach, M. (2008). Youth participation and youth work. *Youth Studies Ireland, 3*(2), 37–53.

Sefton-Green, J. (1999). *Young people, creativity and new technologies: The challenge of digital arts*: Psychology Press.

Sefton-Green, J. (2006). *New spaces for learning: Developing the ecology of out-of-school education*: Hawke Research Institute for Sustainable Societies McGill, South Australia.

Silva, J. E. and Menezes, I. (2016). Art education for citizenship: Augusto Boal's theater of the oppressed as a method for democratic empowerment. *JSSE-Journal of Social Science Education*, 15(4), 40–9.

Sim, N. (2017). *Like oil and water? Partnerships between visual art institutions and youth organisations*: TATE/The University of Nottingham.

Sim, N. (2019). *Youth work, galleries and the politics of partnership*: Springer.

Simmons, R. and Thompson, R. (2011). *NEET young people and training for work: Learning on the margins*: Trentham Books.

Simmons, R., Russell, L. and Thompson, R. (2013). *NEET young people and the labour market: Working on the margins*. In: Youth Studies Conference, 8–12th April, Glasgow (unpublished).

Šinkūnienė, J. R. and Skuolytė, G. (2013). International youth projects as a method of intercultural social work. *International Journal of Liberal Arts and Social Science, 1*(3), 49–62.

Smyth, J., McInerney, P. and Fish, T. (2013). Blurring the boundaries: From relational learning towards a critical pedagogy of engagement for disengaged disadvantaged young people. *Pedagogy, Culture & Society, 21*(2), 299–320.

Sotomayor, L. and Kim, I. (2009). Initiating social change in a conservatory of music: Possibilities and limitations of community outreach work. In: Gould, E., Countryman, J., Morton, C. and Rose, L.S. (eds), *Exploring social justice: How music education might matter* (pp 225–39): Canadian Music Educators' Association.

Standing, G. (2019). *Plunder of the commons: A manifesto for sharing public wealth*: Penguin.

Staricoff, R. L. (2004). *Arts in health: A review of the medical literature*: Arts Council England.

Stevenson, N. (2003). Cultural citizenship in the 'cultural' society: A cosmopolitan approach. *Citizenship studies, 7*(3), 331–48.

Stevenson, N. (2010). Cultural citizenship, education and democracy: Redefining the good society. *Citizenship studies, 14*(3), 275–91.

Talaina Si'isi'ialafia, T. (2018). Channeling positive youth development through the arts: Intrinsic benefits for young people. *Journal of the Arts Faculty of the National University of Samoa, 4*, 49–66.

Tawell, A., Thompson, I., Daniels, H., Elliott, V., Dingwall, N., Rubtsova, O. and Munk, K., (2015). *Being Other: The Effectiveness of Arts Based Approaches in Engaging with Disaffected Young People*: University of Oxford, Department of Education.

Te Riele, K. (2006). Youth 'at risk': Further marginalizing the marginalized? *Journal of Education Policy, 21*(2), 129–45.

Thomson, P. and Hall, C. (2020). Beyond civics: Art and Design education and the making of active/activist citizens. In Addison, N. and Burgess, L., (eds), *Debates in Art and Design Education* (pp 31–44): Routledge.

Thomson, P. and Pennacchia, J. (2015). Hugs and behaviour points: Alternative education and the regulation of 'excluded' youth. *International Journal of Inclusive Education, 20*(6), 622–40.

Thomson, P., Hall, C., Jones, K. and Sefton-Green, J. (2012). The signature pedagogies project: Final report. *Creativity, Culture and Education*. http://old. creativitycultureeducation.org/wp-content/uploads/Signature_Pedagog ies_Final_Report_April_2012.pdf

Thomson, P., Hall, C., Earl, L. and Geppert, C. (2019a). The pedagogical logics of arts-rich schools: A Bourdieusian analysis. *British Journal of Sociology of Education, 40*(2), 239–53.

Thomson, P., Hall, C., Earl, L. and Geppert, C. (2019b). *Towards an arts education for cultural citizenship*: Routledge.

Tranter, R. and Palin, N. (2004). Including the excluded: An art in itself. *Support for Learning, 19*(2), 88–95.

Travis, R. (2013). Rap music and the empowerment of today's youth: Evidence in everyday music listening, music therapy, and commercial rap music. *Child and Adolescent Social Work Journal, 30*(2), 139–67.

Travis, Jr, R. and T. G. Leech (2014). Empowerment-based positive youth development: A new understanding of healthy development for African American youth. *Journal of Research on Adolescence, 24*(1), 93–116.

Trayes, J., Harré, N. and Overall, N. C. (2012). A youth performing arts experience: Psychological experiences, recollections, and the desire to do it again. *Journal of Adolescent Research, 27*(2), 155–82.

Turnbull, G. and Spence, J. (2011). What's at risk? The proliferation of risk across child and youth policy in England. *Journal of Youth Studies, 14*(8), 939–959.

Union, E. (2016). European Union Work Plan for Youth 2016–2018. https://eur-lex.europa.eu/summary/EN/150403_1

Vallance, E. (2017). Arts interventions with young people. https://strathprints.strath.ac.uk/68160/1/Vallance_CYCJ_2017_arts_interventions_with_young_people.pdf

Van de Walle, T., Coussée, F. and Bouverne-De Bie, M. (2010). Social exclusion and youth work – From the surface to the depths of an educational practice. *Journal of Youth Studies, 14*(2), 219–31.

Villaverde, L. (1998). Youth at the crossroads of radical democracy and critical citizenry: An analysis of art, pedagogy, and power. *The Review of Education/Pedagogy/Cultural Studies, 20*(2), 189–208.

Warde, A., Wright, D. and Gayo-Cal, M. (2007). Understanding cultural omnivorousness: Or, the myth of the cultural omnivore. *Cultural sociology, 1*(2), 143–64.

Wilkinson, C. (2015). Young people, community radio and urban life. *Geography Compass, 9*(3), 127–39.

Wilks, L. (2011). Bridging and bonding: Social capital at music festivals. *Journal of Policy Research in Tourism, Leisure and Events, 3*(3), 281–97.

Willis, P. (2005). Invisible Aesthetics and the Social Work of Commodity Culture. In D. a. H. Inglis, J. (ed.), *The Sociology of Art: ways of seeing* (pp 73–85): Palgrave Macmillan.

Willis, P. (1990). *Common culture: Symbolic work at play in the everyday cultures of the young*: Open University Press.

Wright, D. E. (2020). Imagining a more just world: Critical arts pedagogy and youth participatory action research. *International Journal of Qualitative Studies in Education, 33*(1), 32–49.

Wright, R., Alaggia, R. and Krygsman, A. (2014). Five-year follow-up study of the qualitative experiences of youth in an afterschool arts program in low-income communities. *Journal of Social Service Research, 40*(2), 137–46.

Wrigley, L. (2019). (Un)Happy 21st Birthday NEET! A genealogical approach to understanding young people Not in Education, Employment or Training. *Youth & Policy*. https://www.youthandpolicy.org/articles/unhappy-21st-birthday-neet/

Wylie, T. (2015). Youth work. *Youth & Policy, 114*(4), 43–54.

Yardley, E. (2008). Teenage mothers' experiences of stigma. *Journal of Youth Studies, 11*(6), 671–84.

YJB (Youth Justice Board) (2008). *Engaging Young People who Offend.* https://assets.publishing.service.gov.uk/government/uploads/system/uploads/attachment_data/file/356204/Final_EYP_source.pdf

Youdell, D. and McGimpsey, I. (2015). Assembling, disassembling and reassembling 'youth services' in Austerity Britain. *Critical Studies in Education, 56*(1), 116–30.

Young, I. M. (1989). Polity and group difference: A critique of the ideal of universal citizenship. *Ethics, 99*(2), 250–74.

Zitomer, M. R. and Reid, G. (2011). To be or not to be – able to dance: Integrated dance and children's perceptions of dance ability and disability. *Research in Dance Education, 12*(2), 137–56.

Index

References to figures appear in *italic* type. References to endnotes show the
page number, chapter number and the note number (181ch9n5).